10258674

D0513021

LEARNING TO
HISTO

IN THE

SECONDARY SCHOOL

In some hands, history can seem a desiccated and stultifying subject, of dubious relevance and little clear purpose. In others it can be inspirational and immensely rewarding. The purpose of this book is to enable you to teach history in a way that pupils will find interesting, enjoyable and purposeful. It incorporates a wide range of ideas about the teaching of history, with practical suggestions for classroom practice, and ideas for further investigations of particular aspects of teaching and learning in history. The book also covers questions such as how to provide for differentiated learning and how to utilise the potential of new technology in the history classroom.

Terry Haydn is Lecturer in Education at the University of East Anglia. **James Arthur** is Reader and Principal Lecturer in Education at Canterbury Christ Church College. **Martin Hunt** is Lecturer in Education at Manchester Metropolitan University.

Learning to Teach Subjects in the Secondary School Series

Series Editors
Tony Turner, Institute of Education, University of London; Sue Capel, Canterbury Christ Church College; and Marilyn Leask, De Monfort University, Bedford.

Designed for all students learning to teach in secondary schools, and particularly those on school-based initial teacher training courses, the books in this series complement *Learning to Teach in the Secondary School* and its companion, *Starting to Teach in the Secondary School*. Each book in the series applies under-pinning theory and addresses practical issues to support students in school and in the training institution in learning how to teach a particular subject.

Learning to Teach English in the Secondary School
John Davison and Jane Dowson

Learning to Teach Modern Foreign Languages in the Secondary School
Norbert Pacher and Kit Field

Learning to Teach History in the Secondary School
Terry Haydn, James Arthur and Martin Hunt

Learning to Teach Physical Education in the Secondary School
Susan Capel

LEARNING TO TEACH
HISTORY
IN THE
SECONDARY SCHOOL

A companion to school experience

Terry Haydn, James Arthur and Martin Hunt

London and New York

First published 1997
by Routledge
11 New Fetter Lane, London EC4P 4EE

Simultaneously published in the USA and Canada
by Routledge
29 West 35th Street, New York, NY 10001

Typeset in Ehrhardt by Keystroke, Jacaranda Lodge, Wolverhampton
Printed and bound in Great Britain by Page Bros (Norwich) Ltd

British Library Cataloguing in Publication Data
A catalogue record for this book is available from the British Library

Library of Congress Cataloging in Publication Data
Haydn, Terry, 1951–
    Learning to teach history in the secondary school / Terry Haydn,
James Arthur and Martin Hunt.
        p.   cm. — (Learning to teach subjects in the secondary
school)
    ISBN 0–415–15453–7 (pbk. : alk. paper)
    1. History—Study and teaching (Secondary) I. Arthur, James,
1957– . II. Hunt, Martin, 1936– . III. Title. IV. Series.
D16.25.H38   1997
907.1′2—dc21   97–11771
                                                         CIP

ISBN 0–415–15453–7

Contents

Introduction to the series

This book, *Learning to Teach History in the Secondary School*, is one of a series of books entitled *Learning to Teach Subjects in the Secondary School* covering most subjects in the secondary school curriculum. The books in this series support and complement one of the many books designed to help student teachers learn to teach: *Learning to Teach in the Secondary School: A Companion to School Experience* (Capel, Leask and Turner, 1995). These books are designed for student teachers learning to teach on different types of initial teacher education courses and in different places. However, it is hoped that they will be equally useful to tutors and mentors in their work with student teachers. In 1996 a complementary book was published entitled *Starting to Teach in the Secondary School: A Companion for the Newly Qualified Teacher* (Capel, Leask and Turner, 1996). That second book was designed to support newly qualified teachers in their first post and covered aspects of teaching which are likely to be of concern in the first year of teaching.

The information in the subject books does not repeat that in *Learning to Teach*; rather, the content of that book is adapted and extended to address the needs of student teachers learning to teach a specific subject. In each of the subject books, therefore, reference is made to *Learning to Teach*, where appropriate. It is recommended that you have both books so that you can cross-reference when needed.

The positive feedback on *Learning to Teach*, particularly the way it has supported the learning of student teachers in their development into effective, reflective teachers, has encouraged us to retain the main features of that book in the subject series. Thus, the subject books are designed so that elements of appropriate theory introduce each behaviour or issue. Recent research into teaching and learning is incorporated into this. This material is interwoven with tasks designed to help you identify key features of the behaviour or issue and apply these to your own practice.

Although the basic content of each subject book is similar, each book is designed to address the unique nature of each subject. In this book, for example, consideration is given to the importance of pupils' perceptions of history as a school subject. How can we teach history in a way which convinces pupils that it is interesting, important, useful and relevant to their lives? This will not only influence whether they will go on to take history after Key Stage 3, but will also have a bearing on their achievement in history. The book also focuses on the ways in which student teachers of history should interpret the statutory requirements pertaining to school history. Above all, it attempts to bring together theories (or ideas) about the teaching of history with practical classroom approaches and examples.

We, as editors, have found this project to be exciting. We hope that, whatever the type of initial teacher education course you are following and wherever you may be following that course, you find that this book is useful and supports your development into an effective, reflective history teacher.

Susan Capel, Marilyn Leask and Tony Turner
January 1997

The authors would like to acknowledge with thanks the contributions of David Leddington, Christopher Robertson, Ros Ashby and Joe Haydn to this book.

Illustrations

FIGURES

TABLES

TASKS

Important note

From May 1988, all student teachers seeking to gain Qualified Teacher Status (QTS) will be required to demonstrate competence in the areas stipulated by DfEE *Circular 10/97, Standards for the award of Qualified Teacher Status.*

Circular 10/97 replaces the requirements which currently specify the competences for the award of QTS which were laid down by DfE *Circular 9/92,* detailing competences expected of newly qualified teachers.

These documents are centrally important to your training, and define the framework for your induction into the teaching profession. You cannot gain qualified teacher status unless you achieve competence in all the standards specified by *Circular 10/97.*

1997–8 will be a year of transition as training institutions adapt to the change from *Circulars 9/92* to *10/97.* Although there is a substantial degree of overlap between the two documents, there are also significant differences in structure and detail, and there are some requirements which are new.

It is worth drawing attention to an extract from page 2 of the *10/97* standards:

> Professionalism . . . implies more than meeting a series of discrete standards. It is necessary to consider the standards as a whole to appreciate the creativity, commitment, energy and enthusiasm which teaching demands, and the intellectual and managerial skills required of the effective professional.

In view of the importance of the transition from *Circular 9/92,* to *Circular 10/97, Standards for the award of Qualified Teacher Status, Circular 10/97* is attached as an appendix to this book, with permission from the DfEE.

1 Introduction

Almost every person who reads this book will have studied history as a school subject in some shape or form. Most will have encountered more than one history teacher and will be aware of the difference the teacher can make to the experience of school history. In some hands, school history can seem a desiccated and stultifying subject, of dubious relevance and little clear purpose; in others it can seem inspirational and immensely rewarding. The aim of this book is to provide practical guidance in preparing to become a history teacher, and insight into the factors which will enable you to teach history effectively, and in a way which elicits the interest and enthusiasm of pupils. Most people acknowledge that although subject knowledge is important, it is not the only factor involved in being a good history teacher. There is no *necessary* correlation between your prowess as an academic historian and your effectiveness in teaching history to children, although it is difficult to envisage how to teach history without a reasonable base of subject knowledge. Good subject knowledge is a necessary, but not sufficient, prerequisite for effective teaching. Having degree level knowledge of the English Civil War does not in itself guarantee that you will be able to teach it in a way that makes sense to 12-year-olds.

What are the other factors involved in teaching history, and how are the skills involved best acquired? There are differing views as to what are the essentials of good history teaching. One school of thought has argued that the primary duty of the history teacher is to transmit to pupils a knowledge and understanding of the past; others have argued that it is the process of learning which is important, rather than the content of what is learnt, and that 'Education is what remains when we have forgotten all that we have been taught' (Savile, quoted in Noble, 1995).

FRAMEWORKS

Whichever of these positions you incline to, it is important to remember that although you will have a substantial degree of latitude in the way in which you approach the teaching of history in the secondary school, you are not a completely free agent, and that there are frameworks in place which you must take account of if you are teaching history in a state school in England or Wales. Perhaps the most important of these is the National Curriculum for history. In spite of concerns that a National Curriculum would significantly erode the professional autonomy of history teachers (Phillips, 1991), it should be remembered that the National Curriculum is a framework for the teaching of history, not a strait-jacket (see Jenkins and Brickley, 1992; Bennett and Steele, 1995). Although not all history teachers would agree with Nichol's description of the revised National Curriculum for history as a 'flexible, user-friendly beast that you should feel able to mould and train to how you and your colleagues feel history should be taught and learned' (Nichol, 1995), most would agree that it leaves room for (and requires) initiative, imagination and interpretation, in order to teach it effectively.

We are aware that you will be preparing to be a history teacher in different situations and contexts. We have tried to make the content of this book relevant to all student teachers of history, but when talking about the statutory requirements for history have, for ease of reference, referred to the National Curriculum Orders for England and Wales. Those of you who are subject to other regulations should still find that much of what is said is of relevance.

Another essential document in your initial teacher education (ITE) course is the framework of teaching competences laid down by DfEE *Circular 10/97* (DfEE, 1997). Unless you have developed to competence in the four key areas of teaching expertise specified by this circular, it will not be considered appropriate to unleash you on future generations of pupils. The standards laid down by *Circular 10/97* are at the heart of the development of teaching competence, and you should refer to them regularly throughout your course, remembering that in terms of all these competences, there is a continuum between complete ignorance and inadequacy on the one hand, and the (in practice unattainable) mastery of a teaching competence on the other. Part of your professionalism should be to aspire to the highest standards possible in all aspects of history teaching, and to make as much progress as possible towards expert levels of competence, as a student teacher, and throughout your professional career.

Another important framework involved in your development as a history teacher will be the schools and the history departments which you work with during the course of your ITE. History departments are organic and co-operative enterprises, which have a collective responsibility for delivering the history curriculum effectively, and for contributing to whole school policies. You will have to harness your own talents and ideas to those of the department you work in, so as to optimise the quality of experience for you, the department, and the pupils in your care. At its best, it can be a mutually enriching and positive experience for both the department and for the student teacher, but it is not invariably thus, and you will need to deploy personal and professional qualities in addition to technical competence in the classroom.

PERSONAL AND PROFESSIONAL QUALITIES AND THE DEVELOPMENT OF TEACHING COMPETENCE

Very few history student teachers will start their course with expert levels of proficiency and knowledge of all aspects of their subject, and in all aspects of teaching. Most will have some knowledge and experience in certain areas, but will be novices in other aspects of subject knowledge and teaching expertise. Acquiring expertise and teaching proficiency is not just a matter of being instructed into a body of professional knowledge, it requires the application of personal qualities, such as perseverance, resilience, initiative, determination and, perhaps above all, a willingness to learn. In addition to the obvious attributes of professional integrity, reliability, conscientiousness and commitment to the welfare of the pupils in your care, you will need to exercise qualities of adaptability, tact, and a willingness to make the best of whatever situation and circumstances you find yourself in. As a student teacher, you should always work within the aims, policies and practices of the department and the school you are a guest in. An important part of preparing to be a teacher is learning to work as part of a team, and 'fitting in' so that you are in effect a member of the history department, doing your best to make a full contribution to the work of the department in exchange for the time, care and guidance you receive. The relationship should be a symbiotic one, where the student teacher contributes time, energy, imagination and initiative in terms of developing resources, helping with visits, fieldwork, schemes of work, and display work, in exchange for the support and advice which the history department provides. There are many difficult continuums involved in mentoring – the changing balance between pressure and support, encouragement and criticism, direction and freedom to experiment – as your competence and confidence develops. Your task, as a student teacher, is to make the best use of all the resources and support available. This sometimes means reconciling conflicting views and advice as to best practice, and will test your skills of tact and diplomacy, as well as your ability to be 'a good learner'.

HOW DO YOU GET BETTER AT TEACHING HISTORY?

The following are all areas of experience which you will encounter in the course of your ITE. Which do you feel will be most influential in enabling you to develop your teaching competences?

- 'Doing it': your own experience of teaching history in the classroom.
- 'Observing it': watching experienced and accomplished teachers teaching their history lessons.
- Advice: comments from, and conversations with, your history mentor, and/or course tutors.
- Teaching sessions: formal seminars, lectures or workshops either in school or at your higher education (H/E) institution.
- Reading: either prescribed reading, reading books like this, reading for assignments or casual reading of the *Times Educational Supplement* or articles in the newspapers.
- 'Talking about it': with fellow history trainees, in school, at your H/E institution or socially.

All of these experiences *might* make a contribution to the development of your competence as a classroom teacher, but the extent to which they are helpful depends on your response to them. It is important to consider that the process of becoming a history teacher is not purely aggregative, in that the more you do of all the above things the better you will become. One theory which has been influential in teacher education in recent years is that of the 'reflective practitioner' (Schon, 1983). This rests on the proposition that gains in competence and understanding are at least to some extent influenced by the quality of thinking and learning which accompanies the activities undertaken by the student teacher. At its most simple, this encompasses the cliché that 'A mistake is not a mistake as long as you learn from it', and the idea that you must develop the skill of profiting from experiences by reflecting on them and attempting to distil the benefits which might be derived from them into what Labbett has termed 'Principles of Procedure' (Labbett, 1996) for future occasions: what have I learnt from this, what would I do differently next time, how will this affect the way I operate in future? In Labbett's words, 'How have I transformed these experiences into practical suggestions to myself, when planning my teaching during first teaching practice?' It is possible that the comparative utility of these experiences will fluctuate in the course of your development as a history teacher, and that reading about teaching history, for instance, is more helpful when you can place the ideas and suggestions it contains in the context of classroom experience. What is crucial, however, is Labbett's contention that you need to be able to transform reading about educational matters into proposals to inform and test out in your subsequent teaching.

It should be stressed that the idea of the 'reflective practitioner' is only one model about how to develop competence as a teacher, albeit one which has been influential in recent years. Others maintain that the craft of the history teacher is best acquired by the apprenticeship model, of learning it 'on the job', or that academic historians are best placed to deliver the enthusiasm for subject and expert subject knowledge which are at the heart of good history teaching (Lawlor, 1996). As with all theories concerned with education, it is important to be aware that there are usually differing theories and schools of thought as to how education is most effectively delivered, and that these theories need to be tested against your own experience to see which ones appear to be most valid or helpful. Teaching is not like bricklaying, plumbing or learning to play a technically correct backhand drop shot on a squash court; there is no single way of doing it which will work best for all pupils, for all classes, in all schools. There are different views on why history should be taught in schools and how to teach it most effectively, and although teachers retain the ultimate control of how history is taught in the classroom, it is part of their responsibility to be aware of the range of views on why and how history might be taught.

HOW TO USE THIS BOOK

The book is set out in a way which attempts to provide a pragmatic introduction to teaching history in the secondary classroom. An important element of this is the bringing together of theory and practice, so that you are aware of some of the current thinking, problems and differing views on aspects of history teaching, and can relate them to the situations you will encounter in your classroom practice, whether as teacher or observer. The text is also interspersed with tasks or suggestions for points to discuss or reflect on with mentors or fellow student teachers. Where the tasks ask you to engage in activities which impinge upon other people, whether it be structured observation or asking for information, it is important that you first seek the permission of the staff concerned.

The book also provides examples of the sort of activities which might be attempted in your practical teaching. They do not come with a guarantee that they will work perfectly with all teaching groups, and you may well want to amend, adapt or discard them from your teaching repertoire in the light of your experience. Whilst you should feel free to experiment with some of these suggestions, or variations on them, you must remember that in the long term you have got to develop your own ideas for planning for learning in history. Student teachers often find that it takes an inordinate amount of time to plan lessons in the early stages of school experience. There is an understandable temptation to use the resources which have already been developed by the department you are working in, or some of the ideas in this book. There is nothing wrong with this in the short term, and, in a sense, all history teachers have to be 'scavengers' for ideas, materials and activities. What is important is that you progress towards using your own ideas, or adapting some of the ideas you encounter in this book to other historical contexts, or developing extensions and variations to these suggestions and examples. Your short term 'want' is sometimes anything that will get you through Friday afternoon with 9Z; your long term 'need' is to be able to function independently, in generating your own ideas for effective teaching and learning in history. As a general point of professional integrity or etiquette, if you are discussing your use of someone else's ideas or resources, you should acknowledge their provenance.

WHAT DO WE MEAN BY EFFECTIVE LEARNING IN HISTORY?

If you are reading this book, it is presumably your intention to devote at least some of your professional life to teaching history. If you have made this decision you will clearly want to do it well, in a way that will be of maximum benefit to the pupils in your care. The following propositions (and they are propositions, not statements of fact) underpin the content of this book:

There is more to teaching history than simply possessing expert levels of subject knowledge

One of the main challenges of ITE is developing the art of transforming your subject knowledge into effective learning experiences for pupils. There is such a thing as 'pedagogy' – the science of teaching – and it is as important to develop expertise in this as to possess and develop your subject knowledge of the National Curriculum for history. In the words of Jacqui Dean, 'pedagogical content knowledge includes knowledge both of how children learn and of a range of teaching strategies; in short, the teacher's craft knowledge of how to teach . . . History teaching thus involves craft knowledge which is underpinned by academic subject knowledge and shaped by the teacher's concept of the nature of the discipline' (Dean, 1995).

It is helpful for both teacher and pupils to have an understanding of history as a discipline, as well as a body of knowledge

If the study of history is to be of maximum benefit to pupils, it is important that there is a shared understanding of what 'history' is. If pupils are to make sense of the past it is helpful if they understand why history is important and what are we dealing with when we study the past. What is the nature and status of the body of 'knowledge' which is the raw material of history lessons? Although many undergraduate history courses now include elements of historiography, not all history graduates can confidently answer the question, 'What is a fact?', or are familiar with the distinction which is sometimes made between 'substantive' and 'second-order' concepts. If the history teacher is quite clear in his or her own mind about the nature of the discipline, there is more chance that the pupils will have a sound understanding of what they are working with in the history classroom. Although there are those who argue that there has been a tendency to undervalue the importance of pupils' acquiring knowledge of the past, it would seem reasonable to suggest that they should also become acquainted with some of the rules of procedure of the discipline of history.

There are differing views on why and how history should be taught to children

It is your responsibility to be aware of the National Curriculum (or other appropriate) documentation pertaining to history, and the general debate over the purposes of school history over the past decade or so. It can be immensely helpful to keep this debate in mind as you teach history in the classroom. As the non-statutory guidance to the original National Curriculum for history stated, 'a strong sense of *why* history is being taught should pervade all curriculum planning, influencing the selection of content and methods of teaching' (NCC, 1991) One of the most common mistakes made by student teachers when faced with unfamiliar or intractable areas of content is to resort to treating the topic as a slab of the past to be transmitted to pupils 'neat' or in simplistic form, without thinking about what questions it poses, or why it might be helpful to pupils to know about this morsel of the past.

It is helpful to know something about how children learn

Just because you've taught it doesn't mean that they've learnt it. The QED documentary *Simple Minds* demonstrated that in many cases fewer pupils understood a topic after the teacher had taught it than before it was taught – teaching can actually damage pupils' minds. If we decide that something is worth teaching, it is worth spending some time thinking about how to teach it effectively. There is a body of research evidence which gives us some ideas and suggestions about achieving this. It would be churlish to disregard this source of help. Pupils will arrive at your lessons with strongly rooted ideas and preconceptions about many aspects of how the world (including the past) operates. It is important that you try to understand and take account of pupils' preconceptions and ways of thinking if you are to move them on to more sophisticated and powerful ways of understanding both the past and the present. Without taking their understandings into account in your teaching, you may well leave their misconceptions undisturbed.

An important element of preparing to become a history teacher is the attempt to bring together theory and practice

'Theory' might equally be regarded as *ideas* about history teaching. Isaac Newton once said, 'If I have been able to see further than others, it is because I have been able to stand on the shoulders of giants.' Even the most accomplished and inspirational history mentors will have augmented their teaching repertoire with things they have read about, as well as things that have evolved out of their own practice. Theories about how to teach history effectively constitute a potentially important resource in your development as a history teacher. The trouble with theories is that there are different ones, they don't always work, and sometimes they contradict each other. This doesn't mean that they are not worth bothering with. Millions of words have been written about teaching history. Some of them will be helpful and will give you insight, understanding and ideas to improve your teaching. Theories that do not seem to be of use can be discarded.

It is helpful if pupils can be engaged in the process of learning

It has been claimed that the attempt to engage pupils in 'active learning' has been at the expense of academic rigour, and has led to meretricious activities which children might find enjoyable (for instance poster work) but which do little to enhance their understanding of the past. Whilst accepting that there might be times when this is true, as a general rule there is more chance of real gains in learning where pupils are interested and motivated to learn. Successful history teaching depends in part on the ability of the teacher to present the past in a way which makes the pupils want to find out about the past. In the words of Burston, 'The problem for historians and the history teacher, is how to demonstrate the relevance of history to the present in a sufficiently convincing manner to gain the interest of the pupils' (Burston and Green, 1962).

This is not to suggest that history needs to be reduced to constant game playing, poster drawing and group work. 'Engagement' in the process of learning history can be simply listening to the teacher's exposition, and thinking about the past. James Schick claims that in the United States students often express a preference for lectures over other types of class, 'They want the teacher to tell them what's important, to select appropriate facts, to focus on the important issues. They want the teacher to provide all the answers . . . This low-stress arrangement puts as much burden as possible on the teacher and demands little intellectual growth by students. As teachers of history, we must not only revere truth, honour courage, and smash icons, we must require our students to do the same. We must not abet students' intellectual passivity . . . In education, the vital interaction should take place in the student's mind. Without this the potential for learning diminishes significantly. No teaching has occurred if students do not understand' (Schick, 1995).

History in school can be a dispiriting and seemingly pointless experience for the pupils on whom it is inflicted. A recent survey of 10,000 pupils by Barber found that 70 per cent regularly counted the minutes to the end of the lesson (Barber, 1994). But history can also be taught to pupils in a way which gives them knowledge and understanding of the past, insight into some of the most important and difficult questions of human existence, and in addition gives them other educational skills and an enthusiasm to pursue the subject beyond year 9. The aim of this book is to provide practical guidance, structure and ideas for your induction into the profession, and help towards teaching history in a way which will be rewarding and fulfilling for you and your pupils. Effective teaching is not just 'common sense', and to regard it as such is to undervalue the skill and professional expertise of experienced teachers; teaching is a complex and difficult activity. You will be exceptional if you manage to develop to expert levels of competence in all facets of history teaching in the course of your training, but you will hopefully witness expert levels of practice which will make you aware of levels to aspire to. This book can hope to do no more than serve as an introduction, which will assist in providing a sound foundation for your further development as a history teacher. It is because it is difficult that it is also interesting, rewarding and worthwhile.

2 The place of history in the school curriculum

INTRODUCTION

If you are going to dedicate your professional life to becoming a teacher, you ought to be able to justify the worth of your subject's place on the school timetable. The debate on whether or nor to include history on the school curriculum has been both controversial and wide-ranging in recent years, not least because the subject's very relevance has been repeatedly called into question. In 1968, Mary Price's prophetic article, 'History in Danger', set the scene for this ongoing debate largely by drawing attention to the lack of interest pupils were showing in the subject. She was severely critical of the insularity of the emphasis on British history and of the didactic teaching methods which she described as repelling pupil interest and endangering the continued existence of the subject. Price claimed that history teachers had singularly failed to justify or provide a sufficient rationale for the subject's place on the curriculum; that as a result the aims of school history had become irrelevant to a considerable number of pupils and that its future was being increasingly questioned by a wider audience. There was a real danger, she claimed, 'of history disappearing from the timetable as a subject in its own right'. By condemning the relevance of current history syllabuses and the way they were taught Price fuelled the debate among history teachers and called on them to take action in urgently addressing the issues which were responsible for the possible demise of history teaching in schools.

Many of the issues which Price detailed in the late 1960s are still of concern to history teachers and they continue to surround the debate about the nature and purpose of history teaching in schools. Although the original National Curriculum conferred on history the status of a core subject which was to be compulsory to the age of 16 in state schools, a succession of revisions and amendments has meant that history is no longer a compulsory subject post-14, and that once more it is having to justify its place on the curriculum and compete to attract post-year 9 pupils. There have been significant developments in history teaching and learning methods, and a considerable number of innovations and changes in the areas of syllabuses and educational technologies, all of which have impacted on pupils' learning in the history classroom. It is important therefore that you, as a student teacher of history, are aware of these issues and developments and that you acquire the understanding, ability and skills to participate in the professional debate regarding the future of the subject in schools – a debate which has not ceased with the passing of the Education Reform Act of 1988, the formulation of a National Curriculum for history, and the subsequent revision of the original statutory orders in the light of the Dearing Review (Dearing, 1994). The debate on the place and function of history in the school curriculum has become a public one, with over a thousand articles in the national press focusing on why and how history should be taught in schools. You should be aware of this debate, and you should have a clear sense of *why* you are teaching history, and what you hope to achieve through the study of the past, if you are to teach history successfully.

OBJECTIVES

At the end of this chapter you should be able to participate in the ongoing debate about the place of history in the school curriculum and have a sound grasp of the evolution of the present National Curriculum for history through:

* an understanding of the fundamental issues surrounding the introduction of history in the National Curriculum and their implications for the structure and content of school history;
* a rationale for the teaching and learning of history which provides a theoretical basis for its continuing place in schools;
* the development of a critical perspective on the teaching and learning of history within current developments, policies, practices and debates;
* an awareness that there are differing views as to why and how history should be taught in schools.

DIFFERING VIEWS ON THE PURPOSE OF SCHOOL HISTORY

The decision to implement a National Curriculum for history brought about several attempts in recent years to summarise the aims of school history (DES, 1988; NCC, 1991). At one level, these lists were generally uncontroversial, and gained tacit acceptance at least within the teaching profession. The public debate which was unleashed by the decision to introduce a National Curriculum for history did however make it clear that once one got beyond very general statements of aims there were very differing views on what historical content should be taught, and which of the aims of school history were most important. Successive Prime Ministers and Secretaries of State for Education made pronouncements on school history, and there were almost annual lead editorials in *The Times* and many other national newspapers. The national debate on school history, something of a 'Cinderella' subject in the 1970s, served the purpose of raising the profile of the subject; at least it seemed that there was a consensus that history was very important, and that the way in which it was taught would have a significant bearing on the sort of citizens who would emerge from schools.

The debate also raised the question of the connection between the uses of history in general, and history in schools. Marwick (1984) pointed out that 'It is only through a sense of history that communities establish their identity, orientate themselves, understand their relationship to the past and to other communities and societies. Without a knowledge of history we, and our communities, would be utterly adrift on an endless and featureless sea of time.' Without a study of history we would have no sense of context or identity and no sense of progress. Implicit in Marwick's statement is the reality that as the record of the human past is so vast, we cannot learn everything about it, and we must therefore make a selection from the past. The purpose of history is to record those things which have been selected as important in giving us a sense of identity and context. The word 'select' is crucial, since the history curriculum in schools is about selecting those things which, to those doing the selecting, are important. In the words of Tate, 'A fundamental purpose of the school curriculum is to transmit an appreciation of and commitment to the best of the culture we have inherited' (Tate, 1996); or as Woodhead put it, 'I see our task much more in initiating young people into the best that has been thought and said' (Woodhead, 1996). It is at this point – when the business of school history is seen to be one of cultural transmission – that the difficulties in achieving consensus on school history becomes more apparent. Who selects? What are their motives? Are they promoting any particular ideology, explicitly or covertly? Is there any significance in those topics which are not selected? What criteria are used for the selection of content? These are questions which you need to continually ask and assess in your career as a history teacher. The question of who validates the history taught in schools is one of your central concerns as a professional and this has become more acute for you with the introduction of the National Curriculum. You need to be continually aware of the different rationale for the selection of history content and also remind yourself of the 1988 DES discussion paper, *History from 5–16*, which says that 'the content of history courses has to be continually re-assessed and recast'. Debate about history content is far from ended and the National Curriculum should not be viewed by you as a strait-jacket on such a debate. Slater (1989) has pointed out that until recently, the selection from the culture that formed the basis of school history was 'an inherited consensus, based largely on hidden assumptions, rarely identified, let alone publically debated'. He parodied (but with a degree of accuracy) school history as,

> largely British, or rather Southern English; Celts looked in to starve, emigrate or rebel, the North to invent looms or work in mills; abroad was of interest once it was part of the Empire; foreigners were either, sensibly, allies, or, rightly, defeated. Skills – did we even use the word? – were mainly those of recalling accepted facts about famous dead Englishmen, and communicated in a very eccentric literary form, the examination-length essay.

(Slater, 1989)

In addition to the concerns of Price (1968), developments in academic history also percolated through to school level, with the idea of a range of histories, rather than one grand historical narrative, including 'history from below', women's history, and the history of minority cultures. Discussion of what should be essential elements of a National Curriculum for history produced very different ideas as to definitive content. An idea of the scale of these differences can be gained from comparing Pankhania's suggestions in *Liberating the National History Curriculum* (Pankhania, 1994), featuring the oppression of Ireland, the oppression of the Palestinians, the oppression of the native peoples of North America, the oppression of slaves, oppression by the British Empire . . ., with the essentials stipulated by Conquest:

> an educated man must have a certain minimum of general knowledge. Even if he knows very little about science and cannot add or subtract, he must have heard of Mendel and Kepler. Even if he is tone deaf, he must know something about Debussy and Verdi, even if he is a pure sociologist, he must be aware of Circe and the Minotaur, of Kant and Montaigne, of Titus Oates and Tiberius Gracchus.

(Conquest, 1969)

Somewhere between these views was the concern that it would be helpful to those who had to teach history in the secondary classroom, sometimes to pupils who were not devoted scholars or persuaded of the utility or relevance of school history, if the content could bear in mind the extent to which it would be likely to engage pupils in the enthusiastic and committed pursuit of history. Haydn (1992a) pointed out that 'many pupils in comprehensive schools have a prag- matic and instrumental approach to education and a degree of resistance or indifference to some of the more arcane aspects of history . . . interest, relevance and accessibility are the *sine qua non* of teaching history in ordinary schools'. This echoes the concerns expressed in the HMI 1985 discussion paper which stated that 'skills are unlikely to be acquired . . . unless they are related to content that has some inherent interest and appears to relate to the lives of the pupils' (HMI, 1985).

Neither does the belief that history should prepare pupils for citizenship and attempt to promote desirable values and attitudes provide an obvious area for consensus. Not everyone accepts the values which used to underpin the purposes of school history, when its prime aim was seen as providing the moral example described by Willis Bund in 1908:

> to bring before the children the lives and work of English people who
> served God in church and state, to show that they did this by courage,
> endurance and self-sacrifice, that as a result the British Empire was
> founded and extended, and that it behoved every child to emulate them.
> (Willis Bund, quoted in Batho, 1986)

Although this paradigm of school history retained some of its influence until well after the Second World War (see Ministry of Education, 1952) its acceptance has diminished and has not been replaced by an alternative orthodoxy.

Another important point to note is the relation between history for academic purposes and history in schools. An explanation of some of the differences between academic and school history is provided by Husbands (1996). It is important that you are aware of these differences if you are to teach history effectively. We teach it not simply as a preparation for the study of history at university – many of your pupils will not go to university or will go to read other subjects – but because some aspects of the subject are useful to pupils in their lives after school. History is both a body of knowledge and a form of knowledge and some of the historian's rules of procedure may aid intelligent decision-making in life beyond the classroom. Some aspects of the discipline will help pupils to cope with the 'spin' which has become a pervasive part of modern life. In the words of HMI,

> A subject that insists on the critical evaluation of evidence . . . and
> encourages the analysis of problems and the communication of ideas,
> not only contributes to pupils' general education, but develops skills and
> perceptions that increase the employability of young people.
> (HMI, 1985)

HISTORY AND THE AFFECTIVE DOMAIN

Whilst Marwick focuses on the academic study of history, principally at university level, your primary concern will be with school history. Even the question of whether school history should concern itself with the affective domain of values and attitudes is open to question. Is school history to tell pupils what to think or to teach them to think for themselves? John White (1994) sees history as equipping pupils to make life choices based on what they know has gone before them. He claims that the central aim of history teaching in schools is to produce rational, autonomous and critical human beings within a liberal democratic society.

History, as a subject in schools, is therefore subordinate to these overwhelming educational goals. Peter Lee *et al.* (1992), in contrast, view the reasons for teaching history in schools as transformative in that: 'The reason for teaching history is not that it changes society, but that it changes pupils, it changes what they see in the world, and how they see it.' History in this view transforms the way pupils think and cannot be seen as subordinate to educational goals but runs parallel with them, contributing its own distinctive goals to education. There is much that is common to these two perspectives on history teaching; in particular both authors would agree on the aim of pupils acquiring a critical approach to the past and of the development of rational powers of thinking. The main area of disagreement is not necessarily the determining of aims but rather Lee's concern that history may end up distorted if it is designed solely to shed light on the present. He rightly warns against the use of pre-packaged history selected for 'short-term "national interest", political ambition or educational fashion' (Lee, 1994). There is a tension here between those who wish to see school history make a contribution to equality of opportunity, and those who argue that if we use history to 'infiltrate children's minds' (Blunkett, 1996) it ceases to be history and becomes propaganda and indoctrination. It is tempting to be seduced by Hill's dictum that 'History properly taught can help men to become critical and humane, just as wrongly taught, it can turn them into bigots and fanatics' (Hill, 1953), but as soon as we start to enter the realm of values and attitudes, and what constitutes history 'properly taught', we encounter the problems of consensus as to which values and attitudes should be inculcated through the study of history. Slater suggests a position somewhere between that of Lee and White when he states that history

> not only helps us to understand the identity of our communities,
> cultures, nations, by knowing something of their past, but also enables
> our loyalties to them to be moderated by informed and responsible
> scepticism. But we cannot expect too much. It cannot guarantee
> tolerance, though it can give it some intellectual weapons. It cannot
> keep open closed minds, although it may sometimes leave a nagging
> grain of doubt in them. Historical thinking is *primarily* mind-opening,
> *not* socialising.
>
> (Slater, 1989)

There continues to be much debate about the aims of school history. It is therefore important that you consider carefully what you hope to achieve in teaching history and be able to answer the questions: Why teach history? What skills or understanding can history equip pupils with that cannot be supplied by other subjects?

TASK 2.1 THE AIMS OF TEACHING HISTORY

As part of your school experience you will be given a history departmental handbook which will contain the stated aims of the history teaching in your school. You will also have a number of opportunities to observe history teaching by qualified teachers in your subject prior to you being responsible for planning and teaching history yourself. In the light of these experiences consider the following aims for how history may be taught:

- History taught for its own sake, because it is interesting in itself and it is a disciplined form of study that will expand each pupil's knowledge base about local, national, and international communities.
- History taught as a means of social control through the transmission of cultural norms and value systems to the next generations – learning the mistakes of the past and largely preserving the status quo.
- History taught to introduce pupils to their heritage through monuments, historic buildings and towns, architecture, museums, and written sources which chronicle the events of the past.
- History taught to develop the skills of the historian, which enriches pupils' educational experience, including the discipline of study and its value in personal development.
- History taught to instil civil pride and patriotism in one's country.
- History taught to promote virtue and awareness of what is right and wrong.

Which of these aims do you find in the department handbook?
Which of these aims did you observe being implemented in practice?
Which of these aims is your current teaching concerned with?
Which, if any, of the above aims of teaching history are problematic for your teaching of history to pupils and why would this be the case?
Describe any difficulty you might have with any of these aims; discuss these issues with your mentor.

TOWARDS A HISTORY NATIONAL CURRICULUM

History in schools, as Price (1968) indicated, was often taught with pupils adopting a passive role, absorbing a body of knowledge or facts from the teacher.

Change came slowly, but grew out of a perception of danger for the survival of the subject. There was real concern that the subject could be subsumed into a general humanities area. The Schools Council History Project was established in the early 1970s and promoted new teaching methods in order to generate more active learning among pupils and placed greater emphasis on the use of resources in the classroom. The Project was designed to encourage understanding of the nature of history and its fundamental concepts. This process of change was very controversial, for it emphasised making history less a matter of facts to be learnt and more a matter of skills to be acquired. The 'New History', as it came to be called, focused on concepts such as evidence, empathy and cause and used primary sources as evidence in a pupil-centred approach. The case for 'new' history was summarised by P. Lee, R. Ashby and A. Dickinson when they commented, in a paper given at the 1993 BERA conference, that 'the most important single driving force was the feeling that in studying history children ought to have to think as well as remember'. Nick Williams (1986), in reviewing the success of the Schools History Project, commented that whilst history had been liberated from 'the transmission of a corpus of information in a linear and chronological framework' it was also true that 'a sense of chronology had been sacrificed', and he acknowledged that this was something that traditional history did much better.

It was clear that the Project had its limitations, primary among which was the price which had to be paid in terms of content coverage in order to accommodate the time-consuming 'in-depth' source-based and active learning enquiries. Criticism began to emerge that history teachers had gone full circle from Price's criticisms in the late 1960s, from an excessive emphasis on content to an inordinate emphasis on process or skills. A *via media* between the content approach of conventional history teaching, which some viewed as unbalanced, and the approaches which accompanied 'New History', which some believed undervalued content and historical knowledge, was needed, especially as the attacks on the 'New History' mounted. Beattie (1987) highlighted two main criticisms from the political right. First, an increase in what was seen as corrosive and insidious moral relativism, and the contention that there were no 'facts' in history any more since empathy, evidence and imagination were to take on greater importance as the pupils themselves search for bias. Second, that the demand for relevance in history was reducing history to current affairs. Some saw the the real problem as being how to create a history curriculum which would pay equal attention to content and process as well as meeting assessment criteria within the time limits set. The fact that the new GCSE examination in 1988 appeared to adopt many aspects of 'new' history served to polarise the debate still further. Other than the stipulation that each exam board should offer at least one exam based on the history of the United Kingdom, and that syllabuses must be of

TASK 2.2 IS THERE A TENSION BETWEEN SKILLS AND CONTENT IN SCHOOL HISTORY?

Do teaching methods have an influence on the balance between skills and content?

Is the idea of a conflict between skills and content a false dichotomy?

Over a period of one week during your school experience record briefly in a diary the following information: the content of each lesson, and the frequency of the various teaching methods in the classroom that you either observe others using or plan and teach yourself. The following list will help you focus your observation:

- Dictation
- Discussion
- Questions and answers
- Group work
- Individual guidance

- Use of textbooks
- Use of worksheets
- Use of audio-visual aids
- Use of original sources as evidence
- Use of 'chalk and talk'

What is the balance between the skills and content of each lesson observed or taught?

What teaching methods emphasise learning facts most?

What teaching methods focus on learning skills most?

Is there a link between teaching methods and the best way to promote either skills-based history or content-based history? Is there a *via media*?

---

sufficient length, range and depth, deal with key issues and be 'coherent and balanced', there was no requirement to teach any particular areas of historical content. It seemed to many to be a denial of the existence or desirability of a historical 'canon' which all pupils should be taught. Sir Keith Joseph, while Secretary of State for Education, made an important public defence of history in schools in a speech to the Historical Association's annual conference in 1984. He strongly advocated the teaching of history to all up to the age of 16, and his speech remains a benchmark for the place of history in the school curriculum. His concluding remarks are interesting in the light of subsequent legislative developments, for he said: 'history, properly taught, justifies its place in the school curriculum by what it does to prepare all pupils for the responsibility of citizenship as well as the demands of employment and the opportunities of leisure'. He outlined the skills and competences peculiar and distinct to history and identified that 'the knowledge, understanding and skills which the study of history can confer are of great value in themselves'. Whilst he placed British history centrally in the scheme of history he did accept the need for sensitivity to the cultural and social diversity found in Britain today. Joseph also pointed to a key difference between the processes of reasoning which might be used in history as opposed to science, when he noted that one of the purposes of school history was to help pupils to 'use their reason as well as their memories, and to develop skills of analysis and criticism in a situation where there cannot be a right answer' (Joseph, 1984). HMI formalised his outline a year later into a specific framework in which secondary schools might develop history schemes of work, detailing targeted aims, objectives and principles (HMI, 1985). Their aims of history varied from the general, 'to understand the values of our society', to the more focused, 'to look for explanations of change in terms of human intentions, beliefs and motives as well as of environmental factors'. The agenda for establishing a History National Curriculum was clearly set in motion.

THE NATIONAL CURRICULUM

The introduction of the National Curriculum in the Education Reform Act 1988 recognised and confirmed history's important place in the secondary school curriculum as a foundation subject. The government, after advice from its history working group (see Slater, 1991), determined that all school pupils until the age of 16 were to be educated with a compulsory programme of study in history. The working group was guided by the statutory requirements laid down by Section One of the Education Reform Act, which stated that schools must ensure a balanced and broadly based curriculum which promotes the spiritual, moral, mental, cultural and physical development of pupils and prepares them for the opportunities, responsibilities and experiences of adult life. The working party was also to develop appropriate attainment targets (i.e. 'the knowledge, skills and understanding which pupils of different abilities and maturities are expected to have'), as well as programmes of study (i.e. 'the matter, skills and processes which are required to be taught to pupils of different abilities and maturities').

The working group's report did not silence the debate about the purpose of school history, as its Interim Report (DES, 1989) stated: 'there exist many, often strongly held and divergent, opinions about school history'. Debate continued and the new powers of the government to specify what should be taught, to whom, when and what should be understood at certain key points in a pupil's education aroused concern about a 'state directed' history curriculum. The fear was that the government could now determine what was worthwhile knowledge and decide what was to be taught by history teachers. It was inevitable that the government's intentions for history teaching would be seriously scrutinised by history teachers. Lee *et al.* (1992) warned that it would be wrong if the 'interests of serious history teaching and the knowledge and experience of professional teachers were overridden by political or social goals of small groups of politically motivated men and women who have given nothing to history teaching in the past', and concluded, 'History is too important to be left to politicians.' Others made the point that many of the influential figures making pronouncements on the sort of history which should be taught in schools operated at a very substantial distance from the classroom, and were not fully aware of problems posed by teaching history in the secondary school, and that their views on what sort of history is suitable for 'ordinary children' were sometimes unrealistic and inappropriate (Haydn, 1992a).

The implementation and subsequent revision of the National Curriculum for history, in itself a history, as noted in Aldrich (1991), Haydn (1996) and Phillips (1996), seemed to bear out the concern that politicians would attempt to control and direct the content and purpose of school history for political purposes.

In a study of the New Right's campaign on the place of history in schools Keith Crawford concluded that the purpose of the National Curriculum is:

> to help produce a particular kind of society by using history education as a vehicle through which to disseminate a specific set of values and beliefs by attempts to control definitions of the past designed to justify political action, promote particular social trends and develop economic doctrines.
>
> (Crawford, 1995)

Has there been an attempt to hijack history in order to try some kind of social engineering by the Right? Both Crawford (1995) and Little (1990) have attempted answers which are worth considering. Haydn (1992b) suggests that both right and left have attempted to use history for their own ends. A look at the details of the History National Curriculum and the response to it helps to shed light on this question, but you will need to read a selection of the literature surrounding the inception and revision of the National Curriculum for history to gain a fuller understanding of the political debate on the purposes of school history, and to dig beneath the comparatively anodyne and uncontroversial list below.

The National Curriculum Working Group's Interim Report (England and Wales) of 1988 specifically identifies and lists nine purposes of school history:

1   To help understand the present in the context of the past.
2   To arouse interest in the past.

3   To help to give pupils a sense of identity.
4   To help give pupils an understanding of their own cultural roots and shared inheritance.
5   To contribute to pupils' knowledge and understanding of other countries and other cultures in the modern world.
6   To train the mind by means of disciplined study.
7   To introduce pupils to the distinctive methodology of historians.
8   To enrich other areas of the curriculum.
9   To prepare pupils for adult life.

These aims encompass the traditional (1 and 6) and White's citizenship approach (4). There are other general skills and abilities for history listed by Coltham and Fines (1971) which are not directly mentioned by the Report, and these include vocabulary acquisition, memorisation, reference skills, comprehension and communication skills. Booth (1990) responded to the Report with dismay at the emphasis on the 'massive' content which he felt would give no time for other ways of learning through field trips, drama, TV, oral history and the like. He predicted that the attempt to cover masses of content would lead to boredom, dissatisfaction, teacher frustration and rebellion against the proposals by teachers and pupils alike. Booth's hopes that content would be curtailed were not heeded when the final report was produced, speaking as it did of the ideals of 'breadth and balance, to bring pupils to independent thought and giving weight to a sense of chronology to achieve an essential framework' (Final Report, 1990). The Dearing revision of the National Curriculum in 1994 confirmed post-1988 erosions of the status of school history which meant that history would only be compulsory to the age of 14 – a significant setback from the high ground of the original National Curriculum – and made a number of modifications to the programmes of study at Key Stage 3 which detailed what children should learn. There were now six study units which comprised:

1   Medieval Realms: Britain 1066–1500.
2   The Making of the United Kingdom: Crown, Parliaments and Peoples 1500–1750.
3   Expansion, Trade and Industry: Britain 1750–1900.
4   The Twentieth-Century World.
5   An Era or Turning Point in European History Before 1914.
6   A Past Non-European Society.

Bracey (1995) noted that the non-European element of the National Curriculum in history was not only limited, but lacked resources and teacher knowledge in its teaching. Some have suggested that whilst working within the History National Curriculum's programmes of study teachers could interpret these to increase the amount of world history. Despite these suggestions John Slater (1991) felt that history teaching in the National Curriculum should be more accurately described as the teaching of British inherited culture, attitudes and traditions. In 1994, it was decided that there should be no further changes to the National Curriculum for the next five years, which means that you will work within the present curriculum framework, at least for your first few years of teaching.

In comparison with the National Curriculum Working Group's Final Report, and the original statutory orders, the DfE's *History in the National Curriculum* of 1995 is a concise non-discursive statement of the history curriculum. The core document for the teaching of history in schools refers to five Key Elements: chronology, range and depth of historical understanding, interpretation of history, historical enquiry, organisation and communication. One of the functions of the Key Elements is to redefine the relationship between skills and content, and they make it clear that there is an interdependency between the two if there is to be effective teaching of history.

THE NATIONAL CURRICULUM FOR HISTORY

As a student teacher you need to develop and demonstrate competence and a clear understanding of the aims of the teaching and learning of history and of the subject's place in the school curriculum. You need to possess a sound grasp of the National Curriculum documentation which relates to history teaching, particularly the revised orders, *History in the National Curriculum* (DfE, 1995). During school experience you will need to discuss with your mentor the department's

---

TASK 2.3 JUSTIFYING HISTORY TO PUPILS AND PARENTS

Your placement school is organising a year 9 options evening for pupils and parents, and you have been asked to help with a display which points out the benefits of taking history. How would you present the case for school history to a parent whose child 'enjoyed history but didn't think it would be very useful'.

You have urged on a year 10 class the importance of arguing and debating issues in history in class. A pupil states that 'history is a waste of time because it won't help to get you a job when you leave'. What would you say in response to this question? Would you use the same arguments as with the parent or present a different justification for taking history beyond Key Stage 3?

TASK 2.4 AUDITING AND DEVELOPING YOUR SUBJECT KNOWLEDGE

When you have acquired a sound grasp of the National Curriculum, and the main examination options at GCSE and A level, conduct a brief audit of your subject knowledge, noting down any areas of weakness. Keep a record of the steps you make to develop your subject knowledge. This need not be reading and/or note taking, and might include familiarisation with history CD-ROMs, films, audiotapes and television programmes such as *Timewatch* and *The People's Century*. Try to be systematic about this monitoring process and keep a record in such a way as to be able to demonstrate to an external examiner that you have been taking action to develop, enhance and update your subject knowledge.

Read carefully through the requirements of Key Stage 1 and Key Stage 2 history. If you were asked a question at interview about what history pupils were likely to have covered at primary school, could you give a confident and well informed answer?

---

policy and documentation which attempts to interpret the National Curriculum for history, and identify how the key aims in learning/teaching history are reflected in that documentation. You will generally find that history teachers do have views on the purposes of school history which influence the ways in which they teach their subject. There will usually be a variety of the aims enunciated on pages 21–2 which are discernible, but different teachers and departments will see some purposes as more important than others.

HISTORY BEYOND 14

A 1995 comparison of the pupil numbers taking the main subjects at GCSE illustrates history's problem at post-14. English and mathematics had over 520,000 entries each, whilst history finished eighth out of fifteen with under 224,000 entries – some 25,000 behind geography. If under half the number of pupils entering English and mathematics enter history, it is fair to assume that under half the number of pupils study history beyond the age of 14. Further pressure was placed on the subject with the introduction of vocational qualifications, which provided an alternative to GCSEs and A levels. These have already attracted over 25 per cent of those in post-16 education, and credits are also being gained towards these qualifications by 14- to 16-year-olds. History has not been in the vanguard of new developments in GNVQ, and history's contribution to vocational training is at the moment limited and uncertain. Whilst the majority of schools continue to require pupils to choose a humanities option at post-14 the crucial need for history teachers is to provide arguments about history's contribution to the whole curriculum. As Carol White (1996) argues, history must fit into the school's principles and aims, and if these aims include 'the development of tolerance, understanding of other cultures and societies, the promotion of citizenship and understanding of social responsibility then the place of history cannot be denied'. History can also be taught in such a way as to make a massive contribution to the 'Key Skills' which have emerged as one of the most important outcomes of the Dearing Review (1994). History can be taught in a way that encourages autonomous learning, the ability to work as part of a team, the ability to solve problems posed by the teacher, the development of communications skills, both oral and written, and proficiency in IT. It is important that you develop the ability to make clear to pupils the purposes of school history, and to persuade them that the study of history is useful, worthwhile and interesting. Some history teachers are able to convince pupils that in studying history they are addressing some of the most important and difficult questions of human existence. If you can ensure that you keep the purposes of school history clearly in mind in your teaching, you will be more likely to secure the positive engagement in learning that makes teaching a pleasure rather than a chore.

In the context of vocational qualifications and the interests and choices made by post-14 pupils, two central questions for the future well-being of school history in this age range seem pertinent here. First, does history have 'transferable skills'? And second, can history provide pupils with 'interest, relevance and accessibility'? To the first question it can be argued that history does indeed have 'transferable skills' which is what Coltham and Fines (1971) attempted to classify in producing their general skills in history. White (1996) expands on these general skills within the new vocational context when she suggests that the core skills, communication, literacy and vocabulary in GNVQs offer history teachers considerable potential in their planning and delivery.

There is some evidence that teachers have adopted creative approaches to National Curriculum history. Clare Jenkins (1995) claims that whilst working within the National Curriculum, but crucially adopting a GNVQ approach, she was able to motivate less able pupils and revitalise the teaching and learning of history. At GCSE level, she claims that her pupils are not focused on GCSE standards, but on 'skills transferable and valued in adult life'. This may not be a convincing rationale in the eyes of all schools, concerned as they must be with league tables and performance indicators through examinations results. There is also in this approach a danger that it may be divisive: conventional history for the more able and a 'vocational type approach' with its attempt to provide access to the history curriculum to a broader pupil base. Nevertheless, as Slater (1995) says, the National Curriculum does specifically promote enquiry and analysis, and he argues that history teachers should encourage their pupils to be critical of all views and sources they encounter in the subject. These skills, he believes, will be used by pupils long after they have left education and forgotten most of their knowledge of academic history. The academic study of history at A level in schools continues to improve its position both in numbers taking the examination and in the innovative methods used in teaching and examining it. Many history A level syllabuses have been transformed in recent years through course work, personal study and source-based questions. The position of history beyond 16 however, still remains problematic and uncertain, with the threat to many of the innovatory syllabuses and course structures which many teachers have found to be helpful in encouraging pupils to engage with and value the subject.

TASK 2.5 HISTORY BEYOND 14

When you qualify as a history teacher you will be expected to teach history beyond the age of 14. It is therefore important that you observe a number of examination classes in years 10 and 11 and eventually have the opportunity within your placement school to teach these years. You need to familiarise yourself with the syllabuses and teaching methods in your placement school as well as syllabuses used in other schools.

Compile a list of the skills which you have observed being displayed in post-Key Stage 3 history lessons which might be said to be equipping pupils for 'adult life'. List the methods used in post-14 history teaching in your placement school. List the opportunities that you have observed, experienced or discussed in your placement school for cross-curricular approaches to history.

Your head of history in your placement school wishes to investigate the possibility of the department contributing to the school's GNVQ programme, asking you to prepare a short briefing paper for a department meeting on what GNVQs are and what, if anything, history could contribute to their promotion within the school.

It should be apparent that history can make a contribution to the school curriculum in several ways, including the development of 'key' or general educational skills and cross-curricular skills. The study of history could be a vehicle to develop such skills, but the question arises: Why do this through the study of history? It does not justify a study of history, and history would simply become a secondary consideration within this vocational context. What is unique to history is its function of assessing and evaluating the record of human beings through time, and as such it provides insight into many of the situations and decisions which pupils will confront in their lives after school. In the words of HMI, history is valuable because of

> the historian's insistence that the judgements of individuals and groups should be based on evidence, and on constant opportunities to under-stand the predicaments and attitudes of other people. History helps its students living in an open society to decide between alternative attitudes, courses of action with some degree of knowledge, understanding and competence.
>
> (HMI, 1985)

Contrary to the assertions of the tabloid press, there are few history teachers who do not believe that it is important for pupils to develop knowledge and understanding of the past. Many also believe that it can be helpful if this is complemented by an understanding of the nature of history as a form of knowl-edge, and an academic discipline. If you think about the events of the twentieth century, the era of spin doctors, media manipulation, soundbite politics and information overload,

> it does require some little imagination to realise what the consequences will be of not educating our children to sort out the differences between essential and non-essential information, raw fact, prejudice, half-truth and untruth, so that they know when they are being manipulated, by whom, and for what purpose.
>
> (Longworth, 1981)

SUMMARY AND KEY POINTS

You will have seen that the position of history in the school curriculum has over the last thirty years been characterised by painful self-analysis and, at times, a defensive posture. History teachers need to be able to articulate a convincing case for the subject's place in the school curriculum, to parents, pupils, and other teachers. The central issues have been a concern with aims, teaching and learning methods and the future position of history, which were all observed by Mary Price as issues in 1968, and here in the 1990s they are substantially the same. The National Curriculum Orders in History have introduced the framework governing curriculum planning, delivery and assessment for history teaching in the context of the secondary school curriculum. In the end it will be your commitment, expertise and persuasiveness as a history teacher, convinced in yourself about the value of history teaching in schools, that will influence pupils to value and commit themselves to history.

FURTHER READING

Department for Education (1995) *History in the National Curriculum*, London, HMSO.
This government publication is essential reading, and you should obtain your own copy.

Husbands, C. (1996) *What is History Teaching: Language, Ideas and Meaning in Learning about the Past*, Buckingham, Open University Press.
Lucid and interesting explanation of key issues and the difference between the purposes of academic and school history.

Little, V. (1990) 'A National Curriculum in History: A Very Contentious Issue', *British Journal of Educational Studies*, Vol. XXXVIII, No. 4, pp. 319–34.
Arguably the shortest and most admirably condensed summary of the influences on the formulation of the original National Curriculum for history.

Skidelsky, R. (1988) 'History as Social Engineering', *Independent*, 1 March.
Perhaps the most formidable critic of the 'new' history.

3 Planning for learning
Learning objectives

INTRODUCTION

Do you have a clear idea, or plan, of what you are trying to achieve, both within a lesson, and in the longer term, over a series of lessons? Why are you telling these children about something that happened hundreds of years ago?

These might sound facile or obvious questions, but the pressures on student teachers, and the myriad of things you are confronted with in your first experiences in the classroom, mean that it is easy to lose sight of the fundamental purposes of teaching children about the past. One of the most common causes of indifferent or unsatisfactory teaching by student teachers is the absence of clearly thought-out learning objectives for pupils.

Under pressure, student teachers sometimes lose sight of the proposition that there may be other factors behind planning for learning in history, in addition to transmitting knowledge of the past and getting over to pupils what happened. If you are worried about whether they will listen, whether they will be interested, whether they will behave, whether you will remember your 'script', the question of learning objectives might (understandably) not be at the forefront of your mind. One of the questions which is sometimes asked of history student teachers (and their pupils) when external examiners or visiting tutors attend a lesson, is 'what are you trying to do, what is the purpose of today's lesson, why are you doing this?' If all you or your pupils can answer is that it is on the syllabus, or that it is part of the National Curriculum, or that it is important that all children know about the wool trade in the fourteenth century (or whatever), you may not be giving adequate consideration to all the factors involved in planning for learning.

If you can manage to maintain a clear sense of direction and purpose to your lesson planning, and an awareness of the breadth of factors involved in planning, this can have a positive influence on many of the other preoccupations which dwell in the minds of student teachers. In the words of Feiman-Nemser and Parker:

> In learning to teach academic content, beginning teachers must learn to think about subject matter from the student's perspective . . . While

subject knowledge is indispensable in teaching, it does not automatically yield ideas about how to represent or present specific content to students.

(Feiman-Nemser and Parker, 1990)

As noted in Chapter 1, graduate level subject knowledge is no guarantee of a successful lesson; if you explain (for instance), the causes of the outbreak of Civil War in 1642 in the same way that you acquired your knowledge of it at 'A'level, or at university, you may as well explain it in a foreign language for all the sense it will make to many 12-year-olds. Subject application (being able to teach effectively) – is as important as subject knowledge – hence its status as one of the five domains of the 9/92 competences (DfE, 1992). The non-statutory guidance for the original National Curriculum for history stated that 'A strong sense of *why* history is being taught should pervade all curriculum planning, influencing the selection of content and methods of teaching' (NCC, 1991). In spite of the revision of the history curriculum, this is still an essential element of planning for learning in history. It is also important to keep in mind that just because pupils are 'on task' and well behaved, it does not guarantee that valuable learning is taking place. You have to beware that you do not 'fill up their days with dull, repetitive tasks that make little or no claim on their intelligence' (Holt, 1982). A clear grasp of the full range of learning objectives which might be relevant to school history can help you to minimise this danger.

TASK 3.1 PROVIDING EVIDENCE OF PLANNING FOR LEARNING

When you are at a stage of your school experience where you have had at least several weeks of planning, teaching and evaluating lessons, look through your teaching experience file (or that of a fellow student teacher with whom you have a healthy 'critical friend' relationship) from the perspective of an external examiner who is visiting the school to assess your competence. To what extent does it provide supporting evidence that the author is able to satisfy the requirements of the 10/97 competences relating to planning for learning? (B2a–e)

OBJECTIVES

At the end of this chapter, you should have:

*   more ideas about how the purposes of school history might interact with the process of lesson planning;

- an awareness of the teaching competences which relate to planning for learning in history;
- an understanding of how the National Curriculum for history can be used to structure learning in history;
- a clearer awareness of the range of learning objectives which can be relevant to the study of history in the secondary school;
- more ideas about how to relate the structure, content and teaching methods of your lessons to learning objectives.

LEARNING OBJECTIVES DERIVING FROM THE PURPOSES OF SCHOOL HISTORY

As Chapter 2 demonstrated, there are very different views on the purposes of school history, and no universally accepted consensus on either why or how it should be taught. How are you to reconcile this divergence of opinion with the suggestion that what you attempt to achieve in your history lessons should bear in mind the purposes of school history? There are few who would argue that the *only* legitimate purpose of school history is to instil knowledge of the past, and although there are different views on emphasis and comparative importance, the fairly uncontroversial list drawn up in the non-statutory guidance for the original National Curriculum for history (NCC, 1991) proved to be acceptable to most history teachers. You should be relating your teaching aims to the purposes enumerated in this list, and to the framework provided by the statutory orders (DfE, 1995). It is also important that you work within the curriculum policies and guidelines of the school and the department you are a part of.

We would suggest that there are two other propositions which you should not lose sight of in planning for learning:

1 Although developing pupils' knowledge of the past is an essential part of school history, it is possible to teach it in such a way that it is also helpful to pupils in other ways.
2 Although developing pupils' knowledge and understanding of the past should be central to planning for learning, more general educational objectives should also be considered if maximum benefit is to be derived from the study of history.

There may be some lessons where the principal aim is to transmit to pupils information about what happened in the past, but if *every lesson* were to have this objective, and this objective alone, this would limit the benefits which might accrue from the study of the past (they are not all going to go on to take history at university), and is there not a danger that it will be difficult to elicit and sustain pupils' enthusiasm, interest and desire to learn if attention is limited to this objective?

So what other objectives might there be? What should student teachers keep in mind when planning schemes of work and individual lessons?

Figure 3.1 attempts to make the point that there is more to think about than simply subject knowledge in putting together a history lesson. The generally accepted purposes of school history enumerated in the non-statutory guidance (NCC, 1991), and by the Historical Association (Historical Association, 1988) embrace both the development of knowledge and understanding of the past, and the development of pupils' understanding of the discipline of history – what history is, and its rules and conventions. This stems from the belief that some aspects of historical method might imbue pupils with 'transferable skills', which will be of use to them in life after school. Thus at the core of the teacher's

Figure 3.1 Tacit lesson objectives

aims are the twin pillars of knowledge and understanding of the past, and understanding of the nature of history – what history is, and what the rules and conventions of the discipline are. These will be considered in detail in subsequent chapters.

Then there are more general educational objectives; you are not just teaching pupils history, you are attempting to develop oral skills, writing skills, listening skills, the ability to record and recall information and deploy it appropriately. In the section on 'Common Requirements', the statutory orders stipulate that every history teacher is also contributing to children's language skills, and should also provide opportunities for pupils to develop and apply their information technology capability in their study of history (DfE, 1995). There are also the 'cross-curricular' areas which obtrude into the study of history; there are times when the study of history sheds light on pupils' economic and industrial awareness, or provides insight into moral and ethical issues, and links into geography or philosophy. During history lessons, pupils might also develop some of the 'Key Skills' which the Dearing Report noted as being essential elements of education for all pupils – numeracy, problem solving, communication skills, IT, team working and 'learning to learn' (Dearing, 1994).

In planning lessons, there are also pragmatic considerations, which must take into account the nature of the pupils who are to be taught. One is the question of *differentiation* – how can the lesson be structured so as to maximise access to learning, and meaningful gains in learning, for all pupils in the teaching group; another is *progression* – giving thought to moving pupils forward in history, to higher levels of understanding, increased knowledge of the past, and more expert levels of accomplishment in skills of analysis, synthesis, selection and evaluation.

There are also what might be termed 'tacit' or non-cognitive considerations or objectives, and although even the most accomplished and experienced history teachers have to take account of them, they loom particularly large in the planning of student teachers. They include considerations such as classroom management: how will I settle the class down?; how will I draw the lesson to a conclusion in an orderly and effective way?; how can I reduce the chances of child X messing around and disrupting the learning of others?

Some of these 'tacit' objectives are a function of the comparative inexperience and limited repertoire of the student teacher. Because you do not as yet possess a vast archive of successful and proven teaching techniques and ideas on all aspects of the National Curriculum for history, there are times when pupil learning has to be balanced against classroom management and 'survival' strategies in your planning. Student teachers and NQTs have at times to devise 'coping strategies' in order to get through lessons as best they can. If student teachers are honest with themselves, there will be times when some of the learning activities are designed more for classroom management purposes than to advancing learning in history. If you have 'the class from hell', on Friday afternoon, a video extract which the class might enjoy, followed by a worksheet which will 'keep their heads down', and 'keep them occupied', might seem an enticing option, and make for a more controlled and effective lesson than a role-play on the Battle of Hastings. Such strategies may well have diminishing returns in terms of their effectiveness. If you become over-reliant on 'anaesthetic', 'this will pass the time' strategies, pupils may well grasp that child-minding is taking the place of learning, and their behaviour and respect for you as a teacher will deteriorate accordingly. One of the central challenges of your training is to progress as rapidly as possible towards consistently purposeful learning for pupils, as your expertise as a history teacher develops, whilst making appropriate use of 'coping strategies' where necessary. There may well be legitimate reasons for not always focusing on the development of historical knowledge, skills and understanding for the whole lesson or series of lessons. Some pupils may be reluctant scholars, who need to be lured into learning history, and will be 'biddable' to learning history if it is presented in an interesting and accessible manner. A common tactic of many history teachers is to try to devise 'enabling' tasks or scripts, which provide an easy way in to learning historical skills and concepts, or an intriguing or entertaining prologue to the 'serious' history which will follow. If your control of the class you are teaching is not secure, you may have to think carefully about what is attempted and opt for 'settling activities' (such as directed activities related to texts, or taking notes from a video extract), which are more conducive to a quiet working atmosphere, rather than 'stirring' activities (such as drama, 'hotseating' or role-play), which are more suited to eliciting the enthusiasm and commitment of pupils actively engaging in 'doing' history. (For a fuller explanation of stirring and settling activities, see MacLennan, 1987.) There are times when you may need to concentrate on developing a calm and purposeful working atmosphere in the classroom, and history learning objectives are influenced (and limited) by this imperative. There is also sometimes a difficult tension between the long-term need to do interesting and stimulating work which will win the pupils over to the study of history, and the short-term agenda of staying within 'the comfort zone', and sticking to a tried and tested 'survival agenda' which is comfortably within your compass. Tempting though this may be at times, you must remember that by the end of your training you want to have as full a repertoire of teaching experience and methods as possible. Progression in learning is just as important for student teachers as for pupils, and one of the reservations about current patterns of teacher education is the tendency of some student teachers to 'plateau' in their learning (OFSTED, 1996).

In addition to there being many things to consider in planning for learning in history, there are also tensions between some of the factors involved. It is important that you think about these tensions, and discuss them with your mentor, if you are to make maximum progress in the course of your training. 'Tacit' lesson objectives rarely feature in student teachers' lesson plans; it might be helpful to acknowledge them if you are to gain insight into the full range of factors influencing planning for learning. The way forward is not to pretend that they don't exist, but to think, talk and discuss how to get beyond tacit lesson objectives.

Tempting though some aspects of these strategies might be, they do not offer a long-term way forward. Not only is such an outlook ethically indefensible – you shouldn't be teaching history if you don't believe in it – but it is unlikely that pupils will not become aware that you are merely passing (or wasting) time rather than teaching anything of value. As one student teacher noted in her observation of such a lesson, 'A number of pupils expressed frustration at being given yet another drawing and colouring in exercise' (extract from student teacher assignment, January 1997). A popular series of history textbooks pre-National Curriculum, the *History Alive* series by Peter Moss (Moss, 1970), contained many pages of easy to copy cartoon diagrams. If used imaginatively, the books could be very useful; if they were used to get pupils to copy the diagrams and cartoons on a regular basis, they would do little to develop children's historical understanding. There may be a justification for using 'low-value' activities which entice reluctant scholars into learning, but only if something educationally worthwhile is to follow. Your aim should be to build up an archive of worthwhile activities, information, questions and problems on an increasingly broad range of historical topics. You cannot construct a comprehensive archive in the first few weeks of teaching practice, and may at times have to resort to 'low-value' activities as a coping strategy because of classroom management or other concerns, but these should be kept to a minimum, and reduced as your competence and confidence develop.

LOW- AND HIGH-VALUE ACTIVITIES IN THE HISTORY CLASSROOM

Heafford's typology of tasks in modern language teaching (Heafford, 1990) illustrates the idea that some pupil activities might be of more value than others in planning for learning. Word searches, copying from the board and reading round the class are regarded as low-value activities, dialogue in the target language, reading silently and 'doing written work of an error-avoiding nature' are cited as activities of high value.

Why do teachers not always use high-value activities? In some instances, it may be due to limitations in teacher competence – no history teacher has a *comprehensive* archive of high-value scripts, questions, problems and tasks for

---

TASK 3.2 CONSIDERING THE VALUE AND USEFULNESS OF CLASSROOM ACTIVITIES

1 Reading can be done in different ways in the classroom. If you want your pupils to read something, it can be done by either:

(a) pupils taking it in turn to read aloud;
(b) you read the passage or extract to the whole class;
(c) you ask the pupils to read the passage in silence;
(d) the pupils read the passage to each other in pairs or small groups.

What might be the advantages and disadvantages of these options, for the teacher, and for the pupils?

2 Drawing on your experiences and observations in history lessons (both as a pupil and a student teacher), draw up a list of other activities which might occur in a history classroom, and consider what they lend themselves to in terms of usefulness (for the teacher) and value (for the pupils). If possible, discuss your views with other student teachers. It might also be helpful to test out your views on the advantages and disadvantages of the various activities in your teaching to see if 'theory' accords with practice.

---

every historical topic, although good history teachers are constantly extending their repertoire of purposeful and valuable activities or explanations. A key point here is that some activities are valuable because they help to develop pupils' knowledge and understanding of the past, and others are useful for other reasons: for settling a boisterous class down, for instance, or devising an 'enabling' task which will introduce a difficult historical concept in an accessible or striking manner. Although it should be central to planning for learning, developing historical understanding is not the only factor which you have to consider when putting together a lesson or series of lessons (see Figure 3.2). It is important to remember that good teachers often use strategies which might be considered 'low-value' very adroitly, and in a way that leads on to positive learning outcomes.

TENSIONS IN PLANNING FOR LEARNING

In addition to the awareness that there are many factors involved in planning for learning, there is the complication that there is sometimes a tension between them. For instance, your needs as a student teacher attempting to broaden your teaching repertoire by experimenting with new teaching methods might conflict with the reality that you are faced with a teaching group over which your control

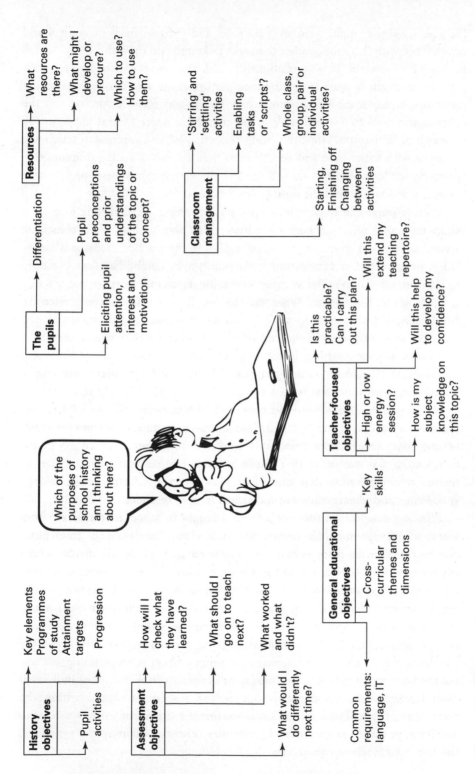

Figure 3.2 Things to think about when putting together a lesson

is tenuous – you might need to 'play safe' and consolidate your control and confidence with this group rather than take risks and end up with a lesson which drifts out of control. If your relationship with the group is poor because they are sick to death of worksheets, drawing pictures, and 'low-value' containment activities, trying something different may be the way forward for you and the pupils. You need to develop skills of judgement in order to find the best way through these tensions. Hopefully, your 'percentages', and sureness of touch will improve with experience and reflection. There are many such continuums in planning for learning, and you will need to deploy perceptiveness, professional integrity and tact to find the right point on them.

Another important tension in planning for learning is reconciling long- and short-term planning. Teachers sometimes think about what would constitute a good next lesson, given the resources available, the teacher's ideas and know-ledge for that topic, and the nature of the pupils to be taught. But they also need to think about planning for learning in the longer term – over a topic, a study unit, a whole Key Stage. What do the pupils need for a comprehensive and coherent education in history? If you were to teach a class right through from the start of year 7 to the end of year 9, what benefits would they have derived from your teaching, in terms of knowledge, understanding, skills and experiences? If teachers do not give some thought to 'curriculum mapping' – within their own subject as well as across subjects – pupils might receive many high quality individual lessons but have studied history in a way which has only bestowed a fraction of the potential benefits which might accrue from the study of the past. One of the reasons behind the formulation of the National Curriculum was the belief that pupils needed a broad and balanced diet of history teaching, rather than one which was driven by the particular talents, specialisms and idiosyncrasies of individual history teachers.

Thus some aspects of the way history is taught in school might derive from whole school planning – the history department may have been the curriculum area assigned main responsibility for ensuring that all pupils in the school experience computer-based data handling activities. The department as a whole will work out how to deliver the National Curriculum for history most effectively, which optional study units to teach, and whether to teach other elements of history as well. Long-term departmental planning will also encompass issues such as progression, differentiation, coherence, continuity, assessment, and the provision of a wide range of learning experiences. Short-term planning, includ-ing the planning of individual lessons, is still generally in the hands of individual class teachers, who decide on resources and teaching methods within the framework of school policies and the department's scheme of work. You have to work within these parameters and guidelines, whilst developing the range and levels of your teaching competence.

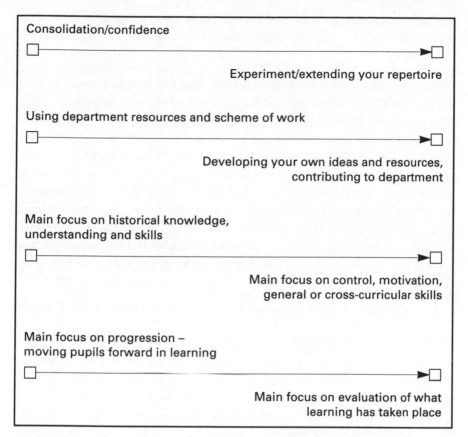

Figure 3.3   Some tensions in planning for learning
Note: This list is not a comprehensive one, but gives an indication of some of the processes involved in planning for learning

STARTING POINTS FOR PLANNING FOR LEARNING

Although there will be a difference in the degree of latitude accorded to student teachers in terms of what and how they teach – some departments will give you a fairly free hand in terms of *how* you deliver the topics you have been assigned – you will have to fit into the schemes of work which have been devised by the department. In some cases you will be asked to contribute, either individually or collaboratively, to the construction of schemes of work, or at least to plan a series of lessons on a particular topic. In addition to considering the documentation which the department possesses, you should consistently refer to the statutory orders for history (DfE, 1995) in order to keep clearly in mind the essential framework which has been provided to aid planning for learning in history.

Given that you are not a free agent in the classroom, and must adhere to school and departmental policies and be guided by the framework of the

National Curriculum for history, there are some factors which might be helpful to consider in putting together history lessons.

1 *Some 'morsels' of the past might lend themselves to particular approaches*
When you first consider the historical topic, event or question you have been asked to teach, think about which purpose of school history it lends itself to. To many experienced teachers, issues such as the Norman Conquest, the Glorious Revolution, Hargreaves' Spinning Jenny and the Holocaust immediately suggest ways into the topic in terms of what questions to ask, and what teaching approaches might be most appropriate. All of these topics pose very important questions, but very different ones. This is not to say that there is one definitive, best way of translating the topic into classroom experience, but that the topic might lend itself to, or easily relate to, a particular key element, second-order concept or teaching approach. A history topic might even be considered as a piece of raw meat – you have to think what you are going to do with it to make best use of it.

2 *It is important to think about what questions or problems are posed by the topic*
What important and/or interesting questions does the topic pose? How can you problematise the topic in a way which presents 'thinking problems' for pupils. When we present pupils with 'evidence' of the past, the purpose is to get them to think about that evidence in a way which develops their historical understanding. Lez Smart goes as far as to suggest, 'No questions, no history' (Smart, 1995). Whether you agree with this statement or not, a helpful way forward for lesson planning can be to think what questions will be posed for the pupils to work on and attempt to resolve, and for you to present and discuss some of the answers which have been suggested (see Figure 3.4).

3 *You should keep in mind, and sometimes draw on, the pupils' ideas about why and how things have happened in the past*
It is important to take account of the understanding and ideas that pupils bring with them to the lesson. They may not know a great deal about the topic itself, but they will have their own ideas about how and why things happen, and if you are to help them to progress to more powerful and effective ideas about why and how things have come to be as they are you need to be sure that you are talking to pupils in a way that engages with their ideas rather than passes over their heads.

4 *A useful starting point for thinking how to approach the topic can be the present rather than the past*
One of the commonly cited purposes of school history is 'to understand the present in the light of the past'. There are few topics in the National Curriculum

which do not have in some way a relation to questions and problems which pertain to the present. Making links between the present and the past can be an effective tool for persuading pupils of the importance and relevance of history, which Burston regarded as one of the central challenges to the history teacher (Burston, 1963). In the words of Ministry of Education pamphlet No. 23,

> The divorce between current affairs and history so that they are
> regarded as separate subjects gravely weakens both. It accentuates
> the natural tendency of children to see history as something remote
> and irrelevant, instead of something which has formed the world
> around them and which is continuously being formed by that world.
> And it accentuates equally the tendency to look at contemporary
> questions as though they had no context in time, no parallels or
> precedents.
>
> (Ministry of Education, 1952)

Making comparisons with the present also helps to clarify concepts and ideas about the past. Husbands makes the point that

> Learning about the concept of kingship frequently involves two
> sets of simultaneous learning: learning about power and its distribution
> in past societies, and learning about power and its distribution in
> modern society. The former cannot be given any real meaning until
> pupils have some more contemporary knowledge against which to
> calibrate their historical understandings.
>
> (Husbands, 1996)

In some cases, this means trying to explain how the present is explained by the past: how the Bill of Rights was an important step towards our present mode of government; why there is conflict in some areas between Catholics and Protestants. In other cases it may be a question of pointing out that many of the major problems and questions of human existence remain the same, but ways of resolving them are affected by changes which have taken place. How do rulers control their citizens, and how do dissidents oppose them? 'Work' is still an important part of the way societies are organised, but the way in which people work, how work is distributed and problems relating to work have all changed over time. The place where we draw the line between what is the state's concern and what is private has changed over time; why and to what effect? In essence, a doctor does the same job now as 2,000 years ago, but the problems which confront doctors have changed. In the words of Bowen (1993) it can be helpful to 'work from the known to the unknown'; to start from the present, and work back to the past.

5 *Sometimes it can be helpful to approach the topic in an oblique or eclectic manner in order to draw pupils into learning*

You do not have to confine yourself to the historical narrative and 'straight' history which is in textbooks and topic books. Sometimes points can be made very powerfully and effectively by the use of analogy, anecdote, cartoon or video extract, before concentrating on the more formal historical record. These are sometimes referred to as enabling or engaging strategies. Their purpose is to secure the interest and commitment to learning of the pupils, or to put over an important idea or concept in an arresting or striking manner. The concept of appeasement might be understood more readily by pupils if it was explained that teachers and parents often use it as a strategy, instead of explaining its use in the Belgian Crisis of 1831 (Ridley, 1972). A common strategy for introducing the idea of long-term and short-term causation and 'trigger causes' (frequently used to explain the outbreak of wars and revolutions), is a short paragraph about a car crash:

> Mr Jones drove home to watch the football match. He was late setting off and so drove faster than usual. His car skidded on an icy corner as he swerved to avoid a dog which had run across the road. He had not slowed down approaching the corner, as there was no street lighting on that stretch of road. One of the car tyres was worn, and Mr Jones had drunk 8 pints of lager before setting off.

(The teacher might at this point describe events leading to the First World War, the Franco-Prussian War, or other crises which lend themselves to this form of analysis or comparison.)

Sheila Lawlor has pointed out that teachers might go too far towards turning learning into meretricious 'fun and games', which removes intellectual rigour from learning, and avoids the reality that sometimes worthwhile learning can require patience and determination (Lawlor, 1989). School history has at times been brought into disrepute by the use of drawing and copying work, word-searches and low-value 'pass the time' type activities. However, you will almost certainly face the reality that not all your pupils are driven by a burning desire to do well in history, and that one of the first steps in putting together a history lesson is to try to engage the attention and commitment of the pupils to the learning activities which are planned, and to ensure that they *understand* what you are talking about. If they are not listening, or if they do not understand, no learning can take place. Initiative, imagination and an awareness of your pupils' abilities and prior understandings are as important as your subject knowledge in planning for effective learning. All history teachers find that some topics offer more obvious opportunities for learning activities than others; many would feel that the Second World War is perhaps a more 'user friendly' topic than 'Roads in the Seventeenth Century' or 'The Wool Trade in the Fourteenth Century', but by adopting an imaginative and eclectic approach to seemingly intractable topics, experienced teachers can often render them just as intriguing and valuable to pupils as topics which are more obviously attractive. As Thompson has pointed out,

> Superficially unpromising topics can promote a lively response and effective learning if they are handled with imagination and sensitivity to the pupil. The significant variable may be not a particular section or kind of history but the approach of the teacher, not any particular content, but the way it is handled.
>
> (Thompson, 1962)

Some topics need to be 'opened out', and interpreted in a broader context. 'Roads in the Seventeenth Century' could be taught in a way which concentrates on transmitting to pupils knowledge of the improvements wrought by Telford and Macadam, or it could examine the question of transport in a broader sense by considering in what ways transport problems have changed over time.

6 *Sometimes, the starting point for putting together a history lesson can be a resource rather than a lesson plan*

Although the traditional 'theory' of lesson construction tends to place the resources to be used after the 'ideas' which are to be addressed in the lesson, there are times when history teachers read a newspaper article, see a cartoon, watch something on the news or *Timewatch*, or visit a museum, which gives them an idea for a successful lesson, or a component of one. They then have to think carefully about how to make best use of the resource, and how to incorporate it into their teaching. Part of planning for learning is being alert to possibilities, scavenging for good resources, and displaying initiative in building up an archive of materials and ideas which can be used to augment the department's reserves.

It is not *just* a question of using a variety of methods, it is also a matter of choosing the teaching method which works best for the facet of historical knowledge and understanding you are attempting to develop.

There are some things that all the topics listed in Task 3.4 have in common: in teaching all of them we will be considering information about what happened in the past, we will be developing children's knowledge and understanding of the past, and there will be some recurrent themes or questions which pertain to the study of many historical topics such as 'Why did this happen?', 'What effect did this have?', 'How do we know about this?', and 'How reliable is this information?'

The following is an example of how the topic of the Industrial Revolution might be approached in terms of 'first thoughts' in planning for learning.

At the end of this topic, I would hope that the pupils would have a better understanding of questions such as:

What do we mean by 'industrial revolution'?

Why was Britain the first country to have one?

In what ways did the Industrial Revolution change what Britain was like? (The difference between feudal/agrarian societies and industrial ones, how and where people lived and worked, changing role of land and commerce and industry on wealth and power in Britain).

What effect did the Industrial Revolution have on Britain's position in the world in relation to other countries? (What part did the Industrial Revolution play in making Britain a great power, what factors make countries 'great', and do those factors change over time?)

What happened when other countries had industrial revolutions?

How does all this affect us in Britain today?

At the end of this topic, I hope pupils will have a better understanding of the following concepts and vocabulary:

resources	colony	capital
feudal system	domestic industry	factory system
technology	raw materials	manufactured goods
'the class system'	division of labour	alienation
supply and demand	monopoly	profit
Luddism	*laissez-faire*	protection
free market	'mixed economy'	nationalisation
regulation	deregulation	balance of payments
labour	trade unionism	trade

Whilst addressing these questions and ideas, in addition to developing the range and depth of the pupils' historical knowledge and understanding, I hope that pupils will develop their understanding of the nature of history as a discipline (in particular that there are differing interpretations of these events), their ability to structure their enquiries into the past and work things out for themselves, and their ability to organise and communicate the results of their enquiries, both orally and in writing.

In order to derive these benefits from the study of the Industrial Revolution, pupils will engage in a variety of activities which will develop their historical knowledge and understanding, and also some more general educational skills (such as oracy, proficiency in information technology and writing skills). In the course of the unit they might work with artefacts, visit a site, do a group presentation to the class on an aspect of the Industrial Revolution, do an extended piece of writing, study written sources, read, listen to teacher exposition, do a data handling exercise and, in groups, produce a newspaper front page on an aspect of the Industrial Revolution.

Figure 3.4 Thinking about how to approach the treatment of the Industrial Revolution in study unit 3, Britain, 1750 to *c.* 1900

TASK 3.3 MAKING IT INTERESTING: APPROACHING UNPROMISING ASPECTS OF THE HISTORY CURRICULUM

Although in theory, outstanding history teachers should be able to render all aspects of the past intriguing and accessible to pupils, the reality is that some topics might offer more obvious opportunities, ideas and resources than others. Ask the history teachers you work with, and fellow student teachers, how they approach less propitious topics, and what engaging and enabling strategies and tasks they use to try and draw pupils into learning.

TASK 3.4 WORKING OUT WHAT KEY QUESTIONS AND CONCEPTS MIGHT BE USED TO FOCUS THE STUDY OF OTHER HISTORICAL TOPICS

The questions posed by study of the Industrial Revolution, and the concepts involved, might be very different from those which arise from a consideration of other historical events. Draw up a list of possible 'key questions' and concepts which might provide a basis for teaching a series of lessons on (a) the Norman Conquest, (b) the outbreak of civil war in England in 1642, (c) the Glorious Revolution of 1688, (d) the Holocaust.

However, different topics offer different *opportunities* to the history teacher, can suggest different 'key questions', and offer insights into very differing sorts of ideas and concepts. Study of the Industrial Revolution will generally enrich the pupils' grasp of economic concepts and the cross-curricular theme of economic and industrial awareness. Study of the events of 1688 might prove an excellent opportunity to develop *political* concepts, and be the point at which to give an *overview* of how government has developed in this country from 1066 to the present day, culminating in an examination of pupils' understanding of the present system of government and the way in which the events of 1688 relate to this. The events of 1066 might not throw as much light as those of 1688, or 1867, on how Britain is governed today, and so instead of focusing on the purpose of 'explaining the present in the light of the past', the main focus might be developing pupils' understanding of evidence, the nature of history, how we know about the events of 1066. Although there are several approaches to the Holocaust (including evidence and the Holocaust), many history teachers use the topic to focus on moral and ethical questions.

The importance of concepts in school history

> Historical knowledge includes an understanding of certain ideas and
> concepts. These are more than glossaries of technical terms, they are
> aids to categorising, organising, analysing and applying historical
> information. They can only be understood when they are used in
> illustrating a variety of different historical circumstances. 'Revolution',
> for example, is a historical idea. But a simple definition will not help
> pupils to understand why the word is applied equally to events in France
> after 1789, in Russia in 1917, or to the history of industry in later
> eighteenth century England, or whether it can equally usefully describe
> events in seventeenth century England. Ideas such as 'left wing' or 'right
> wing' have their value, but only if pupils begin to appreciate their
> limitations and the oversimplifications they sometimes suggest.
>
> (HMI, 1985)

Understanding concepts helps pupils make sense of the world they are living in,
and, in order to make sense of the past, pupils need to understand the ideas and
concepts which emanate from the study of a historical topic, as well as the factual details they are presented with, if they are to 'transform' the learning experience into knowledge and understanding. The HMI document, *History in the
Primary and Secondary Years*, provides a useful, but not comprehensive, list of
the concepts which pupils studying history should develop an understanding of
in their study of the past (HMI, 1985).

In terms of organising planning for learning, many history teachers have
found it helpful to make a distinction between 'substantive' concepts (such as
'liberal', 'capital', 'propaganda' and 'reactionary') and 'second-order' concepts
(such as 'change, 'cause' and 'evidence'). It terms of providing a rationale for
this distinction, it might be helpful to use the analogy of software and operating systems for computers. Substantive concepts relate to themes and ideas
which might recur at intervals in the study of the past, such as 'government',
'revolution', or 'fascist'; second-order concepts are more pervasive and might be
said to underpin, or provide a framework or rationale for, historical enquiry
throughout the syllabus. It is difficult to study any topic in history without
considering what evidence we have and how reliable it is, what caused things to
unfold as they did, and what changes resulted from events. It that sense second-
order concepts are the equivalent of Windows 95, MS-DOS, System 7 or
RISCOS – if you use the computer you are using them all the time.

It should be stressed that not all commentators on school history are convinced of the utility and importance of concepts in the study of history. Several
of the pamphlets from the Centre for Policy Studies argue that the centrality of
a coherent historical narrative and sound grasp of the record of the past have

been undervalued at the expense of themes, concepts and skills (see, for example, Deuchar, 1989; McGovern, 1994). Our belief is that, although it is essential that pupils have a sound grasp of events, the extent to which this factual base is complemented by a grasp of the concepts involved in the study of historical events will add to the pupils' understanding of events, and their significance (see Figure 3.5).

TASK 3.5 LINKING CONTENT TO CONCEPTS

Think of a topic which you will have to teach to a class, and a concept which might arise in the course of covering that topic. How will you structure the work in a way which develops pupils' understanding of the concept, as well as developing their knowledge of the historical content involved. (The concept might, for example, be 'appeasement' in the course of covering Hitler's foreign policy, 'imperialism' in the course of covering Britain in the nineteenth century, 'trade,' in covering the Roman Empire, or 'propaganda' in covering Nazi Germany.)

USING THE STATUTORY ORDER TO PLAN FOR LEARNING IN HISTORY

It is essential to keep in mind that the National Curriculum for history is more than a list of content to be covered. There is a requirement to cover the six study units stipulated, but teachers retain a considerable degree of autonomy in the way in which they might approach these units. SCAA's *An Introduction to the Revised National Curriculum* emphasises that

> How and in what depth to teach material contained in the subject orders is for schools to decide. No priority or methodology is implied in the orders. Decisions on the depth of treatment of aspects of subjects are for the professional judgement of teachers. The Orders should not be interpreted as requiring the same degree of detail in all aspects.
>
> (SCAA, 1994)

An important feature of the Orders is paragraph 7 of Key Stage 3: in addition to requiring schools to cover the six study units, the Orders state that across Key Stage 3, pupils should be given the opportunity to study the past 'in outline, in depth and through a local context', and from a variety of perspectives, 'political; economic, technological and scientific; social; religious; cultural and aesthetic'. There is also the stipulation that coverage should include 'aspects of the histories of England, Ireland, Scotland and Wales; where appropriate, the History of Britain should be set in its European and world context'. There are

Part of a study of the Russian Revolution of 1905 is an understanding of the groups opposing the Czar. The aim of the exercise is to extend the pupils' understanding of the different ways in which the state can be opposed, as well as their grasp of the continuum between terrorism and peaceful protest which can be adopted by opposition groups, both in Russia in 1905 and at other points in history (including the present day). This could lead on to a consideration of which methods of opposition are justifiable, and whether what is justifiable varies according to the way in which the state exercises its power and control, and what are the advantages and disadvantages of the various forms of opposition.

1 Pupils are given an explanation of the events leading up to the 1905 revolution, including the actions and motives of factions opposing or criticising the Czar's regime.
2 Pupils are asked to brainstorm a list of ways in which citizens oppose governments today in different parts of the world, including Britain.
3 Pupils are given two quotes about opposition which are written on the board at either end, with a line drawn across the width of the board to represent a continuum between the two statements.

   Quote A: 'Nothing is ever done in this world until men are prepared to kill one another if it is not done' (George Bernard Shaw).
   Quote B: 'No revolution is worth the effusion of a single drop of human blood' (Daniel O'Connell).

4 Pupils are asked to place the methods of opposition which they have thought of in order, from those which accord with Shaw's view, to those which accord with O' Connell's, or given cards which outline methods of opposition and asked to place them in a continuum between the two positions.

Voting against govmt in elections	Threats of poisoning of water/ food supplies	Hunger strikes	Bomb/sniper attacks on govmt security forces
Placing anti-govmt advertisements in newspapers	Damage to public/govmt property (slashing paintings, setting fire to post boxes)	Drawing up petitions and presenting them to govmt.	Sit-down protests/ blocking public highways Boycotting goods and services
Peaceful protest marches	Hijacking of aeroplanes	Kidnapping and ransom threats	Assassination of govmt agents
Random bomb attacks in cities	Graffiti/poster campaigns against govmt	Non-payment of taxes	Public suicides

5 Pupils are asked to categorise types of opposition. (Some classes or pupils within classes could be given categories, i.e. peaceful/nuisance/violence against self/damage-violence to property/violence against govmt agents/ random violence.)

6 Pupils are asked to position the groups opposing the Czar along the continuum between Shaw's position and O'Connell's, to state which methods of opposition were available to them in Czarist Russia in 1905, and why different opposition groups used different methods of opposition.

The idea of continuums of opposition can obviously be applied in other historical contexts (for example, discontent in Britain after the Napoleonic Wars), and can encompass understanding of the concept of radicalism – including the fact that there can be conservative as well as progressive radicalism.

Figure 3.5 An example of the integration of concepts into learning about the past

also the 'common requirements' that include questions of access for all pupils, use of language, and opportunities to develop proficiency in information technology (DfE, 1995).

Here we see the tension between simply thinking about what would make a good lesson, and planning for a 'balanced diet' of school history which will incorporate a broad range of learning objectives. There is also the question of the time allocation for covering a study unit. You have to think about how a broad and balanced programme of learning in history can be delivered in the notional 45 hours per year which was suggested to advisory groups as the time allocation for delivering the revised National Curriculum for history (although the exact amount will vary from school to school). The focus statement at the start of the Key Stage 3 programme of study indicates the essence of what should be taught over the course of the entire Key Stage.

One of the important facets of the revision of the National Curriculum for history was the concern that 'defining progression too rigidly may be counter-productive and lead to an atomisation of the subject' (Bennett and Steele, 1995). This concern stemmed from the experience of history teachers attempting to implement the first version of the National Curriculum for history, where the emphasis on progression through the '45 boxes' which constituted the attainment targets led to a tendency to teach disaggregated 'little bits' of history, at the expense of coherence and overview (Haydn, 1994).

When you are looking at how to approach a topic (whether it be the Norman Conquest, the structure of medieval society, or popular protest and reform in Britain in the nineteenth century), you should look first to the key elements of the History Order. These are the five central domains of school history which you should be addressing in your planning for learning, and you should consider which of the key elements are most appropriately developed through the morsel of history you are dealing with. 'The key elements and the content provide a basis for setting teaching objectives, for structuring feedback and considering pupils' attainment. The detail of how this is done is for the professional judgement of teachers' (Bennett and Steele, 1995).

The revised National Curriculum for history attempts to provide flexibility for classroom teachers to decide where (and how many) depth studies to pursue, and where overview coverage would be more appropriate. At times you will be linking together work which has been done over the course of the year, in order to help pupils to see 'the broad sweep' of history; at others you will be studying a particular event in considerable detail. This will clearly influence your teaching methods, and the resources you choose.

In order to guard against the risk of thinking too much about 'What would make a good lesson?', at the expense of 'How can I ensure that pupils receive a broad and balanced "diet" of school history?', many departments use planning grids, so that it is easy to check whether and where the different key elements and components of the National Curriculum are being taught. Table 3.1 shows an example of a planning grid for a scheme of work for a series of several lessons on the Norman Conquest.

ASKING AND ANSWERING HISTORICAL QUESTIONS

One of the things which student teachers of history sometimes find difficult is how to ask questions of the past which go beyond recall and comprehension (see Figure 3.6), and which develop pupils' understanding of history as a body of knowledge and as a form of knowledge. If we are to develop the 'thinking skills' referred to in Chapter 1 we must attempt to get beyond questions which simply ask pupils to locate information and write it down, or reiterate what we have just told them.

One way of doing this is to think of the key elements in constructing lessons, and to keep in mind the substantive and second-order concepts referred to earlier in this chapter. Second-order concepts such as chronology, time, change, cause, evidence, interpretation and motive can often be a way of leading pupils into the problems and difficulties which historians face, and which require discussion, debate and thought, rather than pupils consistently being asked to do no more than write down or repeat what they are told.

Sources are not evidence until we start to ask questions of them. It is the asking of questions which renders the study of the past meaningful, and which can help to explain to pupils why historians bother to do what they do and why it might be helpful to understand these processes. So having thought of the questions we wish to pose of the historical content we are teaching, the next stage is to look for sources, stories or ideas which will problematise those questions in a form which pupils can engage with. Although the questions relating to second-order concepts permeate the history curriculum, there are times when

Table 3.1 An example of a planning grid for a series of lessons on the Norman Conquest

Key Questions	Concepts, vocabulary	Historical content	Resources	Pupil activities	Teaching objectives	Assessment opportunities
Why did the Normans invade England?	Invasion, heredity, power, resources	The quarrel for the throne, England before the invasion	Briefing sheet on claims, from *Medieval Realms*, pp. 15–19	Listen to story; groupwork preparing claims for court; presentations	Understanding of motives for invasion and nature of govmt pre-invasion	Oral presentations on claims to throne
What happened at the Battle of Hastings? How do we know? Why did William win?	Evidence, accounts and chronicles	The military campaigns of 1066	Video extract of battle; worksheet on death of Harold; miniature of Bayeux Tapestry	Sequencing exercise; extended writing, 'How and why Harold lost'	Understanding nature of historical record – interpretations	Extended writing exercise on 1066 campaigns
How did William gain control of England with only a few thousand men?	Power, authority, administration, deterrence	From Hastings to 1086; castles; *Domesday Book*	Maps from *Medieval Realms*, pp. 21–2; 'The Normans' software	Mapwork; sourcework exercise from *Medieval Realms*, p. 22; IT suite	Accounts and explanations; taxation; role of individual in history	Sourcework exercise on interpretations
Why were these events important? What difference did it make to life in England?	Kingdom, feudal system, hierarchy	The changed social and political order	Visit to museum; Normans film strip; *Medieval Realms*, pp. 24–6	Construct timeline, newspaper front pages and obituary for class display	Significance; notion of 'turning points', factual grasp of main events and changes	Recap test on main events and key vocabulary

What are historians trying to do when they investigate the past? Why do they bother?

What happened? Events, time periods, time lines, story lines, chronology, accounts, sequencing.

Why did it happen? Explaining things, actions, events, developments, cause, motive, ideas, beliefs.

What changed? **What stayed the same**? Patterns in/of the past, looking for similarities and differences, charting change.

How did what happened affect things? Consequences and signifi-cance for people at the time, for us now.

How do we find out what we want to know? What problems are there in finding out and being sure? What claims can we make? Looking at sources, asking them questions, deciding whether they can be used as evidence for a particular question or for what questions they might be useful.

Why might we get different answers to our questions? Purposes, interests, concerns for reconstructing the past, *why* was this produced? Problems of available evidence, issues of interpretation.

Figure 3.6 Things we want to know about the past
Source: Ros Ashby, 'An Introduction to School History', Workshop, Institute of Education, University of London, 11 February, 1995

you will also be addressing substantive concepts, and trying to develop pupils' understanding of ideas such as *government*, *democracy*, *collectivism*, *oligarchy*, etc. Keeping in mind substantive and second-order concepts can be a way of ensur-ing that you are asking historical questions, rather than comprehension ones. Figure 3.7 gives a small selection of the type of historical questions suggested by Tim Lomas in his Historical Association pamphlet *Teaching and Assessing Historical Understanding* (Lomas, 1990).

In thinking about what questions to pose in teaching elements of the programmes of study, you should consider the key elements, the focus statement which introduces the programme of study for the Key Stage, and the detail given in the outline of the study unit.

THE LINK BETWEEN PLANNING AND EVALUATION OF PUPIL LEARNING

Another important aspect of planning for learning is to consider how you will assess what pupils have learned, in order to think of what elements need to be repeated or reinforced, what pupils might go on to learn next, and what might be done differently the next time you teach the lesson. Although the 'planning loop' of planning → teaching → assessing → evaluating → revised planning will

Cause and consequence

- What was the importance of economic factors in causing the Russian civil war?
- What influence did Robespierre have on the outcome of the French Revolution?
- Why were the children evacuated from this town but not that town?
- Who would be most upset/pleased when the law said that children could not work in the mine any more?
- What long-term factors may have led to the decision to send the Spanish Armada?

Time/Change

- What might a cotton worker have noticed different about conditions at work between 1750 and 1850?
- Look at the picture of the Victorian school. What has changed in most schools since the time of that picture?
- Why did the renaissance happen at the time that it did?
- The events in this story about the murder of Thomas à Becket are jumbled up. Put them in the order which you think makes the most sense.
- Why did it take twenty years before Germany took revenge for the Treaty of Versailles?

Evidence

- What do you think this artefact would be used for?
- Look at the two sources about the Second World War. Where do they not agree with each other?
- Which parts of this newspaper account are just the opinions of the person who wrote it?
- How reliable do you think the author is, even though she was an eye witness?
- Why might the Bayeux Tapestry have been compiled?

Significance

- Why can 1485 be described as a 'turning point'?
- Did the legislation of 1918 solve all the problems of inequality which British women faced?
- Which of these do you think an ordinary villager in the Middle Ages would have felt was more important in his or her life?
- What might have happened if the Jacobites had not been defeated at Culloden?
- Put the following sixteenth-century events in what you consider as their order of importance, giving reasons for your choice.

cont . . .

Similarity and Difference

- Compare the peace treaties after the First World War and the Second World War.
- Why might France have felt differently about Germany in 1918, 1940 and 1980?
- Could the events which caused the French Revolution have produced a similar effect in Britain?
- What differences can you find in the way these two battles were fought?
- How typical was this of Richard the Lionheart's policies?

Figure 3.7 Examples of questions relating to second-order concepts

be considered in more detail in Chapter 10, it is important to keep in mind that effective learning requires you to think carefully about two questions. How much of what you have taught has been learned? Once the pupils have learned something, what should you teach next?

Holt makes the point that these two questions are not always asked:

> I assumed for a long time that my students knew when they did, or did not understand something. I was always urging them to tell me when they did, or did not, understand, so that with one of my 'clever explanations', I could clear up everything. But they would never tell me. I came to know by painful experience that not a child in a hundred knows whether or not he understands something, much less, if he does not, why not. The child who knows, we don't have to worry about, he will be an 'A' student. How do we find out when, and what, the others don't understand?
>
> (Holt, 1982)

Holt goes on to attempt to provide possible ways of exploring the problem of understanding. A key element is that pupils are not simply regurgitating information in exactly the same form as it was given, but are asked to manipulate or analyse the information in some way to demonstrate that they have assimilated it into other, contingent areas of knowledge and understanding. They need to move from being 'knowledge tellers' to 'knowledge transformers' (see Counsell, 1996).

Another example of a format for assessing whether pupils have understood relationships is provided in the National Curriculum Council's booklet, *Teaching History at Key Stage 3* (NCC, 1993) – see Figure 3.10.

In many lessons, you will have what Battersby calls a 'golden nugget' (Battersby, 1996): a key idea or fact that you hope all pupils will grasp, to take away from the lesson with them. In a lesson on propaganda in Nazi Germany, an example of this might be that all pupils understand that propaganda is not

Holt gives the following descriptors of situations where understanding has taken place: 'It may help to have in our minds a picture of what we mean by understanding. I feel I understand things if I can do some, at least, of the following:

1   state it in my own words;
2   give examples of it;
3   recognise it in various guises and circumstances;
4   see connections between it and other facts or ideas;
5   make use of it in various ways;
6   foresee some of its consequences;
7   state its opposite or converse.

This list is only a beginning; but it may help us in the future to find out what our students really know as opposed to what they can give the appearance of knowing, their real learning as opposed to their apparent learning.'

Figure 3.8 Assessing for understanding
Source: Holt, 1982

The following grid is an attempt to assess how well pupils have grasped the relations between the major powers of Europe in 1914. They are asked to give a mark out of 10 to each relationship, with 10 out of 10 representing the most solid and committed of alliances, and 0 out of 10 representing countries which were intensely hostile to each other. In addition to shedding light on their understanding of the two main camps (the Triple Alliance and the Triple Entente), it tests their understanding of the comparative strength of the different alliances and relationships.

Relations between the Great Powers of Europe, June 1914

	Great Britain	France	Germany	Italy	Russia	Austria-Hungary
Great Britain						
France						
Germany						
Italy						
Russia						
Austria-Hungary						

Figure 3.9 Assessing for understanding: an example

The following 0–5 scale is about how much power different groups or people had in the country at a particular time

0	—	1	—	2	—	3	—	4	—	5
No power				Some power						All power

Fill in this table and then stick it in your book.

In a group, put the number from the scale which you think applies to that person or group of people in that particular year on the table, e.g., if you think the King had all the power in 1649 put 5 under 1649 in the first line across. Discuss your group's findings with another group.

	1640	1649	1701
The King			
The House of Lords			
The House of Commons			
The Church of England			
The Army			
The Common People			

Figure 3.10 Worksheet designed to help pupils understand the changes in the distribution of political power, 1640–1701
Source: NCC, 1993

something that only happened in Nazi Germany; its use is widespread and it still exists today, particularly in time of war. As your assurance and competence develops, your lesson evaluations should increasingly focus on the central issue of pupil learning, rather than simply evaluating your own teaching performance. They should move from 'Was I OK?', to 'How was it for them?', considering questions such as:

- How many of the pupils grasped the main points I was trying to make?
- Which aspects did they understand and which aspects do I need to return to?
- How can I try and put this across in another way for those who did not grasp the key points of the lesson?
- How can I reinforce and consolidate what they have learned?
- What points should I move on to for those pupils who have grasped the 'golden nugget' which was the key point of the lesson?
- In what ways might I teach this more effectively next time – what would I change, what would I retain?
- Were they listening to what I was saying or looking out of the window, bored stiff and inattentive?

Planning for learning goes on after the lesson has finished, as well as before the lesson.

SUMMARY AND KEY POINTS

Because of the range of other concerns which preoccupy student teachers when they start to teach, you must make a conscious effort not to lose sight of the learning objectives behind your teaching – there are often other purposes to teaching pupils about aspects of the past apart from transmitting information about what happened. Student teachers often find it difficult to devise genuinely historical questions which go beyond recall and comprehension, to translate their degree-level knowledge into terms which make sense to pupils, and to focus on pupils' learning rather than on their own performance and task management. It is possible for the pupils to be behaving well and to be 'on task', but not necessarily making effective progress in learning. Sound subject knowledge is a necessary but not sufficient condition for confident and effective teaching to take place – it is important, but there are other things to consider in planning for learning.

As well as moving pupils forward in history, you are also responsible for the development of their general educational skills, whether in terms of language, IT capability or cross-curricular themes; you also need to consider your own learning needs, departmental policies and classroom management concerns. Sometimes there are tensions between these concerns. You have to balance these as adroitly as possible – this can require skills and qualities of tact, perseverance, insight and determination!

Initiative and imagination are also important attributes in planning for learning; sometimes it may be necessary to adopt an eclectic approach to the topic, through the use of enabling and engaging tasks, and teacher exposition, in order to draw pupils into the process of learning. This means that one might not always use 'high-value' activities, although it is important to be aware of the danger of using low-value 'pass the time' type activities more than is absolutely essential. Keeping in mind the ideas and concepts which help to generate an understanding of the past can be an aid to posing historical questions and problems.

The National Curriculum for history is a framework for planning for learning, not a strait-jacket; it has several elements, and is not just a guide to subject content. In planning for effective learning you must beware of devising lessons which are entirely content-led or assessment-led. The key elements and paragraph 7 of the Key Stage 3 programme of study (DfE, 1995) are an aid to ensuring that we teach history purposefully, with breadth, balance and variety, in a way which will be of benefit for pupils after they leave school. Different morsels of the past offer different opportunities to the history teacher.

FURTHER READING

Counsell, L. and The Historical Association Secondary Education Committee (1997) *The Twentieth-century World: Planning Study Unit 4 of the National Curriculum for History*, London, Historical Association.
A good insight into how to make sense of vast swathes of content.

Farmer, A. and Knight, P. (1995) *Active History in Key Stages 3 and 4*, London. David Fulton.
Uneven, but some good insights and practical suggestions.

HMI (1985) *History in the Primary and Secondary Years: an HMI View*, London, HMSO.
In spite of its pre-National Curriculum date, an excellent introduction to many of the issues relating to planning for learning in history.

Husbands, C. (1996) *What is History Teaching?*, Buckingham, Open University Press.
Helpful in clarifying the differences between academic and school history.

Lomas, T. (1990) *Teaching and Assessing Historical Understanding* (Teaching of History Series, Number 63), London, Historical Association.
How to teach in a way that asks genuinely historical questions.

Steele, I. (1976) Chapter 4, 'Aims and Objectives in History Teaching', in *Developments in History Teaching*, London, Open Books.
A lucid and succinct explanation of the difference between aims and objectives, and the implications of objectives-based planning.

4 Learning strategies and the use of language

INTRODUCTION

An important aspect of your lesson planning is the selection of the teaching methods you employ for any specific lesson. One of the many skills you need to develop as a history teacher is the ability to select teaching methods which are appropriate for the particular pupils you teach and for the achievement of the learning objectives you have set. Some methods may be suitable for some situations but not for others. The choice of method usually resides with the class teacher for, although the History National Curriculum prescribes the Study Units, identifies the Key Elements which pupils should be addressing, and provides the level description for the Attainment Target, the methods by which the National Curriculum is delivered are left for the teacher to decide.

Most teaching methods have potential strengths and weaknesses. Your skill as a teacher is knowing which approaches are most likely to maximise the learning achieved by the pupils. You need to be competent in the use of a range of styles and methods, sometimes within the same lesson. *Over-reliance on one approach limits the learning potential of pupils* (OFSTED, 1993, 1995). Pupils learn in different ways, and have preferred learning styles in the same way that many teachers have a preference for certain teaching styles and methods. The reality of school life with its pressures on time, the limited availability of resources and the gradual erosion of your reserves of energy as the term proceeds, places some constraints on what is attempted in the classroom. Effective classroom teaching is the art of the possible, and your attempts to provide inspirational learning experiences will need to be tempered by pragmatism. One of the strategies you will learn as you progress is to anticipate these realities of school life by helping to build up a stock of resources for departmental use, and for your own future use. You should gradually be accumulating an 'archive' of teaching ideas and resources, some of which may be adaptable to differing topic areas.

Other factors may inhibit your choice of method, particularly in the early weeks of your school experience. There may be times when it is unwise to move away too abruptly from the methods the pupils have previously experienced.

There may be classes where the choice of methods is influenced by issues of control and discipline.

There is no hard and fast rule which guarantees success

Sometimes adopting a different approach with reluctant learners is just what is needed. As you grow more confident in the classroom, you begin to think more about the quality of learning you are providing and to evaluate the methods and the materials you are using. With that growth of confidence also comes the opportunity to try out new approaches and to take a few risks. Be prepared to experiment even though you may not have seen an approach before. Although your ITE course provides you with experience in more than one school, you will be very fortunate if the amount of observation of experienced teachers you can manage covers the breadth of methods available to the history teacher. *Be prepared to experiment.* If you are trying out a method for the first time and it does not work particularly well, try to work out why this was the case but do not dismiss it forever. Try it again perhaps with a different class and a different topic. *Variety of method is often a key ingredient for a successful scheme of work.* The Key Elements which underpin the History National Curriculum are themselves very varied in their demands and emphasis, and you need to have a range of teaching styles and approaches if all Key Elements are to be successfully developed.

Whatever methods you choose to employ, how you make use of language is often the key to successful learning. It is now more than twenty years since the Bullock Report, *A Language for Life* (DES, 1975), gave an impetus towards a greater concern for the use of language in the teaching of all subjects across the secondary curriculum. Before this publication, language as a key issue in any consideration of the quality of learning had been successfully promoted by educationalists such as Lawton (1968), Barnes *et al.* (1969). The Bullock Report had two central features: (1) reading and (2) language and learning. Available data on reading standards from 1948 to 1971 was studied and some of the conclusions suggested a decline in reading standards in the 1960s, particularly amongst a 'more homogeneous working-class'. While reading ability was a major issue, other aspects of language were explored, as the Report noted that 'the success of the secondary school can be said to depend very considerably on the level of achievement in reading and language. Unless the pupil can read, write and talk competently he cannot benefit from the range of learning, which the secondary school provides'.

Many of the situations the Bullock Report described have a familiar ring today, two decades later. The Report was followed by a range of publications which sought to apply its thinking at subject-specific level. An outstanding example of these is that of Nick Levine's (1981) contribution for the teaching of history to M. Torbé's series on Language, Teaching and Learning. The nature of history, with its abundance of abstract ideas such as 'sovereignty', 'revolution', and 'appeasement', means that the successful use of language is particularly important for history teachers. As Burston noted,

> In history teaching we are dependent to a quite exceptional degree on ordinary language as our medium of communication. History, more than any other school subject, depends upon literacy in its pupils as a prerequisite to success, and increased literacy is perhaps its most important by-product.
>
> (Burston, 1963)

This means that we have to give particular thought and attention to the needs of pupils with very limited or low levels of literacy (see Chapter 7).

As a student teacher, you will soon appreciate how much the ability (or lack of it) of your pupils to read, write and generally communicate their knowledge and understanding will influence the planning and execution of your lessons. In this chapter we will consider four aspects of the role of language in history teaching: teacher talk, reading, pupil talk and pupil's written work. These four activites, which will form an essential part of your classroom teaching, are all dependent on the effective use of language for their success. You will need to be aware of both the problems and the opportunities which will be encountered in the use of language in your teaching.

OBJECTIVES

At the end of this chapter you should be able to:

- examine the subject-specific nature of some teaching methods and skills;
- discuss the potential strengths and limitations of various strategies;
- consider the linguistic demands and the potential difficulties which the learning of history makes on pupils.

PROBLEMS IN THE USE OF LANGUAGE FOR THE HISTORY TEACHER

The whole question of which methods teachers should adopt has received a great deal of publicity in recent times as politicians and educationalists clash in the way they explain deficiencies in pupil progress and give their views on how 'standards' can be raised in schools. Much of the debate, in the language of the politicians and the media, centres around the terms 'traditionalist' and 'progressive'. As noted in the introduction to this chapter the succcssful teacher usually employs a range of teaching methods and approaches. What you will realise from the beginning is that there is a very clear link between what a history teacher believes are the intended outcomes of the teaching and the methods that are chosen to achieve these ends. *Success with any chosen methods must take account of the role of language.*

The limited understanding often experienced by pupils in history lessons suggests that the learning of history makes considerable linguistic demands on pupils. *Language issues can be deceptive.* Edwards (1978) noted the 'frequently occurring paradox' that history teachers can experience. On the one hand the subject would seem to lack 'extensive technical' language and is often dependent on everyday language; yet on the other hand the subject has been identified as one presenting 'unusual linguistic difficulties.'

Consider first the *dependency on ordinary language*. It is easy to make too many assumptions about what is everyday language. What may seem ordinary to a graduate will not necessarily be so to pupils. In your search for words to aid description and explanation it is easy to be over-reliant on phrases that have become familiar to you. Gunning (1978a) used the term 'weasel words'. He said that such words had certain characteristics: they do not always seem difficult and probably are not in some contexts, but can be very confusing in others. In some cases such as the use of the word 'church', 'state' or 'party', teacher and pupil could be using these words differently. To the teacher the 'Church' is describing the institution, to the pupil, a building. Pupils usually apply the concrete meaning of a term rather than its more abstract or generic use. Gunning also noted the danger of using words which seem straight-forward enough but really cover vague or partial understanding. A good example he quotes is 'There was discontent with the Republic', but what does 'discontent' really mean? If pupils are to understand such words they need to be more explicit. Edwards (1978) criticised his own writing when he realised the unhelpful nature of a sentence such as 'Spanish rule in the islands was oppressive.' What does 'oppressive' mean in that context? 'Ordinary language' can also provide problems to pupils when some apparently familiar words had different meanings in the past. For example, 'enthusiasm' was not always viewed as positively as today.

The study of history also requires the use of a host of *abstract terms* and, although the subject cannot claim a monopoly of such terms, because subjects such as economics, politics, sociology and, perhaps, theology are usually studied after the age of 16 it is often through their study of history that pupils will have their first acquaintance with concepts such as 'revolution', 'democracy', 'colonialism' 'representation', 'taxation', 'inflation', and so on.

In addition to the vast array of names of people and events, pupils are faced with *subject-specific labels*, often implying interpretations, such as 'The Glorious Revolution' and the 'Peterloo Massacre'. Furthermore they need to understand and use a range of terms to help them achieve another of the activities of the historian: to categorise and classify. For example, words which help to group together ideas or events to help structure understanding, like 'The Eleven Years Tyranny' 'The Interregnum', or words needed to classify causes and consequences such as 'social', 'technical' and 'economic'. All present real problems for pupils unless they are anticipated by the teacher and adequately explained. Pupils need to be encouraged to use such terms in a way that shows they do understand them and are not repeating other people's language without fully understanding it.

Cowie (1979) noted two further difficulties which the use of language can create for pupils. She noted that history requires the use of a full range of past tenses (perfect, past perfect, past continuous as well as the simple past), which are not often used by pupils in their usual speech. Such *difficulties with tenses* help to explain why pupils usually feel more comfortable with more creative and imaginative tasks than those requiring a more academic exposition. Secondly, she found that many pupils, especially the slower learners, had difficulty with words that place some condition or limitation on statements such as 'if', 'although', 'conversely', 'yet' and 'however'. The greater the emphasis that is placed on historical interpretations and explanations, the more such words are likely to be required.

TASK 4.1 LANGUAGE PROBLEMS IN HISTORY TEACHING

Acquire three or four history textbooks which have been produced at different times in the last thirty years. Select from each book a paragraph and try to identify those words and phrases which could prove to be problematic for the pupils for whom they are intended. Consider the difficulties which might arise from the conciseness of the text, the style and the use of metaphorical language, the use of abstract concepts, of vague descriptive words, of words relating to time and place and the use of quotations from sources.

Select one of the passages and try to rewrite the content so that the potential problems have been eliminated. There will be some occasions when you have to rewrite material to make it accessible to your pupils.

TEACHING METHODS INVOLVING THE DIFFERING USES OF LANGUAGE IN HISTORY

Teacher talk: developing your skills of exposition

As a history teacher it is difficult to avoid the use of teacher talk as a significant element of your lessons. The reason for this is the fact that history is one of those subjects which involves a vast amount of content, so there can be a great deal to talk about. There is and always will be an important place for teacher talk, whether it be questioning or exposition, and the subject offers many topics which can be described in a stimulating way. The development of your skills, both in exposition and questioning, is an essential feature of your competence as a history teacher. However accomplished they become at devising purposeful and worthwhile learning activities for pupils, history teachers must at some point be able to use their skills of exposition and questioning to explain the past to pupils in an engaging and effective manner. They must also beware of believing that if they talk for long enough, pupils will understand. Effective teacher talk is better measured by quality rather than quantity. You must learn to judge how long to talk for, and when to stop.

An important part of your role as a history teacher is to be able to sell the subject, to transmit your enthusiasm for the topic to the pupils. Reluctance to develop exposition skills can encourage the uninspiring use of the textbook or an over-reliance on duplicated handouts. At times you can call on the assistance of a video to stimulate interest in the topic, but there are times when you are dependent on yourself, your knowledge and classroom personality. You need to have a good command of the topic, to have selected from it the significant points you want to stress and the kind of detail appropriate to the age and ability of your class. It is useful to have your notes at hand but try to remember as much as you can. If you appear to be tied to your notes, this serves only to reinforce your inexperience and limits your movement about the class. One of the ways of avoiding frequent reference to notes is to use visual aids, be it the board, the OHP, pictures, or your own creations. These not only serve as an aid to your memory, they help the pupils follow your exposition and also focus their attention away from you. They can also help in reinforcing and recapping key points. Some teachers have found it useful to practice exposition skills at home, not exactly declaiming from the top of the stairs, but possibly using a tape-recorder to help them reflect on their use of language, about any assumptions they may be making about the pupils' understanding, and about how they use their voices. If you feel you have a problem with the way you use your voice, most courses have a specialist available to help you.

You should find that your worries about exposition skills recede as you teach more lessons. Whereas in the early stages of school experience, a ten-minute

TASK 4.2 DEVELOPING YOUR SKILLS OF EXPOSITION

Make notes on the topic you wish to transmit to the class. Then identify those details which will benefit from the use of visual aids or use of the blackboard. Underline those *key* points that you consider to be the ones that need emphasis and which are related most clearly to your lesson objectives.

Record about ten minutes of your exposition and, on listening to the play-back, assess the extent to which you have used your voice to make the topic interesting, relevant and stimulating for your pupils.

For further guidance read Chapter 3 of Capel *et al.* (1995) to help you develop this important skill of communicating historical content.

explanation can appear a daunting prospect, after a while the use of teacher talk can present a different challenge – that is, *how to avoid talking for too long* (with most classes 15 to 20 minutes is a maximum). You must beware of what Labbett has termed, 'discursive intrusiveness' – the belief that if the teacher 'bangs on about it' for long enough pupils will understand. At times, there may well be a negative correlation between the quantity of teacher talk and pupil understanding (Labbett, 1996). You find that there are times when there is a place for self-denial. Although you might be tempted to display your knowledge ('I know it, therefore I will tell them about it . . . '), such loquacity may not be in the best interests of your pupils.

Your competence in exposition must also include an awareness of the advantages and disadvantages of this approach:

1 *The advantages.* Advocates of the value of teacher exposition usually emphasise its efficient use of time, a precious commodity for a subject often restricted to two lessons per week. The material can be thought through ready for presentation, given a logical structure and pared down to the essentials so that due emphasis can be given to key points. Any subject-specific words can be explained as the talk proceeds. The material can be presented with a style and organisation suitable for meeting the needs of assessment, particularly external examination syllabuses. To this many would add the opportunity which teacher talk can give you to sell the subject, introduce humour and anecdotes to illustrate a key point and make the learning of the content personal to the pupil audience. There is little doubt that, with an accomplished practitioner, there are times when this approach can be an effective learning experience, and it is perhaps significant that OFSTED (1995) commented critically on the 'lack of input by the teacher'.

2 *The disadvantages*. This style of teaching does invite questions about the quality of learning that might be involved, particularly if overused or used with content for which this 'transmission mode' is not really appropriate. Criticisms of this mode are most valid when its use may be seen to reflect an attitude towards the learning of history which places the teacher too exclusively in the role of the 'expert', the fount of all knowledge to be covered, and the pupil in the role of the receiver who sits like an empty receptacle waiting for 'knowledge' to be poured in. Teaching through teacher exposition raises fundamental questions about how pupils learn and, specifically, about how they acquire language in a way they can understand and make use of it. The common-sense answer is that there are times when teacher exposition is the most appropriate teaching method, and the art of the expert teacher is to judge when this is or is not the case.

This was a theme of the Bullock Report, noting:

> it is a confusion of everyday thought that we tend to regard 'knowledge' as something that exists independently of someone who knows. 'What is known' must in fact be brought to life afresh by the pupil's own efforts. Instead, pupils need to be given opportunities to use the new content and the language through which it is communicated. They need to be able to re-work it and feel comfortable with it, to graft new ideas, new information and new vocabulary on to what they already know. In short they need to be more active learners than passive recipients of teacher talk.
>
> (DES, 1975)

As Levine (1981) summarises, 'It is the learner's voice we must hear and if they are questioning voices we should rejoice, for learning is a matter of personally engaged struggle rather than detached acquiescence.' Hence, the importance of a methodology which includes pupil talk and expressive and evaluative writing, as exemplified in the sections which follow.

Included within such fundamental questions about how pupils learn, there arise ones which are more specifically related to the learning of history. *How much does the 'transmission mode' encourage pupils to adopt strategies to conceal their lack of understanding?* The ability to repeat what the teacher has said is not necessarily a guarantee that the pupils have understood. A useful maxim to bear in mind is, '*Just because you told them, don't assume they know*'. How appropriate is teacher talk as a means of developing pupils' understanding of concepts? To what extent is such a method likely to overemphasise factual material? Ultimately, although many pupils may be content to settle for their passive role, the limitations of their understanding might well be exposed when they present themselves for assessment.

Use of questioning

A common classroom strategy is that of exposition interrupted by questioning. Questioning is an important skill for any teacher. It has been calculated that teachers spend about 30 per cent of their time asking questions. However, the rate and the nature of oral questioning vary from subject to subject. How you formulate questions and use them is a good indicator of what you think the pupils are gaining from your history lessons. Much has been written since the 1950s about the type of questions used in lessons, which demonstrates the link between objectives and questions. Bloom (1956) made an early contribution to the classification of types of questions, and since then there have been many variants to his original attempt to place types of questions in a hierarchical order, from the easiest to the most difficult. A common list would be recall, comprehension, translation (e.g. transfer from one medium to another, such as writing a description of a picture), analysis, comparison, interpretation, synthesis, hypothetical (invention), evaluation. Opinions will vary about the validity of a hierarchy of types of question, for it is important to stress that some comprehension questions can be very difficult, as will be very clear from a glance at some historical sources, and some interpretations can be relatively straightforward. Garvey and Krug (1977) produced the following taxonomy with particular reference to the use of evidence in history teaching:

1 *Recall questions:* Give details of events, people, places mentioned in the source.
2 *Comprehension questions:* What does the evidence say? Do I understand it? Can I picture to myself the scene that it represents?
3 *Interpretation questions:* How does the evidence compare with my knowledge of the historical context? What was the writer's purpose in writing?
4 *Extrapolation questions:* Does it contradict other evidence? What new light does it shed?
5 *Invention questions:* If you had been there questions? 'What if' questions.
6 *Evaluation questions:* What is the value of the evidence? Is it trustworthy? What is your opinion about the course of action taken?

Such lists give you a useful basis for an analysis of the type of questions you use in your lessons. A familiar criticism of lessons is that too much emphasis is given to what are thought to be the undemanding questions; that is, an overuse of what may be called the 'lower order' questions involving recall, comprehension and translation, with only a limited use of the 'higher order' questions which encourage the pupils to think, such as interpretation and evaluation. Of course, the difficulty of a question depends on the context and materials being used; even so, your aim is to encourage your pupils to think for themselves and to try and use the 'higher order' questions as much as the situation allows. It should be noted that there is also the skill of listening and responding to questions in a way which encourages pupils to volunteer answers.

TASK 4.3 USING 'THINKING' QUESTIONS

1 Using the hierarchy of questions presented on p. 67, analyse a selection of worksheets and try to identify the types of questions that have been asked. What is the distribution of 'lower' and 'higher' order questions? If there are few 'higher' questions, try to formulate some that might be added.

2 Use the same method with the questions on two or three topics in a textbook.

3 When you are planning a question and answer session within your lesson, write out the principal questions you will be asking. Think about the sequencing and how you might include some 'thinking' questions. After the lesson reflect on how you used such questions and on how the techniques you used might differ from the asking of recall questions.

TASK 4.4 ENCOURAGING PUPILS' QUESTIONING

1 When you have taught some lessons, look back on your lesson plans and consider whether there might have been some opportunities for the pupils to do some questioning.

2 Try to list the range of situations that could generate pupils asking questions of yourself, of each other or for interrogating sources. Here is a list to get you started: asking questions of you as Oliver Cromwell; mock trial of Charles I; questioning group reports on a decision-making exercise; questioning the producer/author of a costume drama seen on video; researching family history; questioning a group presentation. Now try to add to these.

3 Think of, and experiment with, strategies for dealing with problems such as:
    (a) the reluctance of some pupils to ask questions;
    (b) how to deal with 'wrong' or inappropriate answers;
    (c) overenthusiastic or attention-seeking pupils wanting to answer all questions.

Questioning should not all be one-way (that is the teacher questions, the pupil responds). *Pupils should be encouraged to ask questions both of the teacher and of each other*. Much can be learned about pupils' historical understanding or lack of understanding from the questions they ask. There is a connection here with your own subject knowledge, because you are more likely to wish to monopolise the questioning if you feel insecure about your knowledge of the topic. OFSTED (1995) noted how, in circumstances that indicated good practice, pupils raised their own questions, developed and tested hypotheses and undertook investigations. A methodology in which pupils undertake their own historical enquiries gives you the opportunity to encourage them to ask questions about the topic and the sources of information they are using.

Reading

It is possible to argue that the role of reading in the teaching and learning of history has paradoxically been one both of great concern and yet of considerable neglect. Concern has been expressed about its suitability for stimulating interest and its accessibility to younger and slower readers. Neglect has resulted in pupils' limited ability to engage upon more extended reading and to use texts effectively higher up the school.

This paradox may be associated with the changing fashions in the use of the textbook. *What lessons can be learned from earlier practices to inform your own use of reading in the teaching of history?* Over a generation ago the typical textbook of the time had little attraction for many pupils. With their lack of illustrations and their terse and concise style, such books attempted to cover a vast range of content. When such books were allied to methods such as 'reading round the class', or the silent reading of a whole chapter followed by a factual test, there is little wonder that the memories of many adults of their school history lessons is one of unmitigated boredom. Many teachers of that era decided it was better to disregard the textbook and rely on resources of their own. Hence by the 1970s it was significant that the Schools Council 'Effective Reading Project' (1978) found that the textbook played a relatively minor supporting role in many classrooms. Teachers had more faith in the spoken word and teacher exposition. The project found that on average only four minutes of a forty-minute lesson was spent on reading, and Lunzer and Gardner (1979) were to note that in 'approximately half of all classrooms reading occurs in bursts of less than fifteen seconds in any one minute'. Explanations of such limited use ranged from the cost of the books, the complexity of the language, the pupils' limited attention and the inappropriateness of much of the content at a time when the content was not prescribed by statute. Thus, with the emergence of the Schools Council History Project materials in the early 1970s, it was not surprising that many teachers had difficulties in coming to terms with the extensive reading which those materials provided, particularly the wealth of source material.

The introduction of the National Curriculum has brought with it a new wave of textbooks, written for the prescribed units. These are in many ways a vast improvement on the books of a generation ago, reflecting not only the technical advances in publishing but also some of the issues of accessibility and the pupils' reading ability. In addition the books are much more task-orientated. With such resources available, the textbook has once more become an important resource for the teacher and can, when used selectively and in association with other approaches, be an effective resource. However, textbooks, no matter how attractive, will not increase the quality of the pupils' learning if they re-introduce the 'bad habits' of the past, namely reading round the class, copying, comprehension exercises which are mainly writing rather than reading exercises and do not necessarily reflect understanding, or reading without purpose or direction which can include setting extensive reading for homework (although help is never given with this skill in class). Hake and Haydn (1995) have also questioned whether the emphasis on sources has reduced the scope for coherent narrative and overview of the past. In their report on history teaching (1995), the OFSTED inspectors noted that the excessive dependence in some schools on a single textbook is also a cause for concern because it can so often result in a narrow teaching style. *As with all resources, you must be clear about why they have been chosen and what questions you need to ask in order to maximise their effectiveness.*

Marland (1977), following the Bullock Report, clearly feels that all teachers, including history teachers, have a role to play in the development of pupils' reading skills. That means not devoting the limited time available to the history teacher to teaching reading skills but to be aware of how the use of reading material in history can contribute to that development. Here are some pointers for your consideration.

First, seek to establish the role of reading in history by taking steps *to build up the pupils' confidence*, taking measures to ensure success. These could include making sure the pupils have sufficient background knowledge, so that the reading makes sense; identifying beforehand the words and phrases that could stop the reader's progress, both subject-specific and non-technical language, and, where significant, the use in the text of structure words such as 'if', 'although', 'nevertheless'; giving the pupils an overview of what the reading involves by summarising the arrangement of the paragraphs. Encourage the pupils to appreciate the value of re-reading. 'A quick reader is not necessarily a good one.'

Second, *make sure the pupils can see the purpose of the activity* (e.g. questions to be answered, diagrams or charts to be completed). Try to ensure that they are given not just comprehension questions but tasks which encourage reflection and opinions on what has been read.

TASK 4.5 THE USE OF READING IN THE CLASSROOM

1 When you are observing history lessons in which use is made of the textbook, make some notes for your reflection on that phase of the lesson:

(a) At what stage of the lesson is use made of reading? Following teacher exposition, following pupil work or as an introduction to the topic?

(b) If it involves reading aloud in class, *who* does the reading? If the pupils, what is the basis for selection? What are the other pupils doing while one reads? Can everybody in the class hear the pupil who is reading? How long are the extracts and for how long does the pupil read before an interruption?

(c) How is the reading used? As a prompt for further explanation and discussion and comment? As a source for questioning pupils? As a source for the tasks to follow?

(d) If the pupils are asked to read silently, for how long? Are they clear why they are doing the reading? What are the quicker readers asked to do while the slower ones complete the task? How does the teacher know all have read and understood the content?

2 Read through your notes and write an evaluation of the strengths and limitations of the use of reading in the classroom.

Third, the revised version of the National Curriculum gives greater emphasis to the use of historical enquiries, particularly involving source skills. Such enquiries can often be individual projects in which the pupils have to display initiative and nearly always involve reading skills. *Ensure that the pupils have the necessary reference skills.* Some pupils can become frustrated and disillusioned if they spend their time unprofitably simply because they lack the appropriate reference skills – the ability to use the indexing system, dictionaries, encyclo-paedias and contents pages. To this we can add CD-ROM materials, which again will require reading ability.

Fourth, *differentiation* is an ever-present issue. *Ensure that the reading material is appropriate for the ability of the pupils.* There will be times when sources are too complex for some pupils and need to be 'doctored' or even rewritten, although some might argue that if such is the case then the source was inappropriate in the first place. However, the greater emphasis on historical interpretations will create occasions when such attention will be rewarding. By contrast, more able pupils can be directed to more extensive reading than is often available in the textbook.

Finally, most teachers are very aware of the *problems of accessibility*. The booklet produced by the Teacher Education Project (1979), *Would You Read This?*, gives a practical guide to the criteria of readability. Even so, Arkell (1982) offers some cautionary advice with the conclusion that you should use readability tests only to supplement your own judgements about suitable reading material. And indeed it is possible that in the worthy attempts to meet the needs of all the pupils, something could be lost. Wilson (1985) has suggested that too much doctoring can leave the reading material a very arid, boring product. There is a case for leaving some difficult aspects of the reading in place if the general tone is likely to be more stimulating and the sense of period is to be retained. It is a question of balancing one need against another. It is not 'cheating' for teachers to provide a commentary as a way of helping pupils to grasp the essence of documents and sources: Fines argues that pupils can cope with quite challenging documents if the teacher helps and guides them through in a skilful manner (Fines, 1994).

Pupil talk

There are occasions when you ask the pupils to be quiet and talking will constitute a breach of classroom rules. Nevertheless, there are other times when pupils need to be encouraged to talk as a means of advancing their learning. Such contributions can include:

- asking and answering questions;
- participating in group discussion;
- reporting back from a group discussion;
- involvement in a debate or role-play or contributing to a presentation to the rest of the class.

For different activities the size of the audience differs, and that difference is often significant as some pupils, who may be reluctant to speak in front of the whole class, will welcome the opportunity within an apparently less threatening situation. Edwards noted how

> in small groups, and in the company of those they know well, the talk is more likely to be 'tentative, discursive, inexplicit and uncertain of direction'. In an atmosphere of tolerance, or hesitant formulation and co-operative effort, the children can 'stretch' their language to accommodate their own second thoughts and the opinions of others.
> (Edwards and Furlong, 1978)

This initial diffidence may be shyness or a fear of being wrong, but may also come from the idea that learning a subject such as history requires the ability to be able to speak in the formal, standard English of the textbook, somewhat alien from most pupils' usual form of speaking. Barnes and Todd (1977) emphasised the need for pupils to be able to re-work new information, new ideas and new vocabulary in their own terms if their understanding is to be advanced. Once pupils have assimilated the new material they are then more likely to feel able to use it in a more formal manner, to a wider audience.

Use of group work

Group work is seen as a useful means of advancing pupils' language development and, with that, their historical understanding. In assessing the value of group work, Brzezicki (1991) gives details of how this approach was used successfully with a year 9 class. He acknowledges that the searching and initial fragmentation of discourse which can characterise some group activities 'does not inspire confidence in some history teachers and therefore limits the extent to which such a strategy would become adopted'. Indeed, the value of the use of group work has on occasions been a source of debate among teachers. One of your tasks when assessing the use of differing teaching methods will be to consider the pros and cons of group work.

TASK 4.6 GROUP WORK

When you are observing a lesson which involves pupils working in groups, with the permission of the teacher:
1 Move around the groups and monitor how they are organising them-
   selves to complete the task. Do individual pupils have specific roles?
   How is the work divided between them? Are the pupils clear about what
   they are doing?
2 When the groups are involved in discussion, stand apart but within
   hearing distance and note the pupils' use of the historical content
   involved and of any subject-specific terms. Do they redefine the formal
   language in their own terms?
3 Move round the groups and try to identify any differences between the
   groups in their approach to the task and in the quality of pupil talk.
4 Write down your observations and conclusions to guide your own use of
   group work.
5 Perhaps later rather than earlier in the course, record one of the group's
   discussions and analyse their interchanges. Compare your conclusions
   with those of Barnes (1976), *From Communication to Curriculum*,
   Chapter 2.

Disadvantages. There can be little doubt that there are circumstances in which the use of group work can adversely affect the quality of learning. Brasher (1970) was quite dismissive of the value of group discussion, arguing that it tended to be discursive, shallow, and did 'not provide the royal road to intellectual advance, which is often assumed'. It was a situation described by one critic as a 'pooling of ignorance'. To these points might be added

- the difficulties of ensuring the pupils maintained 'on task' discussion;
- its use was likely to slow down the coverage of content;
- it was likely to give the pupils too much control of the pace of the lesson;
- at times, the classroom layout of the desks or tables was not helpful to any whole-class teaching which preceded or followed the group work.

Some teachers might argue that such an approach was only effective with able or amenable classes.

Advantages. Nevertheless there are situations when you will find pupils can be more motivated in group activities than being passive recipients of class teaching. OFSTED (1995), in noting the characteristics of good quality learning, refer to pupils 'contributing actively in groups'. Advocates of the use of group work would emphasise the real learning which can take place when the pupils have to use the subject content and language to communicate, and that more can be achieved when pupils are thus engaged than in whole-class teaching. The work of Lee *et al.* (1995) suggests that pupils can often develop more powerful ideas for understanding the past by talking to each other about problems of change, cause and explanation.

Successful use of group activities may be positively influenced by the following strategies:

- Ensure that the pupils have sufficient background knowledge to be able to complete the tasks they have been given. This will influence the enthusiasm with which they set about the activity.
- Think about the way the groups are organised (by ability, friendship groups); choice of this depends on the tasks involved. The use of grouping by ability is not as frequently used as it might be in history lessons. You should explore the possibilities of this and the opportunities it can give you as a teacher to move round the groups asking questions appropriate to the ability of the group.
- Think about how each group may have to allocate tasks or roles (e.g. recording discussion, completing pro formas, presentation of group decisions).
- Be precise in your thinking about the materials the groups will need.
- Give clear instructions. It is fundamental that the pupils have a clear idea of what they are to do and understand the value of what they are doing.
- Employ strategies to maintain the pace of the work. At times there are

several stages to the activity, so time-checks and interim targets can be employed to maintain the pace of the lesson.

- Try to problematise the topic to be discussed in a way that will interest the pupils. A discussion on whether Queen Elizabeth I should execute Mary Queen of Scots won't work very well if the pupils couldn't care less whether she dies or not.
- Perhaps most important of all is the need for any such group activity to have an end product (e.g. a decision or set of conclusions, a presentation or a display).

Role-play

As you gain in confidence and seek to extend the range of methods you can employ, you find there are some topics which are very suitable for the use of role-play. References and examples for role-play activities can be found in Chapters 5 and 6. The method is often at its most useful when pupils have to deal with topics which are conceptually difficult, such as the impact on a community of the religious changes at the time of the Reformation.

Here we offer some guidelines for the preparation of a lesson involving the use of role-play:

1 Research the historical background.
2 Decide on the precise location/time for the role-play.
3 Identify the participants; make a list of the people involved, either real names or fictitious, although the more it is source-based the better.
4 Prepare 'briefing cards' for each of the roles. These include details of the participant and a summary of that person's attitudes on the topic of the lesson. Pupils to be informed of the decision to be debated. (Alternatively the pupils can be assigned roles and they can research the details for themselves. For this they would need to be provided with sources of information.)
5 Teach the historical background, context and precise detail of the setting. Where appropriate use diagrams and maps.
6 Organise the class; allocation of roles to the pupils or groups; give time for the pupils to prepare their case or viewpoint.
7 Proceed with the role-play. Give time-checks.
8 Plenary; reporting back, summarise the significance of the exercise. Set follow-up work, often written work in which the pupil stays 'in role', thus emphasising the important function pupil talk has as a precursor to the pupils' written work.

Remember that role-play does not have to be an 'all singing, all dancing' festival of active drama, with all pupils having to write and act their parts. It can sometimes involve a small number of pupils who have been selected to perform for the rest of the class; it can be done without pupils having to move around the room; and it can be done by simply asking pupils to take part in decision-making exercises based on information sheets or film slides. Some student teachers are reluctant to use role-play, as they envisage that it will entail a full-scale dramatic production. Some of the most effective role-plays are quite modest in ambition, and eminently feasible, without recourse to MGM-scale dramatic production.

Writing

Of the range of activities which take place in the learning of history, writing is one of the most important and, at the same time, the least popular among pupils. Yet it is principally through their writing that their knowledge and understanding is usually assessed. Writing is an issue of some concern. The OFSTED review of current practice in history (1995) commented that 'in a number of cases, where pupils achieved high standards orally, this was not replicated in written work'. Bowen (1995) was more specific when he quoted the OFSTED report on one history department, where the girls were achieving higher examination grades than the boys, and the teachers were advised 'to give further consideration to ways in which boys' written work can be improved to match the quality of their contributions in class'.

The work of Christine Counsell has been influential in recent years in providing teaching strategies for the development of pupils' writing skills in history (Counsell, 1997). Counsell points out that for many pupils history is difficult because it is both vast and complex. Many pupils find it difficult:

- to classify information;
- to organise information and deploy it for a specified purpose;
- to argue and analyse (as opposed to describe and narrate);
- to support their arguments with appropriate detail.
- to distinguish between the general and the particular.

(Counsell, 1995)

Counsell makes the point that one of the key obstacles to pupils' proficiency in extended writing is a lack of awareness that they are confronting an organisational problem. One of the tasks of the history teacher is therefore to assist pupils in the self-conscious organisation and deployment of information and ideas. This can involve the use of the word processor to help pupils to organise ideas and information, and the use of writing frames and 'clever starters' which model ways of structuring paragraphs and provide ways of helping pupils into discursive and analytical responses.

The degree to which the 'scaffolding' of support for writing is provided can vary according to the extent to which the pupils are proficient in extended writing. With a year 7 class which is being introduced to the idea of essay work this might entail writing a first sentence for each paragraph; where proficiency is variable within the same teaching group it might be achieved by providing suggestions for introductory and linking sentences on the classroom walls.

'Some sources suggest that . . . '

'However, others suggest . . . '

'Sources which have something in common are . . . '

'We can't be sure about *x* because . . . '

'A source which sheds some light on this is . . . '

'Another important factor was . . . '

Figure 4.1 Helping pupils to organise their writing
Source: Counsell, 1996

Counsell uses the idea of '*the zone of relevance*', to help pupils to grasp that not all sources of information are relevant (and therefore 'evidence') for a particular question or enquiry. The following statements are given to pupils, and they are asked to place in the 'zone of relevance' the statements which contain information relevant to the question posed.

Question: Why did the fire get out of control and destroy so much of London?

Water supplies were unusually low in 1666	Fire-fighting equipment was not good enough to cope with a large fire	**The zone of relevance**
Houses in London were built very close together		
Someone started a fire in Pudding Lane	Most buildings were made of wood	
Town officials did not believe that it was going to spread and took no action at the start	Throughout London, heating and lighting were provided by fire	

The idea can also be used to develop the idea of 'topic relevance', and 'question relevance', by incorporating statements which have neither topic nor question relevance.

Figure 4.2 Helping pupils to organise information
Source: Counsell, 1995

TASK 4.7 PUPILS' WRITTEN WORK IN HISTORY

With the permission of your mentor, analyse a selection of exercise books covering a range of abilities and ages.

1 Make a list of the different writing activities that have been used.
2 Consider also the evidence the books present of the problems which pupils of different abilities appear to have had.
3 Try to identify those difficulties which would appear to be specific to the completion of written tasks in history.

Curtis (1994) anticipated such comments when she noted 'the difference between written and spoken language, which is at the heart of why certain groups of pupils underachieve in schools'. Most teachers are aware of this mismatch between the quality of oral contributions and the quality of what is presented in writing. Thus, one of the major challenges you will face as a history teacher will be to try to improve the quality of your pupils' written work.

STRATEGIES FOR IMPROVING THE QUALITY OF YOUR PUPILS' WRITTEN WORK

Presentation. You will find that written work in history can cover a wide range of activities which will in turn result in a wide variation in the way they are presented. At times there will be a case for writing standard English, at others rough jottings will suffice. It could be that pupils use different ends of their exercise book for these different writing requirements. So, *you will need to consider how the pupils' exercise book is to be used.* There may be a case, particularly with GCSE classes, for having two exercise books, each serving a different writing function and each intended for a different audience. Rough notes, jottings, draft versions, recording of ideas, summaries of group decisions in one book; more formal writing and recording of information in another. On some occasions work will be completed on separate paper, especially if there is to be a display of pupil work.

Clarity of instructions. A very common feature of student teachers' first lessons is the limited quality of their instructions. To avoid having to stop the class when they have settled to their work to clarify directions and give further guidance, it is important that you have thought through exactly what instructions you need to give. You need to *anticipate the pupils' requirements* about layout, length of work, use of proper sentences, whether they write out the question, ensure they write in their own words and understand the basis upon which you will be marking the work.

Process. Behind these considerations of the mechanics of how written work is presented lies a much more fundamental point about *how you encourage pupils to do themselves justice with their work*, an issue which is central to those concerns noted at the beginning of this section. It can be argued that insufficient attention is given to the processes by which pupils can achieve the quality of work often expected. In the consideration of writing in geography, history and social studies for the *Writing Across the Curriculum Project* (Schools Council, 1978), the point was made that 'we are conditioned to the expectation that all writing will be clearly organised and that if it is not then it is "bad" or "a failure" or "of low standard" '. Curtis (1994) is rightly critical of situations where 'little distinction is made between the purposes of writing – making rough notes, making notes to aid memory for a test or as a basis for a written task'.

Disappointing work may be averted if more emphasis is given to the *preparatory stages* through which the pupil needs to progress before the final product is achieved. Such stages could include activities in which information needs to be collected, sorted and re-sorted. In developing an understanding through exploring their ideas and making the content personal to them, the Project (Schools Council, 1978) argued, writing is being used *as a means of learning* to assist pupils in the gradual process of assimilation. Writing in such early stages will lack clear structure and considerations relating to presentation in standard English. Only after the pupil has come to terms with the historical content, and the ideas and opinions which the National Curriculum and the revised GCSE require, can attention be given to the final product.

THE RANGE OF WRITTEN WORK

You will find it helpful to keep in mind the range of written work that is possible in the learning of history. Curtis (1994) suggests an audit of how writing is used in history involving not only the types of written task undertaken by pupils but also how they are prepared for such tasks. There could be various ways of presenting such an audit. Here, six types of writing are identified and discussed.

Descriptive

You will find such writing is a prominent feature of Key Stage 3.

Types These can include transferring into writing representations such as pictures, maps, diagrams and time-charts; describing historical sites; writing comparisons of photographs and sources.

Use and differentiation Differentiation may be achieved by the amount of completed writing also made available. Many pupils feel comfortable with descriptive writing, but *the slower pupils may need something which has already been written* – for example completing a paragraph begun by the teacher; sequencing activities, which involves rewriting in the correct order statements linked to pictures. You will find gap-filling exercises are frequently used. These can offer useful support, but you should look for every opportunity to move the pupils on from such tasks and encourage them to use their own words. *Many pupils may also need to be encouraged to go beyond description.* A common experience is for pupils, when asked to compare two sources, to describe each in turn without commenting on the differences. Again OFSTED (1995) noted that 'poor achievement was characterised by responses which lacked factual detail . . . or which did not go beyond the literal comprehension of sources'.

Recording

The nature of this writing particularly is determined by its function and the person for whom it is intended.

Types Such writing could include rough jottings, notes for discussion, notes for group presentation or notes taken on a site visit. Alternatively the recording may be notes, which the pupil will need to use at a later date in preparation for an examination.

Use and differentiation Note-making is an activity that plays a significant role in history teaching. OFSTED (1995) noted as a weakness that 'drafting and note-making are not well-developed'. With the re-emergence of the emphasis on knowledge there may be a case for developing skills in note-making, but in such a way that the practice also serves to reinforce and extend pupils' understanding. The emphasis therefore is not on 'note-taking' but on 'note-making', as the pupils use their own words and not those dictated by the teacher or copied verbatim from the board or the textbook. Your task is to help the pupils, in varying degrees according to their ability, to structure their notes. Following initial information, derived from teacher exposition, the viewing and discussion of a video, or the analysis of sources, the abler pupils in all years of the secondary school will be quite capable of making their own notes, given some structure in the form of sub-headings on the board, spellings of proper names and any statistics involved. The amount of information will be extended for the average pupils, whilst with the slower pupils note-making will follow greater re-enforcement and requests to write a complete sentence extending what has been written on the board. The weakest may complete sentences the teacher has begun, but still with some scope for their own words. If reference is to be made to information in books, *try to structure the work so that copying can be avoided.* Pupils are more likely to understand the content if they are required to express it in their own words.

Expressive

The *Writing Across the Curriculum Project* (Schools Council, 1978) stressed the importance of the 'personal' aspect of writing, where pupils are allowed to write with a more personal voice, in contrast to situations where the fear of making mistakes stifles opinion. In the words of Levine (1981) 'to suppress the "self" is to suppress the means of understanding'.

Types. Such writing can include the preparation for debate, comments on a video, on group decisions or participation in a role-play.

Use and differentiation. Differentiation is often achieved by the extent to which evidence is used to support such opinions.

Imaginative

Another writing activity that is released from the more formal, impersonal kind of writing is that which is more creative and inventive.

Types. Such creative efforts can involve writing from the perspective of someone in the past, diaries, reports, eye-witness accounts, letters, plays, provided that the imaginative work is rooted in evidence to create a genuinely historical activity.

Use and differentiation. It is worthy of note that often through this type of writing a pupil can display a greater understanding of the historical context than other writing might suggest. Imaginative work can also cover the consideration of hypotheses: the 'what if' questions. Differentiation is usually by outcome and, again, the extent to which the work is rooted in historical evidence.

Analytical/evaluative

As made explicit in the task which follows, the quality of this type of writing will be greatly influenced by the methodology which precedes it.

Types. Examples of such writing include pupils being asked to group together and classify ideas and data and employ the relevant vocabulary to describe such grouping; the analysis of changes, causes and consequences; the evaluation of sources and interpretations.

Use and differentiation. Such grouping of ideas will encourage the development of more extended writing (again something encouraged by OFSTED, including the skill of learning to think in paragraphs. Gunning (1978b) demonstrated how the challenge of extended writing can be broken down into a series of stages, first working on the content of the paragraphs, then the sequencing, and finally an introduction and conclusion.

Synthesis

This is arguably the most demanding of the written tasks you can set in the teaching of history, where pupils are required to reconstruct an event, create an extended explanation, answer a question at length or present an interpretation – all compositions based on a variety of evidence.

Use and differentiation. For example, if pupils are to compile a comprehensive answer to questions such as 'What was it like living in (your home town) during the Second World War?' they need to be taken through a series of stages of research, recording, classifying and writing if they are to achieve a satisfactory synthesis. Further consideration is given to the writing which results from 'historical enquiries' in Chapter 6.

TASK 4.8 PREPARING A TASK INVOLVING EXTENDED WRITING

During your teaching there will be occasions when it will be necessary for you to set a written exercise which involves extended writing. This will be the culmination of a series of activities. Having selected an appropriate topic such as 'The causes of the English Civil War', try to answer the following questions and then use them in the planning of your lessons to the point where the pupils attempt the task.

1 *Knowledge*
How will I make sure the pupils have sufficient information to enable them to complete the task? What opportunities could there be for the pupils to add to their knowledge in an independent way?

2 *Understanding*
How do I ensure that pupils are familiar and comfortable with the concepts and skills involved? Will I use any pre-writing activities?

3 *Instructions*
What guidance shall I give about the process by which the pupils move to their final draft? How do I make clear my expectations about the layout of the finished work, its length, the way they make use of their knowledge, concern for their use of spelling and grammar, the basis on which their work will be assessed?

SUMMARY AND KEY POINTS

Much of this chapter has concentrated on assuming and anticipating. You have been encouraged to consider what assumptions you may be making in how you choose to cover a topic; assumptions about the contribution to pupils' under-standing when required to listen, read, talk and write. Such consideration will help you to anticipate potential difficulties in the approaches and the materials you choose to use and to employ strategies to help the pupils succeed. This often means, in the words of Marland (1977), helping pupils *through* such difficulties rather than helping them to get *round* them. The styles of teaching you adopt will reflect your understanding of the processes by which the pupils learn.

The *key points* which this chapter has emphasised are that you avoid getting into too repetitious a style with a very limited range of approaches, and that you be prepared to take some risks as your confidence grows. Be careful to vet any reading material before you use it and try to anticipate any potential difficulties it may create. Remember that it is your job to sell the subject, to demonstrate a genuine interest in the past and to ensure that the pupils value the contribution of history to their education. Consider the value of using 'higher order' ques-tions and also of creating situations for pupils to ask questions. Reading can be both under-used and badly used – think carefully about how you can maximise the use of reading materials but be careful not to use the textbook as an easy option. This chapter has attempted to emphasise that pupils often only under-stand historical content if they are given the opportunities to express it in their own way. Hence the importance of activities which include the structured use of pupil talk and opportunities to write in their own words. Finally you are encouraged to carry out an audit of the variety of writing activities you set over a period of time as a means of ensuring you employ the range covered by this chapter.

FURTHER READING

Counsell, C. (1997) *Analytical and Discursive Writing in National Curriculum History at Key Stage 3: A Practical Guide*, Teaching of History Series, London, Historical Association.

Curtis, S. (1994) 'Communication in History', *Teaching History*, October.
An excellent article, which makes many good teaching points and exemplifies them with a case study on the French Revolution.

Levine, N. (1981) *Language, Teaching and Learning: History*, WLE.
This remains a most stimulating and valuable contribution to the role of language in the teaching of history.

5 Developing historical understanding (1)

INTRODUCTION

One aspect of the various developments in the teaching and learning of history which have emerged since the evolution of what has been called the 'new' history is an emphasis on the importance of key concepts in history, particularly the concepts of time, evidence, change, causation and the understanding of events and issues from the perspective of people in the past. This chapter considers how you might set about teaching those concepts which concern chronology, causation and change and the characteristic features of particular periods and societies. It is now generally accepted that the more sophisticated your pupils' understanding of these concepts, when related to historical content, the greater will be the depth of their historical understanding. For this reason these key concepts were included in the assessment objectives of the GCSE examination when it began in 1988. With the introduction of the National Curriculum at Key Stage 3, the study of these concepts was given further emphasis as they were encapsulated in the First Attainment Target when the National Curriculum in history was first implemented in 1991. In the changes which have taken place with the introduction of the New Orders in 1995, these key concepts have been retained within the single Attainment Target, although with less precision than earlier. Even so, their importance continues to be emphasised as they constitute the first two of the five Key Elements, which are designed to guide your planning and teaching. Although the revised GCSE has dropped the assessment objective dealing with 'the ability to look at events from the perspective of people in the past' (DES, 1985), the key concepts will continue to be a major feature of that examination and the assessment targets.

OBJECTIVES

By the end of this chapter you should:

- have some understanding of the contribution of the concepts of time, causation and change to pupils' historical understanding;

- be familiar with some common misconceptions which pupils may have when confronted with these concepts;
- be aware of the problems pupils may experience in understanding the characteristic features of particular periods and societies;
- be in a position to devise a range of teaching strategies with which to develop your pupils' understanding of these Key Elements.

THE IMPORTANCE OF THE KEY CONCEPTS IN THE TEACHING AND LEARNING OF HISTORY

An awareness of the importance of chronology and overview helps to ensure that history is not reduced to dismembered and isolated gobbets of the past, which are not reconciled into a coherent pattern by pupils. One of your responsibilities as a history teacher is to *provide an overview of the past* so that pupils emerge from school history with some sense of the stages which humans have gone through to get to where we are today. When covering particular events or topics, some attempt must be made to put them in their overall historical context if the pupils are to develop a meaningful sense of the past.

One of the most compelling explanations of the importance of these concepts is the greater validity they give to the study of history. Concentration on such concepts helps the move away from an image of learning history as one represented by 'stories from the past', or of factual content which has, in the eyes of pupils, very little connection with their lives and the business of living in the last years of the twentieth century. *The understanding and use of key concepts in history helps to underline the significance of historical events and processes.* Sansom (1987) argued that the application of these concepts, or 'rules of thought', helps to turn information into historical knowledge. It is also possible to assert that, even when a pupil's recall of specific detail diminishes, the understanding that comes from conclusions about the significance of an event or events is the enduring educational outcome.

Your pupils today live in a world of constant and rapid change, and the historical perspective helps them to place such changes into a wider context and to begin to understand the complex and interrelated nature of the causes of change. At the same time there are aspects of life that do not change. Pupils today share a common humanity with people in the past, and there is much to learn from the study of the response of different peoples, groups and individuals to situations that confront them. An emphasis on these concepts also presents a useful guide to the choice of topics within a syllabus, when the amount of time available means there has to be a discerning selection of the content you choose to teach. Finally, as we hope to demonstate in the chapter, your pupils are more likely to succeed in developing this aspect of their historical understanding if they are actively engaged in their use of knowledge.

TEACHING PUPILS ABOUT TIME

It would seem to be a reasonable proposition to suggest that part of the function of school history should be to give pupils some understanding of time and chronology. If pupils are to make sense of history, they need to have some idea about how we 'measure' and reference events in history in terms of when they occurred, and to build up a mental framework of the past. Although secondary pupils will have studied history for at least six years, there may still be 'black holes' in their grasp of fundamental aspects of the concept of time.

It should be remembered that under the original National Curriculum for history, it was possible to get to level 10 in all of the attainment targets for the subject, without knowing what century you were living in, or what AD and BC meant. Time was, at least to some extent, a neglected and forgotten element of the subject, and this was reflected in the textbooks which were published at the inception of the National Curriculum. A survey of over a thousand year 7 pupils found that many did not know which century they were living in, what AD meant, or what words such as 'reign', or 'chronology' meant. When asked about the reasons for these deficiencies, some heads of history suggested that there was an assumption that 'all that had been covered at primary school', or that they had just taken such understanding for granted, or that as it was not part of the '45 boxes' of the original attainment targets it had not been a focus for teaching and assessment (Haydn, 1995). Whatever the reasons, it is important that you do not assume that all your pupils possess a clear grasp of the rudiments of time and chronology. Whereas time was a comparatively peripheral concern of the original National Curriculum for history, its status has been restored in the revised version, and as well as forming one of the key elements, children's understanding of time is a component of all eight of the attainment levels.

One advantage of the National Curriculum has been that all pupils will have had some instruction in history at Key Stages 1 and 2, but as pupils will be of differing abilities, and will have come from different feeder primary schools, it would be surprising if they all arrived at secondary school with similar under-standings about time. One of the tasks of the history teacher is to investigate and develop some insight into what knowledge and understandings pupils bring with them *before* you start to teach the topic or concept in question. Time may well have been approached in a very different manner in various primary schools; some will have learned through family trees and time-lines, others will have started with ancient history and worked forward. Some will already have a sound grasp of dating systems and some idea of a general 'framework' of the past, others may have passed through Key Stages 1 and 2 without having mastered even the lowest levels of attainment in this domain of history.

TASK 5.1 A DIAGNOSTIC EXERCISE ON PUPILS' UNDERSTANDING OF TIME

The following is an example of a diagnostic test of children's understanding of some aspects of time, which might be given to year 7 pupils in order to elicit their grasp of some elements of the concept of time. With the permission of your mentor, and if the pupils have not already been subjected to such a test, give the test to a group of pupils and analyse their responses. The test should take pupils between 5 and 15 minutes to complete. The test attempts to address pupils' understanding of dating systems, their ability to understand and manipulate 'centuries', and their familiarity with some time-related vocabulary. If the pupils have already done a similar form of test, ask your mentor how the pupils performed, and what 'gaps' there were in their grasp of basic time concepts.

History: understanding time

(a) Which century are we living in?
(b) If you look at a newspaper, as well as giving the date it says that it is the year 1997. Why is it called 1997 and not any other year?
(c) Is this year referred to as 1997 in all countries all over the world? Give reasons for your answer.
(d) What do the letters AD stand for before a date?
(e) What do the letters AD mean, before a date?
(f) What do the letters BC stand for after a date?
(g) If the Battle of Hastings was fought in AD 1066, in which century did the battle take place?

What century were the following years in?
(h) AD 1537
(i) AD 637
(j) AD 87
(k) AD 1900
(l) 337 BC
(m) 87 BC

Name any year from these centuries:
(n) 14th century AD
(o) 9th century AD
(p) 3rd century BC

cont . . .

(q) Julius Caesar first landed in Britain in 55 BC. He came back a year
     later. What year was it then?
(r) If someone offered to sell you a coin dated 55 BC would it be worth a
     lot of money? Give reasons for your answer.

Explain the meaning of the following words:
(s) chronology
(t) decade
(u) century
(v) millennium
(w) era
(x) anachronism
(y) Give an example of an anachronism

When the pupils have completed the test, analyse their responses to
examine where there are gaps in their understanding of time. What
activities might you devise in order to rectify any deficiencies in their
understanding of time?

APPROACHES TO TIME AND CHRONOLOGY

The test in Task 5.1 addresses a particular strand of pupil's understanding of
time: that of the 'mechanics' of time – dating systems and conventions, basic
time vocabulary, how time 'works'. Although this is important, there are other
aspects of time which pupils need to address. One of these is an understanding
of chronology, and a developing sense of the order of events in history. Pupils
should develop a mental framework of the past through the study of history.
As the History Working Group's Final Report pointed out, 'A grasp of the
sequence of events is fundamental to an understanding of the relationship
between events, and such concepts as cause and change. Chronology, therefore,
provides a mental framework or map which gives significance and coherence to
the study of history' (DES, 1990). The tendency in recent years to study
'patches' or 'themes' in history, rather than a measured and even (but super-
ficial?) progression from 'The Romans towards the present day', has meant that
not all pupils have a clear grasp of the overall unfolding of events in history.
The nature of the GCSE exam, with its emphasis on the critical examination
of sources, means that it might be possible to gain full marks on a sourcework
question on the Second World War, without necessarily knowing who was on
whose side, and who won. There are also some areas of history where is it
essential to have a clear grasp of the precise *order* of events as a necessary, if not
sufficient, basis for providing a coherent explanation or analysis of a historical

event such as the outbreak of the First World War, or the campaigns of 1066. Understanding of 'Deep Time' – the distant past stretching back to prehistory, the Stone Age and the formation of the earth might also be a facet of time which might be addressed in the course of school history. An understanding of what is meant by the term 'prehistory' can help to give pupils some insight into the nature of the discipline of history itself.

It might be helpful to classify the teaching and learning of time into categories so that you have a clear sense of the various facets of time which need to be addressed in the development of pupils' understanding of the past. For convenience, we have referred to these as T1 to T4:

- T1 = The mechanics of time – dating systems and conventions, time vocabulary, how time works. In the same way that pupils need to understand the 24-hour clock, if they are studying history they need to know 'the clock of history'.
- T2 = The framework of the past: building up a map of the past in terms of a developing sense of what bits of history fit in where. The chronology and sequence of strands of history – for example, the changing nature of monarchy in Britain over the centuries, the evolution of methods of transport, warfare, energy.
- T3 = Building up an increasing range of historical topics or episodes where pupils have a sound grasp of the order in which events unfolded. This might include areas such as the changes in religious policy in England in the sixteenth and seventeenth centuries, the key events and turning points in the Second World War, or an understanding of the chronology of the French Revolution. If pupils have a confident grasp of the order of events *and* can explain why each event occurred, they are some way towards being able to construct an explanation of elements of the past.
- T4 = Developing pupils' understanding of 'Deep Time'. Giving pupils an understanding of the scale of the past, from the formation of the earth, through prehistory to the development of writing and on to AD. Part of this is helping pupils through misconceptions about when humans appeared on earth, and when 'history' started.

Teaching strategies

Your skills of exposition in providing narrative frameworks of the past is an important part of developing pupils' grasp of time and chronology, including an awareness that pupils do not possess the map of the past that some teachers perhaps take for granted. The use of time-lines in the classroom, as well as in exercise books, can be helpful. The development of sequencing exercises – whether on cards, for groupwork, in exercise books, on the blackboard, or on a word processor – can provide activities which require pupils to think through the precise order of events, using inference as well as knowledge. There is however a danger of sequencing for its own sake; that is, constructing arbitrary lists of historical events which have no necessary connection with each other.

The following are examples of exercises which might be given to pupils to develop their understanding of some of these facets of time and chronology.

T1 exercises

(a) The following words are all used to note an amount or length of time. Organise them into the correct order, putting the shortest at the top and the longest at the bottom.

shortest	
	year
	hour
	decade
	second
	millennium
	century
	minute
	week
	month
	day
longest	

(b) The following are all terms which are used to describe periods of time in history. Place them in the column where you think they belong, and then put them in order, with the earliest at the top of the column and the most recent at the bottom.

> Renaissance, Stone Age, Tudor, Pre-Raphaelite, Bronze Age, Hanoverian, Ancient, Pre-Industrial, Plantagenet, Medieval, Modern, Reformation, Victorian, Gothic, Norman, Early Modern, Georgian, Dark Ages, Impressionist, Cubist, Space Age, Prehistory, Regency, Restoration, Windsor.

(This is an example which might be appropriate for very able, or older pupils, but it would be fairly easy to draft simpler versions.) The most able pupils might be asked to identify their own categories

Royal Family	General terms	Architecture	Named after historical events	Painting

T2 exercises

These are simply sequencing and organising exercises. They could be done as card sort exercises or on a word processor. It is comparatively easy to make them harder or easier according to need. These are fairly low level, the idea would be to build in progression by making such exercises increasingly more complex as the pupils' overview of British history builds up over the course of the Key Stage. (For a more complex example, see Chapter 8.)

(a) *Fact or fiction?*

Activity 1: *Divide the following list of 'people' into two columns; those who existed in real life and those who exist only in stories and fairy tales. Then discard or delete the record of those who you have decided are not real people.*

Peter Pan, Adolf Hitler, Queen Victoria, Robin Hood, King Arthur, Roger Rabbit, William the Conqueror, Winston Churchill, Oliver Cromwell, Margaret Thatcher, Superman, Batman, Asterix the Gaul, King Henry VIII, Guy Fawkes, Alfred the Great, Florence Nightingale.

Activity 2: *Look at the list of 'real' people that you have got left on your list. Try to put them in* chronological *order (the order in which they lived – furthest from the present day first on the list, nearest to today at the end). Try to make a rough guess as to when they were alive.*

Before AD 1066	
AD 1100	
AD 1200	
AD 1300	
AD 1400	
AD 1500	
AD 1600	
AD 1700	
AD 1800	
AD 1900	
AD 2000	

(b) *Chronology: 'A scheme of time, order in time'*

Putting things in chronological order means putting them into the order in which they occurred. It is often helpful to be able to do this to increase our understanding of the past and to establish a framework or map of the past which establishes an outline of the unfolding of events through which the past has led to the present.

The following are all periods of history which are part of the National Curriculum. Try to rearrange them into chronological order.

The Vikings, The Victorians, The era of the Second World War, The Tudors, The Romans, The Normans, Ancient Greece, The French Revolution, The Ancient Egyptians, The First World War.

T3 exercises

(a) Reorganise the following events so that they are in the correct order, to form an account of the events of 1066.

Battle of Stamford Bridge
Edward the Confessor died
William of Normandy crowned King of England
Harold accepted the throne of England
William marched from Hastings to London

Harald Hardrada invaded the north of England
Harold Godwinson marched south to Hastings
William won the Battle of Hastings
William landed in the south of England, at Hastings

(b) Place the following events of the Second World War in chronological order, to demonstrate an understanding of how the war developed and ended.

German surrender   Barbarossa
Invasion of Poland   Italy surrenders
Fall of France   El Alamein/Stalingrad
Japan attacked US   Hiroshima
Dunkirk   D-Day
Japanese surrender Phoney War

(Again, the level of difficulty of these exercises can be adjusted by adding or omitting events.)

TASK 5.2 AN EXERCISE ON TIME

1 With the permission of your mentor, try out an exercise on time, and evaluate its results.
2 Try to devise an exercise of your own which might be used by pupils at Key Stage 3 or 4, which is focused on one of these aspects of pupils' understanding of time.
3 Try to devise a pupil activity which attempts to develop pupils' understanding of T4 ('Deep Time'), or ask pupils about their ideas about the distant past.

CHARACTERISTIC FEATURES OF THE PAST

Importance

In the first part of the second Key Element, it is required that pupils should be taught 'to analyse the characteristic features of particular periods and societies, including the range of ideas, beliefs and attitudes of people, and the experiences of men and women; and to analyse the social, cultural, religious and ethnic diversity of the societies studied'.

A useful starting point for your teaching of this aspect of historical understanding is to make sure you are clear as to its purpose. What are the perceived educational outcomes of studying 'the range of ideas, beliefs and attitudes of people' of particular periods and societies? Why is it considered important that pupils analyse the 'social, cultural, religious and ethnic diversity' of particular societies? It is possible that one of the objectives is the expectation that the analysis of societies, diverse in time and place, will produce in Britain a society which is more tolerant and understanding of people who hold beliefs and attitudes which are different to their own. It is through this study that pupils will be encouraged to re-examine or create their own system of values and beliefs. This is where the study of history makes a contribution to the pupil's growing personal awareness by having 'the richest storehouse of human experience and an unrivalled opportunity to reflect on other people's feelings and actions' (Wilson, 1985). The idea here is that school history should be about more than just the pupils' cognitive development; it should also address the 'affective' domain of values and attitudes. This is not an area of consensus amongst history teachers; as noted in Chapter 2, there is a school of thought which argues that the purpose of school history is to teach pupils to think for themselves rather than attempt to inculcate particular values and attitudes, and that the attempt to use history for purposes of socialisation is to reduce it to a form of propaganda.

TASK 5.3 SCHOOL HISTORY AND THE AFFECTIVE DOMAIN

Discuss with the history teachers and history student teachers you work with their views on the idea of school history as a vehicle for developing particular values and attitudes in pupils, such as respect for cultural diversity and tolerance. What other values and attitudes (if any) should school history attempt to cultivate?

Problems pupils might experience

The challenge you have of encouraging pupils to be able to understand past societies with sets of ideas, beliefs and attitudes very different from those commonly held today is one that has been a concern of history teachers for over twenty years. The experience of the GCSE has shown just how difficult that challenge has been with 15- and 16-year-olds and so this will be even more challenging when dealing with pupils at Key Stage 3. Many would agree with Lee (1987) that 'entertaining the beliefs, goals and values of other people . . . is a difficult intellectual achievement'. It is hard, he continued, 'because it requires a high level of thinking to be able to hold such features in the mind as inert knowledge, but to be able to work with them in such a way that the pupil can understand and explain what people did in the past'. Let us try to analyse the problems and difficulties adolescents are likely to experience in trying to understand the characteristic features of societies remote in time and place from their own.

An important part of learning history is the ability to understand the ideas, beliefs and attitudes of different periods and societies. By understanding we mean not just the ability to recall and describe but to acknowledge that for those times and places, such ideas made good sense and did present a rational explanation of their actions. Yet this can create real problems for pupils in the secondary school. For them it is a major conceptual leap when the values and norms of behaviour might be so different from the world in which they live. For them, in the words of L.P. Hartley, 'the past is a foreign country, people did things differently there'. It requires significant adjustments to be made if they are to get to grips with the very unfamiliar ways of people living in the past. To achieve this the pupils need to discard a collection of notions that can detract from the quality of their understanding.

One such notion is the idea, common to many pupils in the secondary school, that people in the past were intellectually inferior to people today and that the further one goes back in time, the more inferior they get. This is not surprising as the evidence of material advances surrounds the modern pupils, and their understanding of the evolution of man would also encourage such thinking. Ashby and Lee (1987) have noted the inability of the pupils to recognise that people in the past could not have known what the pupil of today knows and takes for granted and this can lead them to be contemptuous of past actions. Yet this dismissive attitude has to be surmounted if the pupil is to develop historical understanding. *You need to encourage your pupils to appreciate that what is 'strange' and 'different' is not necessarily inferior.*

Conversely, another notion that can often limit understanding of past societies and cultures, is one where the pupil makes too great an assumption that people in the past were the same as people today, a view that makes little concession to the changes that have occurred over time. Of course, we do have a common humanity with people of different times and places and the assumptions that pupils make are understandable for that reason. The danger is that such thinking is likely to encourage anachronistic representations of the past by the pupil attributing to people in the past, ideas and reactions which could not have prevailed at the time. Even then the short length of time that adolescents have lived and the limited situations they have encountered make it more difficult for them to project their experiences into past situations. Analysis of GCSE coursework would suggest that mature students have an advantage here. *Your task will be to encourage pupils to understand why such ideas and attitudes were held and how these would influence people's actions.*

To do this your pupils need to possess considerable background knowledge of the cultures and religions involved. Much of this knowledge involves abstract ideas, which are themselves difficult for most pupils to understand. The challenge to the teacher is, first, not to make assumptions about the pupils' prior knowledge but also to become skilled in expressing the generalisations in terms concrete enough for pupils to understand. For example, you will find that teaching the Reformation to year 8 pupils can be a difficult task if pupils are to achieve a good understanding of the range of ideas and beliefs of the sixteenth and seventeenth centuries. Additionally, the pupils will find it difficult to communicate such ideas in a way that shows that they clearly understand and are not merely repeating what they have heard or learned by rote. All these problems have profound implications for the teaching strategies you choose when you come to teach this particular aspect of historical understanding.

TASK 5.4 PUPILS' PROBLEMS IN UNDERSTANDING THE IDEAS, BELIEFS AND ATTITUDES OF PARTICULAR PERIODS AND SOCIETIES

1 In your placement schools find out how the History Department seeks to meet the requirements of Key Element 2a (to develop 'range and depth of historical knowledge and understanding about characteristic features of particular periods and societies, including the ideas, beliefs and attitudes of people in the past, and the experiences of men and women; and about the social, cultural, religious and ethnic diversity of the societies studied').
   Which topics are considered appropriate for the development of this aspect?
2 With the permission of your mentor, discuss with a group of pupils the following questions.
   (a) Do you think people in the past were less intelligent than people today?
   (b) What different ideas would people in (the fourteenth century) have in comparison with people today?
   (c) Why do you think ideas and attitudes were different?
   (d) Do you think all people living in (the fourteenth century) held the same ideas?

Teaching approaches

As noted in Chapter 4 you are likely to be successful in developing your pupils' historical understanding if the pupils are more actively involved in their own learning. Whatever the unfamiliar ideas and attitudes are, pupils need to be able to apply them and re-work them in terms which are meaningful to them. *This often means placing the use of such ideas in a specific context which is not too vague for the pupil to handle.* Pupils are more likely to understand ideas and beliefs which are new and strange to them if they are asked to employ them as if they were their own. One example of this might be to ask pupils how they would explain to a fifteenth-century sailor that the world was round, without invoking the use of twentieth-century technology. They need to be presented with experiences and tasks which require them to express such ideas in their own words. Many will find this difficult and many will make mistakes, yet this is an important point for you to consider. By setting up situations and exercises that could lead to anachronistic statements you will be able to assess the limitations of the pupils' understanding better.

Even so, many exercises designed to develop pupils' understanding of particular periods and societies have limited success because the pupils have been given insufficient background information with which to work. Too little background information encourages the far-fetched, fanciful and non-historical. Thus it is important that plenty of attention is given to setting a framework of background knowledge before any exercise is set. This can often involve the comprehension and analysis of evidence, for, as ever, many of these Key Elements overlap. This could be achieved by whole-class teaching and question and answer, or by pupils analysing sources in groups with the task of listing the ideas and attitudes that they think emerge from the sources. Having ensured the pupils have an adequate background knowledge, what else might you consider to achieve success?

1 The best efforts are often those which are set in a very precise time and place. Pupils will find it easier to achieve some synthesis of the information available to them if it has such limitations placed upon it. Lack of precision and vague instructions often characterise the 'Imagine you were . . . ' type of exercise. Such tasks tend to be overused and have at times opened this whole approach to ridicule. Bad examples of this method require pupils to place themselves in a situation, frequently gruesome, and describe their feelings. 'Imagine you are a soldier at the Battle of X' is one such example – some pupils will have 'fought' in several battles from Hastings to D-Day – and the descriptive writing which tends to emanate from such tasks is often more appropriate to the development of skills in written English rather than the advancement of pupils' historical knowledge and understanding. 'You are captain of a sinking German U-boat; describe your feelings', is another example which might not evince responses which were primarily historical. Such tasks only encourage work of very limited value and, what is more, most pupils are aware of this.

Where such approaches were used, and overused, lack of detailed knowledge usually meant that pupils' responses were limited to statements which reflected common feelings, a transmission of everyday experiences and emotions into the past but lacking any real historical substance. As such the result was more creative writing than a vehicle to explore understanding of unfamilar ideas, beliefs and attitudes. *The task set needs to be well-structured.* An example of such precision was an assignment which sought to analyse the ideas and attitudes prevalent in a Lancashire textile town in 1866. Based on a real event, the pupils had studied the destruction by fire of two local mills, the consequences for the town in those days before the welfare state, and also the contemporary attitudes of teachers and the clergy. For this they had used newspaper accounts, personal accounts and extracts from school log books. The exercise was a pupil's view of destruction incorporating the comments, which were made by significant adults, about the disaster.

2 It is usually helpful to consider the 'audience' of the task. This often works best if that 'audience' is also of the period, a contemporary audience, the recipient of a report or petition. *Resolving dilemmas or decision-making can produce useful assignments.* In such exercises pupils are required to describe a difficult choice of action which a person or group of people in the past may have had to make. The pupils have to examine those factors which might influence their choice and in so doing take account that such a decision will involve the application of ideas and attitudes which were different from those prevalent today. For example, the pupil might be asked, as a novice in a monastery or nunnery, to decide whether to take the vows and stay or to leave. What would be the pros and cons of such a decision for a person in medieval times? Such an exercise is arguably better than the more familiar 'A day in the life of a monk', to the extent to which it has the potential to problematise the past. Other examples of decision-making designed to develop understanding of diverse and unfamiliar attitudes could be whether, as a Member of Parliament, to vote against a bill to abolish the Slave Trade in 1789.

TASK 5.5 THE ROLE OF HISTORICAL EMPATHY

The word 'empathy' has been deliberately avoided in writing this section. It does not appear in any of the GCSE or National Curriculum documentation. Yet its use has given rise to a great deal of controversy during the last two decades.

1 To gain something of the flavour of that debate, read and make notes on three articles from *Teaching History*. They are 'Empathy and History' by Anne Low-Beer and 'Some Reflections on Empathy in History' by John Cairns. Both of these are in the April 1989 issue. The third, 'Historical Empathy – R.I.P.?' by Peter Clements appeared in October 1996.
2 Using your notes discuss with your mentor the advantages and disadvantages of using historical empathy in the classroom.

3 It is important to emphasise that such exercises need to be 'rooted in evidence' and as such, while there will be scope for the use of imagination, it must be confined to what can be substantiated by the evidence available and not given a free rein. Peter Lee (1984) has correctly emphasised that historical imagination 'must be tied to evidence in some way and so historical imagination cannot be creative in the same way as in literature, painting or music'.

Historical imagination can be encouraged in many formats such as pages from a diary, which can cover successive days or significant days reflecting change and development. Other well-used tasks are to invite pupils to write a letter in which past ideas and attitudes are revealed, or at times, two letters, where the recipient responds with different views although still consistent with those held at the time. Pupils can be asked to write newspaper accounts, eye-witness reports or petitions for or against some proposal (e.g. a new canal or votes for women). In all cases whatever is written will involve the use of the imagination, but it must be grounded in historical knowledge which can be substantiated by evidence. By using a medium such as a letter the pupils are being asked to transfer sometimes difficult abstract ideas into their own words and into more concrete situations that will be meaningful to them.

More ambitious activities can include an attempt to utilise role-play as a means of developing understanding, following a methodology suggested in Chapter 4. This again can use a variety of formats and can also involve decision-making. Role-play can be used successfully to encourage the understanding of differing attitudes towards enclosures, of a parish's reactions to religious changes in the sixteenth century, to the ideas of a local Board of Health to the news of the arrival of cholera in the town in 1831.

Where appropriate, other evidence that can be successfully incorporated into imaginative work could be a historical site, where the exercise makes use of a familiar landscape (for example a castle, monastery, street or canal). There may be times – perhaps with older pupils, although it has been done successfully by year 7 pupils – when your pupils can be encouraged to reference the sources behind some of the statements. However, they also need to ensure their work does not follow the sources too closely, thus becoming very close to paraphrasing.

4 As will have become apparent, much of the success of such tasks will depend on the preparation you have done to enable you to set the work. You need to be very clear in your mind exactly what is the purpose of the task you are setting, so as to be able to articulate the precise objectives you have in mind. Careful thought here will help the way in which you formulate the task. When you have decided what you want the pupils to do, go back to the objectives and assess whether such a task will enable the pupils to meet the learning objectives you are setting. There have been times when a poorly set exercise has given the

pupils little chance of indicating their understanding of past ideas, beliefs and attitudes. Having precise objectives means you also have to be clear about the assessment criteria you are going to employ when you come to mark the pupils' work. There is a good case here for letting the pupils know what these criteria are, so they can take account of them as they plan and complete their work.

TASK 5.6 DESIGNING A TASK TO DEVELOP PUPILS' UNDERSTANDING OF THE CHARACTERISTIC FEATURES OF THE PAST

It is recommended that you think through the task you are to set your pupils *before* you begin to teach the topic on which it is based. During the process of devising a scheme of work for a series of lessons with a class, examine the content to see if you can identify any opportunities for pupils to show an understanding of the ideas and attitudes that characterised that period. Then:

1 Select the format of the creative task (e.g. letters, diary entries, speech, petition, dialogue, etc.).
2 Consider what *knowledge* the pupils will need to be able to make a good attempt at the task. Ensure that the knowledge will cover not only the context but also the prevailing attitudes and beliefs.
3 Consider the *methods* you will use to make that knowledge available to your pupils. What are to be the sources of their knowledge?
4 Set a two–part task.

Part 1 is the pupils' creative task, for which you will be precise about time, place, the context, the intended audience and possibly even give the names of the people involved. Consider also the instructions you will give about your expectations and the assessment criteria. Check back to your description of the task to make sure the pupils will be in a position to meet your expectations.

Part 2 is to be completed later. Then the pupils are asked to write a few sentences in which they explain how the ideas and attitudes of the people mentioned in their task differ from the attitudes commonly held today. Able pupils might also try to explain the differences.

CAUSE AND CONSEQUENCE

Cause and consequence are arguably the most complex of the concepts under consideration. They are difficult to teach because it is easy to make assumptions about the extent of your pupils' understanding of cause and consequence. Traditionally causes were dealt with as a list of information – any analysis that had been done was achieved by the teacher or the author of the text-book, rarely by the pupils. Pupils were presented with a list of causes and consequences of an event and committed these to memory to reproduce for assessment. There was very little attempt here to encourage pupils' thought about the nature of the concept involved and thus developing their historical understanding. The National Curriculum Council noted that there have been critics of this traditional approach since the early days of this century. Some enlightened history teachers saw the important methodological implications of not relying on the teacher to do all the intellectual work and advocated that 'pupils themselves should be generalising, analysing, judging and explaining' (NCC, 1993).

Common misconceptions about cause and consequence

1 *Pupils can look upon causes as being facts themselves.* Shemilt (1980) noted in his evaluation of the 13–16 Schools Council project that many highly intelligent adolescents treated the word 'cause' as though it refers not to the connection between events but to the properties of one of the events. He also noted the prevalence of the opinion that causes are everything that happened before. For such pupils a cause is something of an agent, which has the ability to make something happen. Thompson (1984) suggested that bad 'traditional teaching helped to reinforce this kind of misunderstanding by treating causes in exactly the same way as events in history'.

2 Shemilt also noted that many pupils are happy to settle for one cause for a particular event; they like the clear-cut conclusion without any complexities. To them any other causes are superfluous. Such simplicity of understanding is attractive but represents a very limited understanding of the concept. For example, if one asked pupils to account for the building of the Turnpike road between Manchester and Rochdale in 1755 some pupils would feel that the fact that the existing roads were bad and in great need of repair to be sufficient for the answer; no additional explanation was necessary. Such a limited response fails to tackle the complexity of the question, where it would be necessary to know who were the people pressing for the setting up of a Trust and for what reasons; whether they had the services of a well-known surveyor available at that time; where precisely would the road be built and did this bring advantages to some of the promoters; what trades or goods would be most likely to benefit and how had it been possible to defeat any local opposition. The challenge for teachers would be how to encourage pupils not to settle for the most obvious mono-causal explanation.

3   Possibly another of the disadvantages of the listing of causes in a traditional manner was that it failed to present any analysis which took account of the order in which the causes might have had their effect and the inter-play between events and causes. The Balkan Wars of 1912–13 did not directly precipitate the First World War but they contributed to the demands for self-determination and the heightened resistance of the multinational Empires towards this development. At times a distinction was drawn between long- and short-term causes and similarly long- and short-term consequences, but this was often a means of categorising information rather than a basis for discussion about the nature of the concept or indeed how distant a long-term cause had to be to qualify for this category.

4   We also have the problem of causal determinism. Scott (1990) indicates that this can occur when pupils liken the concept of causation in history to a scientific interpretation. This is encouraged when words such as 'catalyst' are used (it may be better to use words like 'triggers'). Confusion with *scientific causation* can lead to an almost mechanistic interpretation of causation. It is possible to see here the beginning of the attraction of adolescents towards the conclusion that some historical events were 'inevitable'. It is almost as if, given a certain combination of causes, an event was 'bound to happen'. The outcome is not only predictable, it is inevitable. This 'scientific' view of causation at least has the merit of logic and not least the importance of the interrelationship of causes. However, only the more sophisticated pupil is likely to be able to distinguish between the scientific and the historical mode of causal explanation and is able to understand the 'uniqueness' of a historical event, the sheer unpredictability of events involving both individuals and groups of people. *One of your tasks will be to encourage pupils to be sceptical about claims that an event was inevitable.*

5   This 'uniqueness', which is such an important feature of historical content, stems from the central fact that history is the study of human beings in the past, and human beings are themselves unique and unpredictable. Consequently historians have to concern themselves with motivation, which is itself an important aspect of the concept of causation. Pupils should be able to discriminate between understanding motive and cause and not see the two as synonymous.

6   Nevertheless, there may be something of a paradox here which could be confusing to pupils. While emphasising the 'uniqueness' of events and their causes, the nature of the learning process often means there is a need to categorise and assimilate language which describes categories and concepts. Consequently an important function of learning the concept of cause and consequence will be to enable pupils to understand and use words such as 'social', 'political', 'economic', technological' and other adjectives we may wish

to use to describe categories of causes, mindful of the fact such terms can be employed in the explanation of widely different events.

TASK 5.7 IDENTIFYING PUPILS' ASSUMPTIONS ABOUT CAUSE AND CONSEQUENCE

1 When you have covered an appropriate topic, present the class with a list of causes and events. Then ask the class, in pairs, to identify which are the cause and which the events and to give reasons for their choice. Consider then the teaching points you will make at the conclusion of this exercise.

2 With a class, or a group of pupils, discuss the following questions:

(a) Do you think the (selected event just covered) was inevitable, i.e. was bound to have happened?

(b) How might you decide which cause was the most important? (Is there always a most important cause?)

(c) What do you understand by the terms short- and long-term causes?

(d) Why might it be difficult to work out the consequences of an event?

In the light of this discussion, what points will you need to emphasise when teaching these concepts?

Strategies for teaching the concepts of cause and consequence

To remove many of the misunderstandings noted above, you should be prepared to invest time in the careful study of causal connections and give pupils the opportunity to work out their own ideas and thinking. The concept of causation is best approached *after* the details of a topic have been considered. Here are some of the teaching and learning strategies which you might adopt.

Matching exercises

There are various ways in which such exercises can be approached. Often pupils are presented with two columns – one of events, another of causes – and the task is to match items from one column with another and then explain the reasons for the choice.

Group work using causation cards

Example. With a year 9 class. After a detailed study of a topic on the coming of the railways, the pupils were placed in groups and each group received a set of cards on each of which was written a possible cause of the building of a specified (local) railway line. Each card was numbered to facilitate discussion:

1 Dissatisfaction with canal companies' freight charges.
2 Availability of a labour force prepared to move around the country.
3 Civic pride/rivalry.
4 Demands for the faster transport by many trades and industries.
5 Successful trials of steam locomotives.
6 Appointment of skilled engineer.
7 Leadership of local business people.
8 Use of wrought iron rails.
9 Defeat of opponents (canals, turnpikes, rival railway companies, land-owners, coach firms) in Parliament.
10 Courage, foresight of bankers.
11 Spirit of the Age (progress, eagerness to improve, enterprising climate).
12 Earlier experience of railroad traction using horses.
13 Discovery of steam power.
14 Existence of Iron Industry capable of meeting requests of engineers.
15 Availability of hard-working skilled engineers.
16 Dissatisfaction with the speed of land transport.
17 Knowledge and skill in capital accumulation, share-holding, joint-stock capital.

Having received these cards the groups were asked to perform a series of tasks, each followed by a class discussion. These tasks included the categorisation of the cause on the cards. With most groups it would be necessary to identify the categories and to explain these beforehand, but with some able groups it is a useful challenge to ask them to create their own categories. In the following feedback discussion the results of the groups are compared, and from this activity it is possible to create a spray-diagram in which the categories of causes are grouped together. Later, this spray-diagram could assist the writing of a short essay on the reasons for the building of the specified railway as outlined in Chapter 4 (see p. 82).

A further activity was to ask the groups to identify from the cards those which they considered to be short-term and long-term causes. An extension of this, in an attempt to deal with the issue of the ordering of the effect of the causes, could be to ask the pupils to try to place the causes along some imaginary or real time-line. Finally the pupils were asked to consider which causes were the most important and which the least important. The NCC (1993) advises teachers to make sure that pupils use sensible criteria when making such choices through the application of logic and the assessment of evidence.

With able pupils, who have some familiarity with the use of causation cards, once a topic has been covered it may be possible for them to devise their own cards and for groups to compare the results. It is possible to use this approach with older pupils when the selection of particular causes as being the most important is seen to indicate something about the attitude of the historian towards causation. Questions such as which cards might a Marxist historian be likely to choose as the most important can be considered. In this there is a link with Chapter 6 on historical interpretations.

'Why then?' activities

It is important to keep asking this question, particularly in those circumstances when the long-term causes have been in place for so long. If the condition of the French peasants was worse in 1722 than it was in 1789, why did the Revolution take place at the later date? Also, why not in 1722? This is useful to dissuade pupils from the attraction of the inevitability of events.

The recent research of Lee *et al.* (1996) provides not only interesting information on the development of pupils' ideas about causation and explanation, but excellent examples of 'pupil-friendly' tasks which address some of the complexities outlined above, particularly with regard to the interrelationship of causes, and pupils' ability to discriminate between fact, reason and cause.

CHANGE AND CONTINUITY

For many decades history teachers have been aware of the underlying importance of the concept of change and continuity, but only in the last two decades have the reasons for its importance been articulated in pedagogic terms with attention to the way change in particular may be misunderstood by pupils and students. Again much of the research which underpins this emphasis comes from the Schools History Project (SHP). Attractive textbooks associated with this module have been produced by Joe Scott (1987) and are organised in such a way that the concepts of change and continuity are given a clear and comprehensive emphasis. These textbooks offer plenty of ideas about utilising these concepts, which can be adapted to other content areas.

Common misconceptions

As in the case of the concepts of cause and consequence, you will find that it is possible that your expectations of your pupils' understanding of change and continuity may be too high. You need to be aware of the possible misconceptions which pupils may have if you are to succeed in developing their historical understanding.

Thompson (1984) concluded that 'change' is a historical concept that adolescents initially find difficult to entertain in any but everyday use. Pupils can understand change in relation to different times, but their appreciation of the nature and scope of change varies very much from pupil to pupil. A feature of Shemilt's research (1980) was to note how many pupils saw change as an episodic rather than continuous process. One change (event) was not seen as in any way connected with changes (events) preceding it in time. This limited understanding tends to be reinforced by a syllabus which is itself episodic, which moves from one topic to another with little apparent relationship to that which precedes or follows. There is a case to be made for a syllabus which does have a chronological base so that the process of change can be better addressed.

Shemilt also noted that the difficulty pupils may have with the idea of historical change seems to stem from their inability to imagine the daily life which gives the events their meaning. History lessons can so often present pupils with a succession of events with little reference to the context in which they occurred, and as a result the pupils are not sure of what precisely it is that changes. Hence, the value of making such changes personal by the use of role-play or writing from an individual perspective.

TASK 5.8 RELATING THE CONCEPTS OF CHANGE AND CONTINUITY TO PUPILS' OWN LIVES

1 Set some of your younger pupils the task of asking an old relative or neighbour the following questions:

(a) What has changed today from the time when you were young (travel, transport, entertainment, shopping, types of employment, prices, education)?

(b) Given the choice, would you have preferred to be young today or was it better when you were young. Give reasons for your choice.

2 As a class devise a chart comparing *then* and *now*.

3 Use the data as a basis for discussing some of the misconceptions relating to continuity, the speed of change, change and progress, and the reasons for change.

4 Then, project the exercise back into the historical topic you are teaching (e.g. if you were to have asked the same questions to some old people living in 1070, what might their answers have been?).

You may also find it rewarding to find out how pupils interpret the idea of 'progress' over time. It is quite common for young people to assume that the changes that occur over time are all for the better. Consequently there is value in stopping to consider whether this was always the case. What were the consequences of the discovery of gunpowder? Did this represent progress? Such questions prompt a consideration of some of the wider issues that the study of history can generate, showing that the subject is fundamental in the Humanities.

A further misconception that often needs to be corrected is that because of the pupils' tendency to compartmentalise their history (the episodic approach), they may assume that changes occur at once. Suddenly there is a change from the domestic system to the factory system. Yet what can make the concept even more confusing for pupils is the fact that while some things change others do not. Change is not clear cut and to that degree requires a level of understanding which is quite sophisticated and not easily achieved by many pupils.

Strategies for the teaching of the concepts of change and continuity

1 *Emphasising the overview*. It is important to make sure the pupils are able to see how the content covered or to be covered presents an overview or framework from which a discussion of change and continuity may develop. It may be useful to present an outline framework at the beginning of a topic or scheme to assist understanding and then return to the framework when the content has been covered, to ask questions relating to change and continuity. Such a framework can also be used for reference while teaching a topic to aid the understanding of particularly complex content.

> *Example*. A topic which will benefit from an overview is the French Revolution, which may be said to be a series of revolutions. To assist under-standing it can be helpful to create a time-chart which emphasises this succession of changes. Such a chart could also form the basis for a wall display. How much detail is included will depend on the ability level of the class, but the idea of an overview is to ensure that the changes are not obscured by too much factual 'clutter'. As the topic is covered in more detail, the chart is a useful reference point for the pupils.

Too often there has been a tendency to move from one block of content to another without sufficient emphasis on the overview which helps to show the significance of the study. The National Curriculum Council (NCC, 1993) noted that it would be wrong to see the study units at Key Stage 3 as static 'patch studies'. The term 'zero-ing' has been used to describe the rush to start a new topic just when the point has been reached when that content covered can be usefully developed to address some of the key concepts and offer further challenges to the pupils. Emphasising the overview also helps both teachers and pupils to distinguish between what has been called 'durable' as opposed to 'disposable' data.

2 *Imaginative presentation of changes in the form of illustrated time-charts, time-lines, diagrams or graphs.* These may be drawn to highlight periods of slow or rapid change and again help to place the content under study in an overall context. There are times when it may be necessary to limit the precise accuracy of presentation in order to make general points in some imaginative diagrams.

3 *Comparative exercises.* For some time 'similarity' and 'difference' have been identified as concepts in themselves. However, it is possible to use these terms more as an effective strategy for teaching the concepts of change and continuity. They are often used most productively at the beginning of a topic. They often make a relatively straightforward entry into the discussion of more demanding concepts such as causation. The use of 'similarity and difference' approaches nearly always involves pupils in making comparisons, which in turn can encourage varying degrees of analysis. Such comparisons often work well with pictures or other visual materials, but can also involve with effect cartographical and statistical material. You will find that most of the textbooks of recent years make good use of comparisons, and so material for their use is not too difficult to find. Even so, there is always scope for your individual initiative in the acquisition of appropriate resources. *Evidence from the local environment and from local history can add to the interest of lessons, as can skilfully chosen analogies from aspects of contemporary life closer to pupils' own interests and experiences.* While most emphasis may be placed on the differences, it is also important to look for similarities.

There are a variety of ways in which comparative exercises can be used to further the pupils' understanding of the concepts of change and continuity (see Figures 5.1, 5.2). One is the *then–now technique.* This is most likely when pupils have some familiarity with the present-day example, especially involving the use of physical evidence. Contrasting a modern-day street with a photograph of the same street in Edwardian times encourages plenty of discussion about what has changed and what has remained the same. Booth *et al.* show how comparison of pictures of a Victorian and present-day kitchen can also bring out many facets of continuity and change (Booth *et al.*, 1987).

4 *Comparison of the implication of change for identified people living at the time or at contrasting times.* There is plenty of potential here for simulation exercises, role-play and the use of 'radio' plays. For example, for topics such as enclosures, the change from the domestic system to the factory system; religious changes of the sixteenth and seventeenth centuries.

Town populations : comparison of the sixteenth century with recent times

As part of a lesson on towns in the sixteenth century, the following two lists were written on the board.

Sixteenth century	Recent times (1977)
1 London (200,000)	1 London (7,030,000)
2 Norwich (15,000)	2 Birmingham (1,050,100)
3 Bristol (12,000)	3 Leeds (734,000)
4 York (11,500)	4 Sheffield (547,000)
5 Exeter (9,000)	5 Liverpool (536,000)
6 Newcastle (9,000)	6 Manchester (491,000)
7 Chester (5,400)	7 Bradford (464,200)
8 Hull (5,000)	8 Bristol (409,000)
9 Coventry (4,000)	9 Coventry (340,000)
10 Manchester (3,500)	10 Nottingham (282,000)

After first identifying the changes featured in these lists, the pupils were asked to consider why such changes had occurred, and how to account for the disappearance of some towns and the appearance of others.

Figure 5.1   An example of a then–now exercise

Effects of enclosure

This time pupils were given two maps, one showing the open fields, common lands and meadow and the nucleated village of pre-enclosure times and the other showing the effects on the landscape of the introduction of enclosures. The pupils were first invited to identify the similarities and differences between the two maps as a basis for a study of the changes which had taken place and the reasons for those changes.

Figure 5.2   An example of a before–after exercise

5 *Encouraging speculation.* Teachers may gain useful insights into how pupils are assimilating the concept by asking them to consider what changes might be experienced by people living at a certain time when they were thirty years older, or by the time of their grandchildren.

> *Example.* Year 7 pupils have spent two or three lessons extracting information from the local census returns for 1861. From this information they have been able to construct bar charts showing the different occupations of the people living in 1861, the age and gender distribution and details of the inhabitants' places of birth. As an additional task the pupils were set the following tasks:

- Make a list of those jobs or occupations which you think would *grow* in number in the next thirty years – that is, by 1891.
- Make a list of those jobs or occupations which you think would *decline* in number – that means, there would be less of them, by 1891.
  Give reasons for your judgements.

The answers given would be quite informative of the pupils' understanding and also could be checked by a comparison with the 1891 census returns.

TASK 5.9 ASSESSING THE SIGNIFICANCE OF THE MAIN EVENTS, PEOPLE AND CHANGES STUDIED

In this chapter great emphasis has been placed on the importance of drawing out the significance of the historical events you teach. This is one of your most important tasks as a history teacher, hence its status as the concluding part of Key Element 2.

1 Select one major event from three of the Study Units for Key Stage 3. Try to create a spray-diagram (some call them spider-charts) which shows the significance of the event (e.g. The Black Death, the battle of Bosworth, the defeat of the Spanish Armada).
2 When observing a history lesson in your placement school, try to identify what you think is the significance of the topic being taught. How much is this being communicated to the pupils?
3 After the lesson, with the permission of the teacher, ask a few pupils some questions about the lesson. They could include: What was important about the topic? What were the changes that resulted from the event? And, most challenging, how do they think the study of that event and its outcomes might contribute to their understanding of the present?
4 Make some notes on the pupils' responses and consider the implications for your own teaching.

---

6 *Use of hypothetical questions.* Although there has in the past been some reluctance by history teachers to ask questions which invited speculation on what did not happen, it can be a useful way to emphasise the significance of a change or indeed lack of change. For example, consider what might have happened if Henry Tudor had been defeated at the Battle of Bosworth, or what might have been the result had the Spanish Armada been successful in 1588?

7 *Sequencing activities* (such as those suggested earlier in this chapter on chronology, in which pupils have to reorganise events in the order in which they occurred). The best of these are where the selection of detail allows pupils to

think through decisions using inference and their general understandings, rather than exercises which are purely reliant on memorisation. Such activities are a further example of how the concepts covered by this chapter interrelate, as the concepts of change and continuity owe much to an understanding of chronology.

8 Following the completion of a topic, inviting discussion on what the pupils consider to be significant *turning points* in the events which have developed.

9 *Spot the anachronisms.* This can be both an amusing and yet revealing activity. Pupils are presented with a picture or a passage of writing which contains several errors of an anachronistic nature and are challenged to identify the deliberate mistakes. Alternatively they could be asked to identify which of two accounts is genuine and give reasons for choice.

CONCLUSION AND SUMMARY OF KEY POINTS

The teaching of the key concepts covered in this chapter aims to provide you with some ideas and examples which have the potential to serve as a basis in constructing some stimulating and successful lessons. That success will be helped if you have a good understanding of the likely problems many pupils may experience in handling these key elements. The challenge for you is to keep reinforcing the significance of the events you cover and the wider relevance of the concepts involved. In that way you help your pupils to realise that history is not just about the acquisition of knowledge but how you apply that knowledge.

FURTHER READING

Lomas, T. (1990) *Teaching and Assessing Historical Understanding*, London, Historical Association.
A useful supplement to this chapter, which has a particular emphasis on the types of questions you might ask your pupils.

Sansom, C. (1987) 'Concepts, Skills and Content: A Developmental Approach to the History Syllabus', in C. Portal, *The History Curriculum for Teachers*, Lewes, Falmer Press.

6 Developing historical understanding (2)

INTRODUCTION

In this chapter we will consider the teaching of two more Key Elements in the History National Curriculum: interpretations of history and historical enquiry. The first of these is much more a newcomer to the 11–16 curriculum, the latter more established, although the greater emphasis on enquiries rather than source skills may be seen as a welcome advance. Because 'interpretations of history' is a more recent development, we are giving it more emphasis in this chapter. This is not to understate the importance of historical enquiry as an important facet of school history. The National Education Training Targets (NETTs) stress the need for pupils to become flexible and autonomous learners; the Dearing Review noted the ability to be a 'good learner' as one of the 'key skills' in education for the twenty-first century (Dearing, 1994), and OFSTED reports on school history have consistently praised those departments where pupils have been given the initiative and responsibility to become autonomous learners (OFSTED, 1993, 1995).

It can be argued that for many years teachers have encouraged their pupils to be aware that the way the subject matter of history is presented is replete with interpretations. The very terms in which some people and events are described encourages discussion of the reasons why such words are used. Why was 'The Glorious Revolution of 1688' so called? Who called the period between 1629 and 1640 'the Eleven Years Tyranny'? Why was the extension of the franchise to just over another 200,000 men called 'The Great Reform Act'? Who decided that Alfred was Great, Elizabeth I was Good, and her sister Bloody? It is also reasonable to ask how much the use of words such as 'revolution', 'progress' and 'civilisation' involve interpretations. Consider the use of the word 'reform'. Today pupils might well consider how the word 'reform' can be uncritically used in news bulletins implying 'a change for the better', even though it is a matter of opinion whether that is the case.

However much we may have considered the nature of interpretations in the description of people and events in the past, only recently has this aspect of historical understanding been formalised within the history syllabus. Having made its first appearance in the original orders for the National Curriculum, it is included in the assessment objectives for the revised GCSE. The prominence now given to the teaching and learning of historical interpretations is a further example of the emphasis of how the processes by which history is communicated may be used as a basis for developing your pupils' historical understanding. Encouraging pupils to be aware of the way historical events, people and situations may be differently interpreted, reduces the opportunities for the imposition of 'one version' history with all its potential dangers. An under-standing of why such different interpretations occur might make a valuable contribution to the further development of a democratic society. At the same time the range of historical interpretations can give you the basis for producing some interesting lessons, using materials which might not have been considered appropriate a few decades ago.

OBJECTIVES

At the end of this chapter you should:

- have a clear understanding of what is meant by both historical interpretations and enquiry in the context of the secondary school curriculum;
- have some understanding of the potential problems for both teachers and pupils when studying historical interpretations;
- be familiar with the wide range of interpretations and reconstructions which can provide material for the study of this element;
- be aware of some of the strategies and approaches that can be used for the teaching of interpretations of history;
- have gained some ideas for setting up an enquiry-based project.

INTERPRETATIONS OF HISTORY

How can we define historical interpretations?

You may find it helpful to be clear in your own mind about what is meant by historical interpretations when used in the context of the secondary school. You need to be clear about how this aspect of the teaching and learning of history is distinguished from that range of skills associated with the use of sources. Sometimes the distinction has been made that interpretations are only linked to secondary sources, yet the distinction between primary and secondary sources can sometimes be blurred and often depends on the purpose for which the source is used, rather than when the source was produced. It is perhaps better to think of an interpretation, as Bennett (1995) has suggested, as 'a conscious interpretation of the past, which normally draws together different sources of information'. Furthermore, that 'conscious interpretation' will be found in a greater variety of representations than those normally covered by the 'use of sources', for example, historical stories and novels, museum displays, as well as pupils' own interpretations. Such variety increases the potential for adding interest to history lessons.

Potential confusion also lies between 'interpretations' and the use of the 'characteristic features of past societies' covered in the previous chapter. The concern of 'interpretations' is *not* the knowledge of ideas and attitudes in the past, which may be very different from those prevalent today. It may, however, be necessary to explore how the ideas and attitudes of the past are related to different interpretations. Tony McAleavy (1993) made the point when he wrote, 'an interpretation of history is a conscious reflection on the past and NOT the ideas and attitudes of participants in past events'. Pam Harper (1993) takes this point further when seeking to distinguish between contemporary perspectives portrayed by the use of role-play and interpretations of history. 'For example,' she wrote, 'activities where a class is divided into two and a role-play of the story of the Boudiccan revolt from the point of view of the Iceni or the Romans will not in themselves enable pupils to work towards an understanding of inter-pretations of history. *Only if pupils spend time analysing their interpretations of events* and compare them with the available evidence of the revolt will such work be related to historical interpretations.' In other words, interpretations are a *second-stage activity* that usually follow the study of the content and the completion of activities to develop an understanding of that content.

TASK 6.1 IDENTIFYING THE USE OF HISTORICAL INTERPRETATIONS

1 During your school experience discuss with your subject mentor how the department seeks to meet the requirements of this Key Element within the Study Units. Note which topics have been chosen as being suitable for the development of the pupils' understanding of interpretations. Find out what range of approaches are planned and discuss how these may differ according to the ability of the pupils.

2 Collect a variety of textbooks which have been written for the Key Stage 3 Study Units and investigate the materials and tasks designed for the study of historical interpretations. Note any particularly useful examples for future reference.

So, to summarise our definition, interpretations of history can be presented in many forms; they represent a deliberate and thoughtful attempt to reconstruct and explain events in the past; to be of any worth they must be rooted in genuine evidence, and normally that means they are drawn from several different sources of information.

The problems of teaching historical interpretations

The emergence of historical interpretations as an aspect of learning history in all years of the secondary school presents both problems and challenges to the teacher. You find that your lessons are more successful if you are able to anticipate the problems your pupils might encounter. Consider the following.

Knowledge

If the study of historical interpretations is to be a valuable learning experience, pupils must have a reasonably detailed knowledge of the topic which is the subject matter of the interpretations. They need a factual basis to enable them to understand the interpretation in the context of events and a basis for making worthwhile comparisons. As greater demands are made of the pupils, for example, to assess and evaluate interpretations, these could be of very limited value if the student is insufficiently informed on the subject matter.

However, the way in which that content is initially presented or 'discovered' by the student could influence later work on interpretations. It may be a case of what information to give and what not to give. If you are planning exercises involving historical interpretations, the ways in which the groundwork of necessary information is presented will need careful consideration. Basically, the question is: *What do the pupils or students need to know and understand in order to complete work on interpretations with success?*

Accessibility

Perhaps the most far-reaching and possibly frustrating problem for teachers seeking to teach historical interpretations is, as with the use of sources, that of accessibility. The principal barrier to understanding is that of language – complex sentence structure and unfamiliar words have for many years presented a problem for teachers and examiners alike, as indicated in Chapter 4. To this may now be added the adult language of historians as they present their interpretations of people and situations in the past. At times such interpretations rest on nuances and shades of opinion too subtle for some pupils. While the variety and range of interpretations can add to the interest and stimulation of the study, the language of poetry or folk songs can also present problems of accessibility. Cartoons and satirical drawings may again be too subtle and complex for some pupils. In all cases the challenge to you as a teacher is to try to make such interpretations and representations accessible to the pupils without distorting the meaning, or in the case of assessment, removing too much of the skill or understanding one is trying to assess. The problem of accessibility, therefore, is linked to that of differentiation.

Conceptual leaps

The revised Attainment Target for the History National Curriculum presents a more logical and acceptable progression in the description of a pupil's developing understanding of historical interpretations. That progression of knowing, describing, explaining and evaluating, which can be extracted from the level descriptions, follows a well-established model. Even so, for many pupils that progression is not necessarily smooth or predictable. For most pupils there is a significant conceptual leap from describing to suggesting reasons and on towards giving a comprehensive and weighted explanation. Whereas many will feel comfortable in describing the differences between the interpretations by analysing the data presented to them in a variety of media, they will then struggle to explain those differences, particularly when they have to draw upon information not immediately before them. Many might settle for the obvious, for example, 'because they were written by different people living at different times', which, while correct, is not the depth of insight one might be looking for. In order for pupils to make such conceptual leaps, it is necessary to ask what the pupils need to know to enable them to make such leaps. *What questions do they need to ask and what activities are most likely to help them to move to the higher level of explaining and evaluating?* The leap from explaining to evaluating is considerable, if the evaluations are to achieve that balance and sophisticated appreciation of the value of an interpretation to its historical context, rather than a random and arbitrary decision.

Background of the interpretations

Closely linked to the problem of the conceptual leaps, implying a progression of understanding, is that of the pupils' knowledge of the background of the 'interpreters' – those responsible for an interpretation. In current parlance, there is a need to know 'where they are coming from'. That background information might be correctly but superficially expressed as 'He was a royalist', or 'She was a French Protestant' or, with older pupils, 'He was a Marxist historian', but such information would need to have a fuller explanation, which requires further layers of knowledge. Should it be necessary to determine that an interpretation of a much earlier event reflected the spirit of the times of the person responsible for the interpretation, then that requires knowledge not only of the event being interpreted but also of the times of the interpreter. Clearly the need for knowledge of the background of the interpretation places a real problem for the teacher: the need to refer to the attitudes and events sometimes centuries ahead of the topic being interpreted.

Conveying genuine understanding

When presented with such problems as described above, one approach chosen, particularly if the pressure of external examinations is involved, is for teachers to present user-friendly packages of interpretations for the pupils to recall and reproduce within the examination room. Then, what is being assessed is an awareness of the differing interpretations and the ability to recall accurately. It is a problem that has existed for many years with the assessment of concepts such as causation. If asked the causes of an event, the candidate reproduces the list from his or her exercise book copied from the blackboard ('The twelve reasons for the decline and fall of Napoleon', 'six reasons why France lost the Franco-Prussian War'). Does this really indicate an understanding of the concept? The challenge for you as a teacher is how to create situations which can genuinely assess an understanding of historical interpretations, an *application* of principles and knowledge rather than diligent recall. How can you set up activities which enable your pupils to work out and explain different interpretations rather than present them with a pre-packaged summary of recognised interpretations?

Confusion of certainty and uncertainty

A problem inherent in the study of historical interpretations is that while for some it encourages valuable insights into the nature of events, people and issues in the past, for others there is a danger that such a study could promote a rather negative attitude towards history as a subject. For the latter they need to be assured that they are learning something that is accurate and 'correct', knowledge that they can now 'possess' to put alongside their knowledge of other subjects. To them, if history is too frequently presented as a mass of uncertainty, represented by different viewpoints, they may become disenchanted with the subject. You need to constantly emphasise that what is accepted forms the framework of our historical knowledge and assure your pupils that a great deal of what they learn falls into this category, at the same time stressing that what

TASK 6.2 INTRODUCING PUPILS TO THE PROBLEMS ENCOUNTERED IN THE STUDY OF HISTORICAL INTERPRETATIONS

1 Choose an event to which your pupils could relate (e.g. an incident in a supermarket, or in a football match).
2 Compose different interpretations of the incident. You could include: participants, onlookers, officials, higher officials who were not present, a newspaper reporter who was not present.
3 Select pupils who in turn read out one of the interpretations.
4 Place the pupils in groups, each group having a set of the interpretations.
5 Ask pupils to consider the following questions and record their conclusions:

- What can we be certain actually happened?
- In the statements what are facts and what are opinions?
- What are the differences between the interpretations?
- How can the differences in the interpretations be explained?
- Taking each interpretation in turn, what are the points for and the points against the interpretation being a reliable account?
- What more would you want to know about the people who gave their interpretation of the incident?
- Which interpretation does your group think is the most reliable?
- What have you learned from this exercise about the difficulties a historian might have when faced with different interpretations?

Then, repeat the exercise, as far as practicable, with different interpretations of an event you have taught.

really adds interest to the subject are the questions such uncontested knowledge raises. We accept that the Normans won the Battle of Hastings in 1066, what may be open to interpretation is how much that event affected England and Wales in the years that followed. Perhaps for this reason, in your schemes of work for Key Stage 3 you need to structure work on interpretations according to the ability of the class or pupils within a class. You need to be aware that unless the question of interpretations is presented appropriately, it may serve merely to confuse and demotivate pupils. Pupils and students need to be able to understand the educational outcomes that arise from such study and be able to recognise their relevance for the world in which they are growing up. For all these risks, the successful use of informed scepticism and the ability to make discerning and considered judgements about alternatives will be extremely helpful to pupils in life after school, and is one of the justifications for the place of history on the school curriculum.

DEVELOPING PUPILS' UNDERSTANDING OF HISTORICAL INTERPRETATIONS

Explaining the purpose

There are times when studying the different interpretations might seem to some pupils a rather arcane and dry exercise, irritating in its uncertainties and lacking the interest of the original story. To counter this possible reaction, it is both advisable and educationally useful for pupils to be able to appreciate the value of such exercises. Your pupils always need to be encouraged to see the relevance of the aspects of the historical study they pursue to the world in which they are growing up. An important element of this is to compare the varying interpretations of past events to current ones and be able to show how sometimes what may be presented as an unequivocal truth is really an inter-pretation. Some current issues may be too complex for some Key Stage 3 pupils; ideally the teacher should have examples of interpretations of differing levels of complexity. Many Key Stage 3 pupils will be able to understand why and how people who once wrote of Nelson Mandela as a terrorist are now prepared to accept him as a great leader. Films such as *Braveheart*, and *Michael Collins* may raise complex issues in terms of the multi-layered interpretations involved, but they also offer significant opportunities to the history teacher (in terms of engaging pupils' attention as well as their potential for exploring interpretations).

The range and diversity of historical interpretations

An important feature of this Key Element is the need for pupils to appreciate the breadth and variety of interpretations. Because they may regard history as a school subject with content that has to be learned, it is easy for them to fail to appreciate just how widely used history can be and that much of its use involves somebody's interpretation. The use of popular fiction and television-based historical dramas such as *Robin Hood* or *Ivanhoe* can be helpful in this respect; King John gets consistently bad reviews in these media. References to interpretations which are familiar to the pupils form a useful starting-point for the development of their understanding. This can be extended to include historical stories and novels, drama, cartoons, museum displays, guides to and displays at historical sites, popular views about the past as well as your pupils' own interpretations.

TASK 6.3 ENCOURAGING PUPILS TO UNDERSTAND THE RANGE AND DIVERSITY OF HISTORICAL INTERPRETATIONS

Study the following school-based activities. In most history departments the topic of Thomas à Becket will be covered in year 7. Consequently any suggestions for activities involving interpretations must only consider those appropriate for such young pupils. All but the most able will lack the chronological understanding for any historiographical approach. The example and the activities set out below therefore have as their main objective the task of familiarising the pupils with the range and sometimes the unusual nature of interpretations.

Example:
After studying the topic of Thomas à Becket and Henry II, the pupils in groups may be given the following chart:

Types of interpretation of the murder of Thomas à Becket

Type	Example
Textbook Novel Play Biography Information technology Brochure Film Eye-witness account Drawings Academic study Poetic play Saga Mosaic Personal records	

The groups will also receive a set of cards, the contents of which are listed below. With such pupils it will normally be necessary to go through each of the cards giving some explanation of their contents.

Activity 1
The first task for the pupils is to match the description on the cards to the type of interpretation listed in the chart. For most it is a matching exercise with reasonably easy clues.

Activity 2
As the development of the pupils' chronological understanding is an important feature of the year 7 syllabus, the pupils, again in groups, could be asked to place the cards in chronological order. As with all group activities involving cards, it is useful to number each card to facilitate the feedback session. After the teacher has made sure that the cards have been placed in the correct chronological order, the pupils might be asked to describe how the representations of the earlier cards differ from the more recent ones and try to explain the differences. Such an activity will also contribute towards the further development of the pupils' understanding of the key concepts of change and continuity.

Activity 3
The pupils could be asked to place the cards in three separate piles (or three columns in an exercise book). One pile would be for those interpretations which they felt would be pro–Becket, the second anti–Becket and the third neutral. In each case they could be asked to explain their choice. What were the 'clues' on the cards which helped them to make their decision?

Activity 4
Although the pupils are only 11 or 12 years old, they should not be denied the opportunity to consider some of the higher order questions, which they can tackle in their own way. The teacher could ask them to select the card which represents for them the most accurate interpretation and the least accurate, again, giving reasons for choice. While some will make guesses with little substantiation, the range of responses will give useful data on how much individual pupils have begun to understand some of the issues arising from the study of historical interpretations.

1 *An Illustrated Story of Becket*	2 *The Life and Martyrdom of Saint Thomas Becket* by Father John Morris, S.J., written in 1859	3 *Mediaeval Realms, 1066–1500,* by J.F. Aylett, published in 1991
A book produced about 1235, which told the story of Becket's life with pictures of the main events.	Morris was a Jesuit, that is a member of the Catholic Society of Jesus, begun by Ignatius Loyola.	A school textbook which gives more detail than most, covering four pages.

4 *Guide Book to the City of Canterbury, including the Cathedral* (1996)	5 *Icelandic Saga,* edited by Eirikr Magnusson. Produced in its present form in the early 1300s	6 *God is My Right,* a novel by Alfred Duggan, published in 1955
The Cathedral is a main point of interest for tourists. The guidebook retells the story of Becket's murder as a background to the visit.	A Saga is a long poem usually describing heroic deeds. It is a feature of Scandinavian literature. Based on a 'Life of Becket' which has been lost.	Duggan lived from 1903 to 1964. He wrote many historical novels. His writings were based on his religious beliefs. He also wrote a book based on Becket's letters.
7 A description by Edward Grim, written about 5 to 7 years after the murder	8 *Murder in the Cathedral*, a play written in poetry by T.S. Eliot in 1935	9 *Life of St. Thomas, the Martyr of Canterbury*, by Garnier of Pont-Sainte-Maxene, written about 1175
Grim was one of the eye-witnesses of Becket's murder. He was a clerk at Canterbury who attempted to shield Becket and was severely wounded. He spent a lot of his time finding out facts for his account.	T.S. Eliot lived from 1888 to 1965. He became a British citizen in 1927. He was very much concerned with the religious aspects of the event and whether Becket wanted to die for his beliefs.	Garnier, like Grim (card 7), was a clerk in the Church. He was also a wandering author, who lived on his ability to write. He went to Canterbury to check his facts. He got on well with Becket's sisters.
10 Mosaic in a cathedral on the island of Sicily, near Italy	11 *Becket*, a play by Alfred Tennyson, written in 1884	12 *The Becket Controversy*, by Thomas Jones, published in 1970
A mosaic is a pattern or picture made up of small pieces of glass and stone. The Normans ruled Sicily in the 1100s and were responsible for many mosaics there. The mosaic of Becket shows he was highly regarded. Both of Becket's parents were Norman.	Tennyson lived from 1809 to 1892 and was a highly respected poet. The play was one of three showing the battle of the English people against the Pope in Rome. The play was put on the stage in 1893 and was a great success.	One of several books published to mark the 800th anniversary of Becket's death. A detailed study which goes over all the evidence from the time of the event and looks at how that evidence has been used by the people who have written about Becket and Henry II.

13 *Murder in the Cathedral*, a film produced in 1952	14 *Mediaeval Realms*, a CD-ROM produced by the British Library, 1996	
This film, made in England, was a film version of Eliot's play (card 8). Great efforts were made to make the cathedral appear exactly like it was at the time of the murder, and the people's clothes as they would have been in 1170.	Interactive multi-media. This CD-ROM includes 17 sources relating to Becket. Some sources are written ones, others are pictures. Some were written near the time of the murder, others as late as the 1400s.	

Now consider the following questions. Do you think the activities are consistent with their objective? What problems might you need to anticipate in order to increase the chance of success of the activity? What further questions could be asked of the pupils?

Additionally, you might consider a topic area with which you are particularly familiar and try to devise a similar exercise.

Identifying and explaining differences

You find that there is a logical sequence as you take your pupils to a point where they are in a position to begin to explain differences in interpretations. Your first task is to ensure your pupils understand the content of the interpretation. This might require some editing of the original statement or prompting to note the significant details of, for example, a picture or a poem. Then the pupils can be set the task of comparing the differences and the similarities. Once these have been identified you can begin the real task of explanation. At this point your pupils can begin to apply the questions set out below. What is important is that your planning takes into account what the pupils will need, while *allowing pupils some scope for initiative and insight.*

TASK 6.4 SETTING AN EXERCISE TO IDENTIFY AND EXPLAIN DIFFERENCES OF INTERPRETATION

Presented below are two extracts which show two very different interpretations of Thomas à Becket. On the left-hand side of each extract are the actual words of the author; on the right is an attempt to make the content more accessible.

Using these extracts work out a sequence of activities for your pupils to enable them to begin to offer explanations of these differing interpretations and to make some attempt at evaluating them. You will find some background details about John Morris in the material of Task 6.3. You should find these further extracts from John Harvey of use:

> 'Again and again kings with a truly regal achievement to their credit are found to have . . . their memory besmirched by historians.'

> 'Becket got what he asked for, but Henry, as generous and as just as he was free from petty spite, was left burdened with murder and sacrilege for the remaining twenty years of his life.'

Interpretation 1: From John Harvey, *The Plantagenets* (1959), p. 45

'Nothing could be more misleading than the notion of a saintly man of God ill-treated by a tyrannical potentate. It was said that Henry was never known to choose an unworthy friend, but Becket's worthiness is a matter of opinion. Extraordinary mixture of well-to-do-man-about-town, witty and extravagant, and self-willed, self-torturing, and it must be said, self-advertising churchman, Thomas Becket won for himself an outstanding place in history by his genius for manoeuvring other parties into the wrong.'	*The idea that Becket was a saintly man of God, who was harshly treated by a cruel king is far from the truth. People said Henry always chose good friends, but whether Becket was a good friend is a matter of opinion. Becket was an unusual mixture of well-off man-about-town. He was witty but wasteful. He was stubborn, self-torturing and, it must be said, a churchman who was keen to show off. Thomas Becket won for himself an outstanding place in history because he was a genius at making other people appear to be in the wrong.*

Interpretation 2: John Morris, S.J., *The Life and Martyrdom of Saint Thomas Becket, Archbishop of Canterbury* (1859), p. 91	
'The personal hostility which King Henry was now beginning to entertain against St. Thomas, soon found vent in an attack upon the liberties of the clergy. This was a part of the King's policy of self-aggrandisement in which he had been restrained by the Saint, whilst he exercised influence over him.'	*The personal hostility, which King Henry was now beginning to show against Saint Thomas, was soon seen in an attack upon the rights of the clergy. This was a part of the king's policy of increasing his own importance. Before that, in the days when the Saint was able to influence the King, Thomas had been a restraining influence.*

Asking questions about interpretations

An important part of the teaching of historical interpretations is the development of pupils' skills in asking questions about an interpretation. It is possible to identify a sequence of questions which would provide a useful basis for such questioning; a set of questions, which pupils could be encouraged to apply to a range of interpretations and a range of topics. The following list is taken, with some adaptations, from Pam Harper (1993).

- Who produced it? What was his or her starting-point?
- What do we know about the person who produced it?
- Why was it produced?
- Where was it produced?
- What sources were used and how valid were they?
- Who was the intended audience?
- What was the purpose of the interpretation?:
  (a) to amuse or entertain?
  (b) to sell the past or an image of it?
  (c) to inform?
  (d) to create myths?
  (e) to search for truth?
  (f) to justify or explain the present?
  (g) to influence current and future policies and discussions?
- Are some interpretations more believable than others?

You will need to be careful in your use of these questions, selecting those which are appropriate for the materials you are using and for the abilities of the pupils you are teaching. You need to ensure that pupils have access to the information needed to answer the questions. Less able pupils could be given more structure and support in their materials and information.

Explaining why historical interpretations might change

In order to meet the requirements of the Key Element relating to historical interpretations, pupils need to be able to explain 'how and why some historical events, people, situations and changes have been interpreted differently' (DfE, 1995). Part of that explanation involves an understanding of how changing circumstances might influence an interpretation. To summarise these changing circumstances it is possible to create a spray–diagram. Figure 6.1 shows some factors; no doubt there are others. Able pupils could be asked to try to design a diagram before being given a final version. Having drawn the diagram, pupils might be asked to write a sentence or two explaining each point. Most would find it useful to have some examples of each point also.

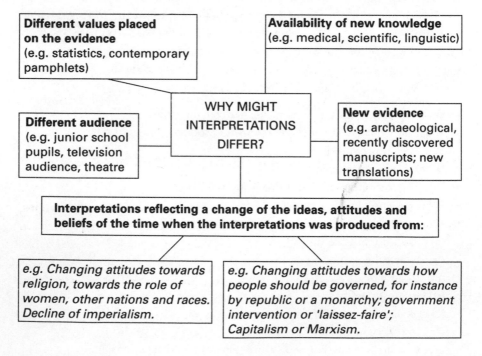

Figure 6.1 Why might interpretations differ?

Approaches to the teaching of historical interpretations

The teaching of historical interpretations is more likely to be successful if there has been a sufficient investment in the preparatory activities *before* the interpretations can be considered. Figure 6.2 gives some indication of the stages through which the teaching of interpretations can move.

Figure 6.2 summarises some of the points made in the chapter to this point. Stages 1 and 2 represent the preparatory stages for the study of interpretations. The knowledge of the topic and the identification of the interpretation are vital preliminaries for the successful completion of the higher levels of analysis, explanation and evaluation. The key question is: *do the pupils have sufficient information from which to be able to draw meaningful conclusions and to make valid comments on the interpretations they are studying?* Without sufficient knowledge the pupils will become frustrated and lose motivation. It has been suggested that only when the activities described as stage 3 and above are reached is the real study of interpretations underway. Only if pupils spend time analysing their interpretations of the events and comparing them with the available evidence will such work be related to the assessment of pupils' understanding of interpretations. Further knowledge about the authors of the interpretations and the context in which they were working would be needed for the pupils to be able to tackle successfully stage 4 – an explanation of interpretations.

Examples of approaches

These are presented to some extent as approaches for an ascending order of ability.

The use of a variety of children's books, old-fashioned history textbooks and popular historical story books

For pupils who have had little experience in considering historical interpretations, the use of history books intended for a younger audience than themselves can provide a useful introduction. The NCC (1993) described the use by year 7 pupils of a view of William the Conqueror based on a Ladybird book by L. Du Garde Peach, published in 1956. Pupils were asked to compare that interpretation with their own knowledge and try to explain the limitations of the Ladybird view. Similarly, a year 8 class could be presented with the following extract from *The Story of Queen Elizabeth* (Ladybird, 1958) by the same author.

> Queen Elizabeth reigned over England for forty-five years. When she
> came to the throne England was poor. When she died, England was rich,

Stage

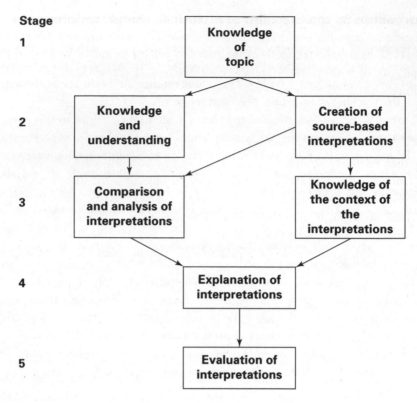

Figure 6.2 Pathways towards interpretations of history

prosperous, united and happy. Her reign saw the beginnings of
what came to be the British Empire. The fighting sailors of her reign
and the great victory over the Spanish Armada, made England one
of the greatest countries of Europe. Much of this was due to the
character of Elizabeth herself. She never despaired and she never
gave in.

Again, pupils could consider whether all these statements are confirmed by
their knowledge and discuss why the author has chosen to present such an
interpretation. This encourages a useful discussion of the relationship of an
interpretation to its intended audience. With able pupils it could also be the
starting-point for an enquiry into 'How accurate is "The Elizabethan
Legend"?'.

The study of historical interpretations can also generate a revived use for
some old textbooks. Quotations from some such books, written in the late
nineteenth century or early twentieth century can tell as much about the
times in which they were written as the topic about which they were written.

This particularly applies to comments about the British colonies and other countries, where the books often had an imperialist and condescending tone. Others sought to use the study of the past as a vehicle for moral lessons for the pupils; as such they encourage the consideration of the author's purpose in writing a historical textbook.

Drawings

Another relatively straightforward approach to the study of historical interpretations is through drawings and artistic reconstructions. Returning to the Ladybird books, these are attractively illustrated, and it may be useful for pupils to think about such pictures as interpretations. How much do the pictures showing the social background of the times present a sanitised, attractive representation of what was often dirty and unhygienic? How much is the artist influenced by the nature of the audience? Similarly, artistic reconstructions in textbooks can be the subject of such questions.

An alternative approach to interpretations through drawing is to encourage the pupils to draw their ideas about a topic. This can offer useful clues about the pupils' understanding of that topic. Wilson (1985) has shown how successful this can be with pupils of generally low ability. Apart from using drawings as a welcome alternative to the symbolic meaning of language, encouraging pupils' drawing helps them to realise that what they produce is the product of their own imagination – 'history not necessarily as it was, but as they think it is'. The comparison of each other's interpretative drawings and the ensuing explanation of the differences enable the pupils to be operating at stage 3 of Figure 6.2. Furthermore, as Wilson also points out, 'this subtle distinction between fact and interpretation is less clear when children are presented with visual material, which is the product of the imagination of others, including the illustrations of modern text-books' (Wilson, 1985).

Use of historical fiction

In more recent years teachers have overcome some reluctance to make use of historical fiction in their history lessons. It has become generally accepted that such literature can be a useful aid to pupil interest and understanding. *By following the experience of individual characters placed in past situations, it is easier for many pupils to begin to comprehend situations very different from their own experience.* Any concern about the lack of authenticity of such a medium has been dispelled to a degree by the good fortune of having had in the past half century some excellent writers of historical fiction for young people, writers who, moreover, spent many hours of solid historical research on the background of their novel. The very nature of such fiction means that it represents an author's interpretation of an event or past environment. So, while extracts from such literature, with the wealth of detail that is often included, are an excellent aid to understanding in themselves, they can also be used to develop further pupils' understanding of historical interpretations. Consider the following description of exploited child labour in the factories of the early industrialisation. The passage is taken from a novel, excellent for this purpose: *The Devil's Mill* by Walter Unsworth.

> If Jeremy was overawed by the machinery and the noise, he did not fail to notice his fellow apprentices. What he saw was not encouraging: thin, ragged children with pinched faces, some only seven or eight years old and so tiny that they had to stand on stools to reach their machines. The boys wore only shirt and trousers, though the mill was damp and cold, the girls plain, pinafore dresses. All were barefoot, with unkempt hair, and incredibly dirty.
>
> Though these things in themselves were bad enough it was the faces of the children which alarmed Jeremy. Pale, sickly, their faces had set into a look of utter hopelessness. He felt a cold chill of apprehension to think that these were his companions of the future and he wondered whether he too would become like them.

Such a passage could precipitate the use of some of the questions about interpretations listed above. It would be particularly useful for pupils to consider not only the purpose of the author and the intended audience but also the extent to which they think it represents an accurate picture of such factories. Furthermore, such a passage could be used to introduce the topic of child labour in factories, then followed by the use of contemporary sources to examine whether the passage was supported by the evidence. Alternatively, the use of the extract could, as in the procedure indicated by Figure 6.2, follow the study of child labour and so enable the pupils to move from analysis through to evaluation.

Completion exercises

The understanding of historical interpretations can be greatly helped by the use of completion exercises often in a tabular format. They have several advantages – it is usually clear what the pupils have to do, the requirement to fill in columns or to complete a diagram or a sentence helps to pinpoint a specific idea or issue in the material being studied, whether it be documentary, video, pictorial or physical evidence. Most importantly, the completion of tables etc. usually asks pupils to make decisions without at that stage requiring much writing. 'In which column shall we place a tick?' Having made a decision, they can then be asked to explain it and, in so doing, move them up the stages of our diagram. The extent to which completion exercises can help less able pupils can also be noted as a means of helping them to analyse two conflicting sources. The use of tables and charts can help pupils towards organising their information in a way which will assist them towards deploying it for some form of analysis or judgement.

TASK 6.5 USING COMPLETION EXERCISES

Study the following tasks. At what point do you think the pupils are considering 'historical interpretations'? They involve relatively simple tasks for year 8 pupils studying 'The Making of the United Kingdom'. The approach is to present the pupils with a comparison which requires them to make a series of decisions. Having done this, they have to try to give reasons for their choices. The later questions reflect an incline of difficulty represented in Figure 6.2.

Example:

Read carefully the following two passages about 'Bonnie Prince Charlie' and answer the questions which follow.

Source A

'Charles was an idle spectator of the Battle of Culloden at a safe distance. He took the first opportunity to flee and to preserve his life – a life perhaps more worthless and miserable than that of the most wretched of fellows.'

Source B

'At the Battle of Falkirk, the presence of Charles encouraged the Highlanders. He praised their courage. He made them pick up their muskets [guns], which lay thick on the ground and, ordering them to follow him, led them to the brow of the hill.'

1 In the right-hand column of the following table, mark *either* 'A' (for Source A) *or* 'B' (for Source B) against those words which agree with that source.

cont . . .

What was 'Bonnie Prince Charlie' like?	'A' or 'B'?
idle good at encouraging his followers cowardly brave inspiring courageous good leader useless	

2 Using the words in the table, complete the following sentences.

Source A says Charles was _____

_____

Source B says Charles was _____

_____

3 One of the sources was a statement by a Highland officer who fought
   with Charles, and the other comes from a newspaper which was
   published in London in 1746. The newspaper was called the *True
   Patriot*. Read the sources again and complete the following:

   A Highland officer wrote Source   _____
   The *True Patriot* published Source _____

4 Try to give reasons for your choice to the previous question.
5 Why do you think these sources give such a different description of
   'Bonnie Prince Charlie'?
6 Do you think Source A or Source B gives the more accurate description
   of Charles? Explain your choice.

Decision-making, recorded in tabular form, may also be used to indicate how differing interpretations could emphasise different causes of an event.

Use of video, film

Amongst the most stimulating aids to the understanding of historical interpretations is the use that can be made of videos and films. These vary greatly in their nature. The BBC schedules for schools for history at Key Stage 3 include a programme on Oliver Cromwell, subtitled, *Hero or Villain?* The Teachers' Notes, available from the BBC, include suggestions for the use of the programme in the classroom. The teaching materials provide source-work and map-work. Pupils are encouraged to develop their own interpretations of Cromwell.

The use of film material does raise legitimate questions about the use or neglect of historical evidence, the purpose of the interpretation and, again, how the nature of the intended audience can affect the interpretation. A familiar anecdote on this theme may be retold of how the film director, Eisenstein, in his reconstruction of the Bolshevik Revolution of 1917, did more damage to the Winter Palace when shooting the film than was ever achieved during the actual revolution. Clips from that film have been used in documentaries and news programmes for many years since the film was made in 1922, to the extent that Eisenstein's reconstruction is often assumed to be the actual event. Pupils will be familiar with various historical 'epics' and costume dramas frequently repeated on television. Such reconstructions could be useful starting-points for the study of a topic. Useful discussion will focus on the degree of artistic licence involved to add drama to the reconstruction.

The use of comparisons

There is some evidence that pupils will respond positively to tasks inviting them to make comparisons. An analysis of 149 GCSE scripts showed that, out of a total of seven source-based questions, the two which targeted the comparison of sources gained the highest percentage of good answers. As you will have appreciated in reading this chapter, the study of historical interpretations is by its nature likely to encourage the use of comparisons. Furthermore, such comparisons can be made at a variety of levels, so that most abilities can achieve some success. Beginning with clearly contradictory pictorial representations and clear-cut, forthright opposite views, comparisons can become increasingly more subtle and complex. Even when this is the case there are times when the language can be simplified to meet the needs of a wider range of ability. Furthermore, the potential problems of the use of adjectives in the study of historical interpretations can be noted again when pupils are placed in situations where they are asked to articulate their own interpretations as a basis for comparison. Less able pupils may need a list of adjectives from which to select the ones they believe are appropriate.

Much can be gained from the pupils' own interpretation of pictures. For example, a photograph of a painting by A.F. Tait of the Stockport Viaduct (1842), soon after its completion, was passed round a year 9 class studying the nineteenth-century industrial town. Individually, they were asked to write down one or more adjectives that came to mind when they analysed the photograph. In the following feedback, a variety of contrasting interpretations emerged. Most saw a smoky, grimy factory town beneath this massive viaduct, while others produced words such as 'romantic', and 'magnificent'. These differences generated a useful discussion about the painter's purpose, about how people in 1842 might have felt about the new viaduct and its railway, and why so many pupils had emphasised the dirty aspect of the town. The discussion then moved on to consider further comparisons reflecting different viewpoints.

Successful lessons may be based on giving different sets of evidence to different groups within the classroom. In their discussions the groups are asked to produce a set of conclusions based upon the information available to them. When their responses are fielded and recorded, one of the points that emerges from the ensuing discussion is the conclusion that interpretations will differ because they draw upon different evidence. A lesson using such an approach was given to a year 8 class studying the Moghul Empire. The groups were asked to answer the question, 'Who won the battle of Panipat?' Two different duplicated and contrasting sheets were in use, some pupils had Sheet A, others Sheet B. Sheet A was fictitious. The different views were later recorded in a chart on the board. The teacher then analysed the results and asked the pupils a series of questions about the conflicting interpretations. Destroying the fictitious sheet before them, the teacher then asked the pupils to consider the significance for historians of having only one side of evidence on which to base their interpretation of events (David Gourley and Ryder Hargreaves developed this idea at Burnage High School). *Again it is worth re-emphasising the importance of the follow-up work in re-informing the significance of issues that had emerged from the discussion.* Sometimes student teachers do not allow sufficient time for this important follow-up to the activity, assuming that the group activity itself will be sufficient for the objectives of the lesson to have been met.

Use of drama

The use of a variety of forms of drama can provide a valuable approach to the study of historical interpretations. Any printed play is itself an interpretation, and there are times when material on a historical topic could be appropriately used in the classroom. Another approach could involve playlets (usually read out as radio plays rather than acted), about three or four pages only in length, written by the teacher. It is surprising how quickly such materials can be produced and how often such an effort is rewarded with a successful lesson. This is an increasingly popular way of dealing with some of the conceptually difficult topics which occur in the 'Making of the United Kingdom' unit. To retain consistency with the definition of an interpretation established earlier in the chapter, such a playlet should also include some indication of the sources on which it is based.

Once pupils have become familiar with the format of a play, some classes can be given an opportunity to write their own playlets. This should not be too onerous a task. The real work on interpretations will occur when the pupils are given an opportunity to compare the results and to try and account for the differences.

Use of role-play

Another increasingly popular but valuable approach used in history teaching is that of role-play. Its main purpose is usually to help the pupils to comprehend complex issues in formats that they can understand by making situations more personal and immediate. Such an approach can also be used to help the understanding of historical interpretations.

The use of familiar media formats can also be used to good effect. A year 9 class was asked, in groups, to prepare a radio programme on the Peterloo Massacre. Different pupils within the groups were to be interviewed, presenting different interpretations of the event. Each interpretation was based on a collection of primary sources made available to the pupils. The discussion which followed the group work then sought in sequence to (1) identify, (2) explain and finally (3) evaluate the differences that emerged.

Historical Enquiry

The fourth Key Element in the National Curriculum is entitled 'Historical Enquiry'. It is interesting to note the emphasis on the word 'enquiry' and the inclusion within this element of what was the third Attainment Target, the 'use of sources'. This change of emphasis will hopefully help you to encourage pupils to use sources not as discrete and often arid exercises, removed from their context, but as a means of mounting a set of enquiries. In other words, 'sources' may be seen as an aspect of 'resources' available to aid the development of historical understanding. For this reason the use of sources and the skills involved are included in Chapter 9.

The renewed emphasis on pupil enquiries and investigations is to be welcomed. The limitations of some of the coursework produced for the CSE examination before the GCSE probably helped create a deprecatory attitude towards the history 'project' if it involved a 'scrap-book' of copied extracts and cuttings. This created an understandable dislike of 'projects' if they were so lacking in rigour and challenge. However, pupil enquiries, if they are well-organised, can offer plenty of challenge and scope for individual initiative. SCAA (1996) emphasises the point in noting that 'independence in carrying out research and in making historical judgements is an important characteristic of work at higher levels'. Local history can offer many opportunities for pupils to pursue their own historical enquiries, and if used appropriately some of the more thoughtfully designed history CD-ROMs can provide a useful resource for pupil investigations. The British Library's structured investigations based around their CD-ROM, *Medieval Realms*, are a good example of this (British Library, 1994). OFSTED reports have stressed the desirability of pupils being empowered to find things out for themselves, and develop into autonomous learners (OFSTED, 1995). The Dearing Review of the National Curriculum also stressed that the ability to work and learn independently was one of the 'key skills' which needed to be emphasised and developed (Dearing, 1994).

The use of historical enquiries would help towards meeting OFSTED (1995) comments about the need to give pupils more responsibility for their own learning. Their inspection reports, analysed by Bowen (1995), also notes that in addition to the underuse of libraries that 'too often pupils appear to be given access to only a limited range of texts and the teaching of research and retrieval skills is not developed sufficiently'. You find that there are great opportunities for differentiated work if you can encourage pupils to use their initiative to complete enquiry-based projects.

TASK 6.6 ENCOURAGING THE USE OF ENQUIRIES IN LOCAL HISTORY

Local history sources can provide the basis for many stimulating enquiries for pupils of all ages and abilities in the secondary school. They are particularly useful if your locality can provide examples which help your pupils to understand national history. Fieldwork, site investigations and the use of local history libraries can give an extra dimension to the learning of history.

The following activity for year 7 classes can help to develop their understanding of the use of sources for a series of enquiries. As with all valuable lessons involving enquiries, appropriate materials need to be accumulated. For this activity you need to acquire a set of census returns for, say, 1861 for the area in which you are teaching, then:

- divide the data into approximately equal amounts for six groups. A population of 800 people would result in two A4 pages of data per group;
- explain to the class that they are going to find out what occupations the people living in their area had in 1861;
- using the entry for a particular household, explain each of the columns and give the class some details of how the census returns were acquired;

- appoint two pupils whose task is to move round the groups collecting and collating the data.
- appoint another pupil who will then use the data to create a bar chart on the board;
- the groups will complete the following sheet and the collators complete their totals (suitably amended for your area and data):

Group.............................

We have found that in ...... in 1861 there were:

Total of all groups

1	_____	servants or house servants	_____
2	_____	labourers; farm labourers	_____
3	_____	laundresses; washerwomen	_____
4	_____	housewives; housekeepers	_____
5	_____	gardeners	_____
6	_____	cotton factory workers (winders, weavers, spinners, calico printers, dyers, agents)	_____
7	_____	farmers	_____
8	_____	craftsmen (blacksmiths, stone masons, wheelwrights, joiners, shoemakers, carpenters)	_____
9	_____	warehousemen	_____
10	_____	salespeople (beer-house keepers, butchers, grocers, saleswomen, provision dealers, hosiers)	_____
11	_____	jobs related to travel (railway porters, carters, grooms, coachmen, carriers, footmen, paviours)	_____
12	_____	craftswomen	_____
13	_____	professional jobs (teachers, police, nurses, clerks, cashiers)	_____
14	_____	merchants, manufacturers	_____

An important part of the investigation will be a discussion of the final bar chart and the questions that can emerge. Further enquiries using the same data could include an analysis of the age range of the population and an investigation into their places of birth.

The Peasants' Revolt: an individual enquiry-based project

The following is a suggestion for an enquiry-based project on the Peasants' Revolt. It would follow a more conventionally taught scheme on the Black Death, which has encouraged the pupils to consider key questions in history such as 'What was the Black Death?'; 'What were the causes?'; 'Why are there different interpretations of the causes?'; What can we learn about attitudes of people at the time from the study of the Black Death?'; 'What were the results of the Black Death?'; 'What was the significance of the Black Death?' (as set out in Figure 10.3). The following scheme would seek to provide data for the application of the revised level descriptions of the Attainment Target.

Introduction: The pupils are presented with a relatively brief overview of the topic, concentrating mainly on the principal events. The pupils are then told that they are to produce their own projects on the Peasants' Revolt. Each will have a pack of information and access to a range of books, published at different times. The pupils are told the criteria which will be the basis for the marking, but not the level descriptions. Use of initiative and independence will be rewarded.

Preliminary task: The pupils, having heard the overview, are required to browse through the information pack and then try to create a list of questions or separate enquiries, following the example of the questions from the study of the Black Death. These lists themselves will contribute to the assessment, because what the pupils choose to include can be quite instructive about the pupils' own historical understanding. These lists will be returned with comments and the pupils will then be ready to continue with the next stage of the project.

The project work: This is as much about process as product, and there will be limits on the amount of time spent on each of the enquiries. For example, one of the more obvious enquiries will be into why the revolt took place. Pupils will have a deadline for its completion. One of the dangers of using the 'enquiry approach' is that you can lose some control over the pace of the lesson, hence the setting of short-term targets. Pupils may also find it helpful to present information in lists or diagrams, where applicable. In the not too distant future much of the material for their enquiries will be accessed through the use of networked computers. This will also push the subject towards individual enquiries. Pupils could be asked to hand in separate enquiries as they proceed to ease the marking and ensure all are making progress.

Conclusion: The whole project is completed and handed in. There may be a case for reviewing the products in some whole-class teaching so that all can benefit from the individual enquiries.

SUMMARY AND KEY POINTS

The teaching of interpretations of history gives you the opportunity to plan and deliver lessons which can be imaginative, interesting and which can problematise the study of the past in a way which engages pupils in historical enquiry. We have seen that it is important that the pupils have a clear understanding of how the study of historical interpretations differs from source skills and also that they know why we consider them to be important. This Key Element poses some difficulties to the new teacher, who needs to be aware of the possible learning difficulties pupils might experience. The chapter has stressed that problems can arise through insufficiency of content, the pupils' limited comprehension, their need to have the confidence to move from describing to explanation and, where appropriate, on to evaluation. At the same time you need to emphasise to your pupils that there still remains much about the past about which we can be certain. Your pupils need to understand why it is important for them to study historical interpretations. Success is more likely if you try to use a range of types of interpretations, including some, such as television advertisements, that your pupils will be surprised can form part of their history lessons. This in turn encourages you to employ a range of media and of teaching styles.

The chapter concludes by emphasising the point that the development of source skills is likely to be more successful if they are seen by the pupils to have a purpose. Such skills are to be seen as the means by which they can carry out historical enquiries rather than as exercises in source skills, divorced from their context and without any evident utility.

FURTHER READING

Fines, J. and Hopkins, T (1993) *Teaching for Attainment Target 2*, London, Historical Association.
A useful introduction, although written before the introduction of the New Orders.

McAleavy, T. (1993) 'Using the Attainment Targets at KS3: AT2, Interpretations of History', *Teaching History*, July.
Establishes and discusses some of the key issues presented by this new development in the teaching of history, which are supported further in the following NCC publication.

NCC (1993) *Teaching History at Key Stage 3*, York, NCC.

Pendry, A. *et al.* (1997) 'Pupil Preconceptions in History', *Teaching History*, no. 86, January, pp. 18–20.

Towill, E. (1997) The Constructive Use of Role Play at Key Stage 3', *Teaching History*, no 86, January, pp. 8–13.

7 Pupils with special educational needs in the history classroom

INTRODUCTION

During your school experience you will be faced with the challenge of meeting the learning needs of all the pupils you are assigned to teach. It is an inescapable fact that you will be expected to teach history to pupils with varying levels of ability and motivation. You will experience pupils with poor memory, short concentration spans, poor writing and reading skills and limited powers of discussion in dealing with historical concepts. You may also experience exceptionally able pupils. It will thus be necessary for you to adapt the history study units, your planned classroom activities, your teaching strategies and resources in an effort to meet the individual needs of the pupils in your class. The History National Curriculum is explicit in stating that the subject should be taught in a way which makes it accessible to 'the great majority of pupils in the Key Stage, in ways appropriate to their abilities' (DfE, 1995). There will be very few, if any, pupils in most mainstream schools for whom the National Curriculum will be disapplied. Failure to identify and respond to the special educational needs of pupils inevitably results in pupil underachievement, and possibly dissaffection, leading to poor classroom behaviour. A school which has a selective intake or adopts a streaming policy does not escape responsibility for identifying pupil learning difficulties. Pupils will not only differ in ability, but in interests, social class, self-concept and self-esteem, ethnic background, creativity, preferred learning styles, and the extent which they deem history to be any use to them. All of these can impact on teaching and learning in the history classroom and therefore you need to be familiar with the principles of teaching pupils with special educational needs, and strategies for getting the best out of all the pupils in your care.

OBJECTIVES

At the end of this chapter you should be able to understand the educational context in which teaching and learning take place with regard to pupils with learning difficulties. You should also develop an ability to recognise possible learning difficulties presented by the study of history, to identify factors which are preventing pupils from performing to the best of their ability in the subject, and be able to adopt appropriate teaching strategies to help them through their learning difficulties, with both able and less able pupils. You will need to understand the range and variety of learning difficulties you are likely to encounter in school and be able to understand some of the reasons for those difficulties. This means that as you are observing or teaching pupils you need to make a conscious effort to understand why many pupils find aspects of learning history difficult. The chapter aims to:

- provide an overview of the current situation with regard to teaching history to children with learning difficulties in mainstream classrooms;
- provide a definition of special educational needs for the history teacher;
- provide an introduction to the Code of Practice on the identification and assessment of special educational needs as it relates to the teaching of history;
- provide an introduction to differentiated learning and the various teaching strategies and methods to enhance the learning of history for pupils with learning difficulties.

THEORETICAL BACKGROUND

Special Educational Needs (SEN), as an educational term, came into use in the 1960s, partly as a reaction to the negative terminology and categorisation of 'disabled', 'retarded', 'backward' or 'handicapped' pupils, and as a response to the increasing awareness and frequency of learning and other difficulties affecting pupils. The meaning of the term was developed further by the Report of the Committee of Enquiry into Special Education of Handicapped Children and Young People which was chaired by Baroness Warnock (DES, 1978). The Report adopted a more positive approach to SEN, with greater attention given to pupils with SEN in mainstream schools, and advocated a move towards educating pupils with SEN in mainstream schools where possible. The Report recommended that provision for pupils with SEN should be based on the assumption that about one in six at any one time, and one in five at some time during their schooling, will require special education provision in one form or another. As you will know from your school experience, the exact percentage of SEN pupils in any one school will depend on a number of factors, not least the school's annual intake of pupils. The number within any one particular class will also vary according to the school's approach to streaming and mixed-ability teaching.

Many of the Report's recommendations were incorporated into the Education Act 1981, but the definition of SEN was limited simply to any pupil who experienced a learning difficulty which called for special educational provision to be made. A very good guide to the principles found within the Act can be obtained from a reading of Brian Goacher's book (1988). The Act required local education authorities to make special educational provision through an individual statement which set out the pupil's needs and the provision being made. The statement contained an action plan which had to be implemented in school and was monitored and reviewed. Parents were to be consulted and had the right of appeal. The process was certainly time-consuming and the responsibilities of the various bodies concerned could often seem confusing. The Education Reform Act 1988, which established the statutory right of all pupils to a 'balanced and broad curriculum' by means of a National Curriculum, and from which pupils with SEN would only be made exempt under special circumstances and for a limited period of time, placed greater pressure on this process. The 1981 Education Act had stipulated that the aims of education were the same for all; the 1988 Act made this an entitlement for every pupil. There was now a statutory duty on teachers to include SEN pupils within the National Curriculum. It was clear that there were wide variations in the proportion of pupils given statements and in the types of need deemed eligible. There also seemed to be a diversion of attention away from pupils not statemented, and additional resources were concentrated on statemented pupils to provide them with support. Nevertheless, understanding of the range and breadth of learning difficulties faced by pupils was enhanced by these developments.

The publication of the Code in 1994 resulted from the Education Act 1993 and attempted to improve and clarify the procedural situation with regard to pupils with SEN. The Code recognised the needs of the 18 per cent of all pupils in schools with SEN but without statements, as well as the 2 per cent with statements. Schools now had a statutory duty placed on them to take the Code into account when identifying, assessing and making provision for pupils with SEN. The Code requires all subject teachers to identify pupils with SEN in their classes, and it significantly places accountability for developing appropriate SEN policies and provision firmly with schools, not local education authorities. One of the most positive aspects of the Code was 'the focus on children with SEN but without statements' (Hornby, 1995). The Code also emphasised early identification and assessment of SEN and devised a five-stage process with each stage representing a certain level of need for a pupil. The stages comprised:

1 the pupil's SEN is recognised;
2 the provision of greater differentiation for the SEN pupil;

3 outside specialists are used by the school;

4 the need for a statutory assessment is considered;

5 a pupil is assessed for a possible SEN statement.

The Code makes it clear that 'the needs of most pupils will be met in the mainstream without a statutory assessment or statement. Children with SEN (with or without statements) should, where appropriate – taking into account wishes of pupils and parents – be educated alongside their peers in the mainstream' (DfE, 1994). This means that pupils with SEN will normally be taught with their peers rather than being withdrawn from lessons for small group or individual work with a specialist teacher. Nevertheless, teaching and learning would have to be planned at the individual level, with the development of an individual education plan for pupils with SEN.

Provision for SEN was to be one of the aspects of educational quality which would be monitored by OFSTED. The 1995 OFSTED report on the teaching of history makes a number of references to SEN pupils and the provision being made by history teachers. It found that insufficient attention was being given to pupils for whom reading and writing was difficult, and it mentions the inappropriate use of resources and tasks for pupils with varying abilities and that history teachers do not always make best use of support staff to help provide access to the curriculum (OFSTED, 1995). The implication for history teachers is that they will need to make increased efforts to ensure that the full programme of history study units are accessible to pupils of all abilities. This includes pupils with the potential for exceptional achievement, to which topic we will return later in this chapter. It is one of the factors which you will need to take account of in your planning for learning in history (see Chapter 3). Above all, the Report recognises that the failure to identify pupils with SEN is often aggravated by the use of unsuitable teaching strategies. You should have the advice and support of the school's special educational needs co-ordinator (SENCO) to whom you should make yourself known at an early stage of your school experience.

However, in the course of your school experience, and with the help of the teachers you work with, you should be able to identify and recognise mild or moderate learning difficulties in pupils through your assessment of their work, and through careful observation and conversation with pupils. You need to keep in mind that pupils struggling with tasks that are beyond their capabilities may not have SEN, as the problem may lie more with your teaching methods or assessment techniques, or the limits to which you have been able to persuade pupils to commit themselves wholeheartedly to the task in question. You need to recognise that history contains many abstract terms and concepts which, if not introduced at the right level, will cause ambiguity and confusion in the minds of all pupils, not just those with SEN. The linguistic demands of history as a subject are also high, and you need to be constantly aware, not just with SEN pupils, of both the language you use in communicating with pupils and the demand placed on pupils' use of language. You also must guard against history lessons becoming reading and writing exercises for pupils who already have difficulty with these skills – increased literacy is a by-product of history teaching, not its main aim.

RECOGNISING PUPILS' SPECIAL EDUCATIONAL NEEDS

At some point in your school experience you should have opportunities to discuss SEN issues with the SENCO, who is responsible for implementing the school's SEN policy. The SENCO would be the person to consult in the case of a pupil recognised with signs of SEN. Recognising learning difficulties is clearly the first step to addressing them, and the Code describes the following categories of learning difficulties:

- a physical disability;
- a problem with sight, hearing or speech;
- a mental disability;
- emotional or behaviour problems;
- a medical or health problem;
- difficulties with reading, writing, speaking or mathematics work.

TASK 7.1 YOUR SCHOOL'S SEN POLICY

During your school experience find out what the school and department policy is concerning the identification of pupils with SEN, including exceptionally able pupils.

Does the school have a whole-school approach to SEN with a written statement of policy? How does the history department interpret the school's SEN policy in terms of individual education plans and departmental strategies for pupils with special educational needs?

Referring to the list of learning difficulties recognised by the Code observe one history class and try to identify any learning difficulties that the pupils have. In particular look at:

- ability;
- motivation and interests;
- maturity;
- preferred learning styles;
- behaviour;

- reading and writing skills;
- listening skills;
- communication skills;
- memory.

TEACHING HISTORY TO PUPILS WITH SPECIAL EDUCATIONAL NEEDS

The lack of focus by history teachers on SEN was acknowledged by the Historical Association at its 1978 annual conference, and by the publication of a pamphlet by Cowie (1979) which provided useful suggestions on the use of oral history, appropriate textbooks, visual materials, together with television and video programmes suitable for pupils with special educational needs. However, research has tended to confirm what most history teachers already experienced. Wilson (1982a) found that low achievers often lacked motivation in their study of history and that these pupils questioned the relevance of history, and expressed dissatisfaction with the teaching methods employed in the classroom. These are the same concerns that Mary Price (1968) identified about all pupils in the 1960s and which have been discussed in Chapter 2. Cowie (1979) had also identified these problems with SEN pupils in that they find it difficult to 'see links, find relationships, make contrasts, generalisations, or discriminate' in history. McMinn (1983) found that teachers had better results from their teaching when they taught historical content rather than historical skills to pupils with SEN, an approach which would deny full access to the National Curriculum history study units if it was to be adopted by history teachers today. Pupils are offered a series of opportunities to acquire different skills through being introduced to different historical content. As Hull (1980) rightly says; 'History is not . . . a cumulative subject. We do not depend for the understanding of one concept or item in the syllabus upon the essential mastery of an earlier concept.' There obviously needs to be greater attention given by the history teacher to clarifying learning objectives and learning methods.

The aims of the History National Curriculum, as Ware and Peacy (1993) point out, are exactly the same aims we have when teaching SEN pupils history. Consequently, you will need to ensure access to the National Curriculum for all of your pupils by means of a flexible, but carefully structured approach to learning and teaching. This will require you to make professional assessments of pupils' existing knowledge, understanding and skills, an appreciation of their previous experience and development and an awareness of the resources available to you in the classroom. Careful judgement will determine the appropriate level of work, task or expectation that you need to set to progressively challenge your pupils. As Hull states:

> if we can present our subject clearly, regularly exercise skills in which pupils of lesser ability become reasonably competent and give them a structure for their work which they can understand, we have a real possibility of arousing the pupils' interest and restoring confidence and self esteem.

(Hull, 1980)

We need to provide all pupils, of whatever background or ability level, with the opportunities to demonstrate what they know, understand and are able to do. In other words, the good classroom teacher differentiates by ensuring that pupils are given tasks which are appropriate to their level of attainment. This does not mean a separate or different History National Curriculum. An understanding of what educational achievement entails is essential to successful work with pupils with SEN. Hargreaves (1984) makes the point that there are at least four aspects of educational achievement that teachers need to keep in mind:

- dealing with the capacity to remember and use facts;
- practical and spoken skills;
- personal and social skills;
- motivation and self-confidence.

It may be instructive to think back to the subjects you were 'good at', or 'did well in', as a pupil. Was part of your success due to confidence and self-belief? How can this be developed in pupils who may not be naturally 'gifted' in history? Teaching is in part, instruction – in this case, explaining the mysteries of the past to pupils – but is also about encouraging pupils to learn and making them feel that they can learn and improve. One of the skills you will need to develop is the art of devising activities which will push pupils to the limits of their ability, but which are within their compass, to provide both access and challenge. As OFSTED have noted (OFSTED, 1993), one of the abuses of history has been to give pupils with special educational needs mechanical and undemanding tasks, which have no intrinsically historical purpose and are in effect tests of comprehension, transcription or presentation.

TASK 7.2 LEARNING FROM PUBLISHED SEN RESOURCES FOR HISTORY

Either from your placement school or from the resources centre at your ITE institution, look through one of the textbooks or resource packs designed for pupils with SEN, and examine how they attempt to retain genuinely historical activities whilst ensuring that materials are rendered accessible to pupils. Examples include Heinemann's 'Foundation History' series (e.g. Kennedy, 1994), Oxford's 'Access to History' series (e.g. Robson, 1993) and the Schools History Project materials published by Murray mentioned above.

Having looked through the materials, try to devise an exercise for pupils with SEN for one of your teaching groups which attempts to *adapt* some of the principles and strategies used in the published materials.

TASK 7.3 AN EXAMPLE OF A TASK DESIGNED FOR PUPILS WITH SEN

The following exercise, taken from Harrington and Chaplin (1990), attempts to introduce pupils to some aspects of problems of evidence. It uses the device of an 'enabling' example, drawn from a non-historical context, to provide a way in to dealing with historical sources.

Evidence: how to look at sources

Look at this primary source:

'At Pentecost was seen, in a village in Berkshire, blood welling from the earth . . . ' (from the *Anglo-Saxon Chronicle*, AD 1100).

Do you think this is true? Give a reason for your answer.
Do you always tell the whole truth?

People in the past were the same as us. They did not always tell the whole truth either.
People today have different likes and dislikes.

Write down something that you like, and something that you dislike.
Now see if your classmates agree with you?

Because we are all different, we all have different opinions. People in the past were the same.

Now look at these two primary sources about the same man, William I;
'he was a wise man, very powerful . . . he was mild with good men . . . '
'A hard man . . . sunk in greed . . . may God show mercy on his soul and pardon him his sins' (both quotes from the *Anglo-Saxon Chronicle*, 1087).

Do the sources both agree?
If both sources are from the same book, and about the same man, why are they so different?

In what ways might you have to adapt this exercise, or provide additional support for pupils with SEN in order to make it accessible to all pupils in a year 7 class, including pupils with very limited reading skills?

The quality and availability of published resources for less able pupils have improved in recent years, with several publishers providing specialised text-books for less able pupils (see for instance, Robson, 1993; Kennedy, 1994). Many of these books provide suggestions for work which is accessible to pupils of limited ability, but which address historical understanding. One way of focusing on history rather than comprehension is to keep in mind the questions which historians pose of the past; in the words of Husbands (1996), 'the questions we think it important to ask about relics of the past'. This can often be achieved by focusing questions on the second-order concepts such as change, cause and evidence which underpin so much of the study of the past (see Chapter 3). The Schools History Project has put together resource packs particularly designed to support pupils with special educational needs, and which make imaginative and thoughtful use of picture packs (see, for instance, Shephard and Brown, 1994).

Differentiation is the key to addressing SEN with pupils in mainstream classes. History teachers often set a variety of work in their classes corresponding to the different levels of pupil ability – differentiation by task. Just as often they will set similar work for their classes which produces a variety of outcomes – differentiation by outcome. To be effective, history teachers need to be competent in both types of differentiation by looking at tasks between different abilities of pupils and then using a series of developed and increasingly complex questions to assess the pupil's knowledge. An 'incline of difficulty', as Hilary Bourdillon (1994) describes it. The questions used should start as simple process questions (e.g. Who?, What?, When?), and move to more complex 'key' questions (e.g. Why?, How?), and so on. Differentiation is therefore the process of identifying with each pupil the most effective strategies for achieving attainment in the History National Curriculum. As Wilson (1985) says: 'Surely it is differentiation by input (in terms of planned teaching strategies, selection of resources and planned pupil activity) according to pupils' individual needs which is most relevant to the teaching and learning process.' Certainly the Final Report of the History Working Group places the main emphasis on differentiation by outcome, as it states:

> History is accessible and of value to all pupils although assessment
> techniques and arrangements have not always been appropriate to pupils
> with SEN . . . It is important that due regard is taken of the difficulties
> faced by individual pupils, especially in ensuring that they are not,
> inadvertently, excluded from showing what they can achieve by the
> nature of the tasks set for assessment purposes.
>
> (DES, 1990a)

Ask yourself whether or not the level of difficulty in the textbook or worksheet is suitable for all of the class? What can you do to provide the 'scaffolding' which will help less able pupils to answer the same questions put to able pupils? This might be done by giving the pupils individual attention, putting support material on the classroom wall for consultation, allowing pupils to work cooperatively, or breaking down the task into smaller components through the use of

TASK 7.4 MOTIVATION AND SEN IN THE HISTORY CLASSROOM

Even if you do not have 'special educational needs', you have probably experienced the feeling of not wanting to try particularly hard at something that you feel you are not very good at (dancing, maths, piano, cross-country running, public speaking?). By the time pupils reach secondary schools, many pupils are aware that they are not 'good at history', do not consider it one of their favourite subjects, or do not feel that it is 'useful'. This can affect the extent to which pupils attempt to do well at history – there is often a connection between SEN and motivation, extending to what is sometimes termed *failure avoidance* – 'if I don't try, no one can say I'm no good at it'. This can be presented as a continuum between those pupils who are keen to do well in history, and pupils who have an aversion or indifference to achievement in history.

Attitudes to learning history

A common misapprehension of student teachers is to ascribe levels of attainment in history to ability rather than ability plus motivation. How many of your pupils are trying to do their best in your lessons? To what extent have pupils with SEN 'given up'?

Over the course of two or three lessons, and after taking in and scrutinising the work produced by pupils, assess the extent to which pupils are trying to do well in history, and consider the relationship between ability and motivation. Pupils might be at any point on the following continuum:

- *Disconnected*: the scale of the pupil's learning difficulties means that there is no real learning connection between you and the pupil other than the fact that you are in the same room. He may well not even be aware of what you are trying to do.
- *Disruptive*: pupil is actively hostile to what you are trying to achieve in the lesson, and attempts to distract others from learning and spoil the lesson.
- *Disaffected*: pupil is generally unpersuaded of the purpose of school/education as a whole and has made a conscious decision not to bother with whatever it is that you are trying to do. This attitude is not particularly related to history as a school subject.
- *Disengaged*: pupil makes no effort to cooperate in the enterprise of learning or do the work involved – if you didn't make the pupil work,

he/she would literally do nothing, but in a passive rather than hostile 'anti-learning' manner.

- *Desultory compliance*: pupil does the bare minimum required to satisfy what are perceived to be your 'demands', no pride in work or desire to do well, will do enough to try and get you not to bother him/her – looking out for a sort of tacit deal (you leave me alone and I won't bother you).
- *Diligent*: basically conscientious and will make a reasonable attempt to do the work set to a fairly high standard.
- *Driven*: passionately keen to do well, to the extent of obsessively (and sometimes pointlessly) long homeworks. Wants to become exceptionally accomplished at the subject, 'come top', obtain the highest grade, be recognised as excellent in the field.

Over the course of your school experience, consider how the proportions of pupils in the various categories change, discuss the relationship between SEN and motivation with the teachers you work with. What strategies do they use to encourage pupils with SEN to work to their full potential?

TASK 7.5 DIFFERENTIATION

As preparation for this activity you should read Lewis (1992) on the practical listing of the types of differentiation in Vol. 19, No. 1 of the *British Journal of Special Education*. You should then observe a particular pupil throughout a lesson or shadow them through a whole day of lessons. Make notes and comment on their performance in a range of activities in each of the classes.

From your notes try to identify:

- the extent to which pupils were on or off task;
- how interested they were in each lesson;
- how many contributions they made in the lesson;
- the quality of their written work;
- the extent to which they appeared to understand the purpose of the tasks they were engaged in;
- how they responded when they encountered difficulties with tasks assigned to them;
- to what extent pupils were able to work things out for themselves.

What do your notes tell you about differentiation? Try and meet with the school's SENCO to discuss the SEN policy in the school.

directed activities related to texts (DARTS), tables and charts to help them organise their thoughts, or a writing frame to help them to structure their responses (see Chapter 4). Remember that another aspect of differentiation is the question of the climate for learning which you create in your classroom. Are all pupils supported and encouraged – including the quiet, well-behaved ones? Do they want to do well in history? How many of your pupils with SEN are trying as hard as possible to do well in history?

It is important to remember that there is more to differentiation than whether it is to be achieved by task or outcome. Lewis (1992) notes twelve forms of differentiation, and these do not include the important question of the relationship between teacher and pupils which is also a crucially important determinant of whether pupils will perform to the best of their abilities. Effective teaching of pupils with SEN depends on skilfully developed and accomplished social interaction with pupils, which will generate a positive approach to learning, as much as planning, preparation and resources.

SOME APPROACHES TO TEACHING HISTORY TO PUPILS WITH SEN

The nature of history as a school subject lends itself to a variety of approaches. It has been suggested that pupils with SEN can cope with more demanding history if it is presented at a concrete level, or if it is seen as relevant or even if it exploits their interests. Many history teachers have consequently used story-telling, the media, drawings, discussion, field trips, model-making, role-play, drama, information technology and visual displays in an attempt to make history more concrete for pupils with SEN, although differentiating and varying teaching methods to appeal to SEN pupils in such ways has worried some. Ware and Peacy (1993) have asked: 'How can history be made more accessible without distorting its complexity? Concrete examples, such as those provided by dressing up in period costume or visits to historic sites, are required to give access, but history cannot be reduced to such experiences.' Perhaps one answer to such concerns is to use such strategies as *starting points* which will help to draw pupils into an understanding of the past. Starting with the present day and tracing historical problems back in time is one way of doing this. Bearing in mind that your task is to ensure that each pupil shares in the same statutory entitlement to the History National Curriculum, consider the following practical suggestions for producing materials, especially worksheets, in your history teaching. These suggestions draw on the work of Hull (1980), Clarke and Wrigley (1988) and Wilson (1982b) which you should consult for further ideas.

Presentation

The materials or resources you use should seize the pupil's attention with a high ratio of picture to print. Instructions on worksheets should be clear and simple. You may need to break down instructions to assist understanding. Visual support in the form of pictures and objects can make historical ideas more accessible and even serve as a 'mental peg' for pupils. Worksheets should have good spacing and sections broken with diagrams and illustrations.

Language

It is often the case that pupils with SEN have a lower level of language development than that of their peers. As far as possible, therefore, try to ensure that your exposition and your worksheets use simple and clear terms and instructions. If you introduce new words, then they should be explained. Remember that history can make an important contribution to the acquisition of literacy skills. You will need to test the readability of worksheets and repeat key words frequently. Remember that your supporting explanation of written materials and individual help given to pupils can help to make more difficult written materials accessible.

Content

The content should always demand some 'mental effort' of pupils. Be careful not to ask too much too soon. Choose exciting examples or lively accounts to illustrate historical themes and concepts. Do not use too many concepts in any one lesson, and if you use abstract terms, try to explain them; also, give examples or analogies where possible, and check for understanding (see Chapter 3). You also need to ensure that there is adequate provision of materials to support learning – this can include supplementary materials on the classroom walls, or on the teacher's desk.

Teaching

Use a variety of teaching styles and promote learning by appropriate classroom organisation. Pupils learn in different ways; a variety of teaching techniques provides for pupils with different preferred learning styles. Some pupils like group work and oral work, others like the teacher to explain things to them, or to work on their own. Pupils may require repeated reinforcement of points made and you need to be aware that pupils with SEN can become adept at appearing to understand. You need to ensure that time is spent monitoring the progress of individual pupils on a given task. But there is a tension here; at times, for

TASK 7.6 BUILDING UP A REPERTOIRE OF APPROACHES TO TEACHING PUPILS WITH SEN

Some student teachers tend to see SEN in terms of pupils with specific learning difficulties such as dyslexia, hearing impairment, or a generally low level of cognitive ability. You will realise that SEN has a much broader definition, and includes any factor which is preventing a pupil from performing to their potential in history. During your school experience, if possible, observe a number of lessons of mixed-ability classes and observe which strategies the classroom teacher uses in working with pupils who have the following learning difficulties: poor organisational skills, lack of confidence, poor presentation, poor language skills, isolation from other pupils, poor spelling, poor memory, lack of interest, short concentration span, physical impairments, poor organisational skills, poor general knowledge, reluctance to contribute orally.

Discuss with your tutor the approaches which can be used to help pupils through their learning difficulties. You may find the booklet by the Association of Teachers and Lecturers recommended in the further reading section of this chapter useful.

Read John Hull's article in *Teaching History* entitled 'Practical Points on Teaching History to Less Able Secondary Pupils' (October 1980). You will see that he lists a number of examples of how to exercise historical skills which include:

- analysis;
- vocabulary acquisition;
- synthesis;
- inference;
- comprehension;
- memorisation;
- sequencing.

Choose one of these skills and design a lesson plan and worksheet for year 8 which incorporates one of these skills as its aim.

reasons of classroom management, you may need to stand back from the pupils to take stock of the overall working atmosphere in the classroom. Your speech in class must be pitched at the appropriate level for the pupils to understand. Use open questions to permit some response from the pupils which you can build upon. You can help by explanation, breaking tasks down into smaller steps, reading through materials for pupils, providing a first sentence or introductory paragraph, providing examples, encouraging pupils, providing constructive feedback and making pupils aware of what is required to do the task well.

The use of differentiation in planning and preparing lessons will be integral to your approach, and you will need to structure the use of resources to achieve historical goals. In all of these endeavours you need to promote a sense of achievement on the part of the pupil, and foster a sense of progress. You need to remember that the use of activities such as imaginative writing requires first that the pupils be able to describe and record. In the same way, if you produce worksheets with missing word sentences to be completed by the pupils then you should ensure that they can read the incomplete sentences. The use of project work is popular with history teachers, but it is also a demanding and

---

The following pupil tasks were designed to enable pupils to discuss with each other ideas about cause and explanation They have been given to pupils of widely differing ages and abilities (Lee *et al.* 1996a).

The fact, reason and cause task

Box A
The Romans were able to take over most of Britain because . . .

Box 1
the Roman Army trained a lot and the Roman soldiers were used to fighting

Box 2
the Roman Emperor Claudius decided to invade Britain in AD 43

Box 3
the Romans wanted to make sure that they could get tin and pearls from the Britons

Box 4
Claudius wanted to show that he was a great Emperor

Box 5
the Britons lived in different groups which sometimes fought each other

Box 6
the Emperor Claudius had a limp

Lee, Dickinson and Ashby also use box structures which allow pupils to explore and discuss the relationship between causes (Lee *et al.* 1996b). These tasks not only shed light on pupils' historical understanding, they provide engaging pupil activities which can be used with pupils of very differing abilities.

Figure 7.1 Exploring pupils' ideas about cause and explanation

sophisticated exercise with many elementary skills needed first. It needs to be carefully structured if you are to avoid the potential danger of achieving differentiation by 'removing the history' and allowing some pupils to do work which is primarily copying and drawing. Lovey (1995) provides some excellent teaching strategies for reading and writing difficulties experienced by pupils. She also has much to suggest about improving spelling, memory and organisational skills. Judy Sebba's (1996) book is worth consulting, since it details a number of teaching strategies to increase access to history through drama, information technology and group work. The work of Lee, Dickinson and Ashby has provided examples of pupil tasks which are accessible to pupils of differing ages and abilities, and which invite pupils to think about quite complex aspects of historical understanding (see Figure 7.1).

MEETING THE NEEDS OF ABLE PUPILS IN THE HISTORY CLASSROOM

The terms to describe pupils who are exceptionally 'gifted' are usually either 'able' or 'talented'. Whilst there is no one definition of what constitutes either of these terms, they can be recognised in pupils who possess outstanding general intellectual ability. If the school provides scope and opportunities for pupils to exercise their talents, then we can often readily recognise artistic, dramatic, musical and physical talent in pupils, but academic ability needs careful and continuous assessment. Some teachers do not accept the term 'gifted', nor do they agree that the ablest pupil may sometimes have different needs. However, as with less able pupils, more able pupils need to be identified, and their needs of realising their full potential in history met. Like the less able pupil, the more able pupil also needs a variety of levels of challenge and approach. There is research evidence to suggest that the needs of able pupils have not always been met (Mason and Essen, 1987), and the competences outlined in *Circular 10/97* are quite explicit in requiring student teachers to be able to 'identify pupils who are very able and set appropriate and demanding expectations for all pupils' learning' (DfEE, 1997).

This is not always easy for student teachers, preoccupied as they understandably are with a host of other concerns, including factors such as whether they are in full control of the classroom, which can seem a more pressing priority. The problem is also complicated by the fact that able pupils sometimes pretend to be average in order to be accepted; they are not necessarily crying out to be extended. In spite of these difficulties, it is essential that you direct some of your attention to the needs of the able pupil in the history classroom, both in terms of their identification and in the provision of teaching strategies which will enable them to fulfil their potential in history.

Marjoram (1988) provides a list of indicators for history teachers to enable them to recognise the 'gifted' history pupil. These include the pupil's ability to memorise quickly, the ability to follow complex directives easily and show great intellectual curiosity. Able pupils are normally rapid readers, they have a broad attention span, have keen powers of observation and imagination, and have reading interests which cover a wide range of subjects. Marjoram (1988) says able pupils will 'possess superior powers of reasoning, of dealing with abstractions, generalising from specific facts, understanding meanings and seeing into relationships'. More comprehensive taxonomies can be found in Laycock, (1957), who lists twenty characteristics of able pupils, and Belle Wallace (1985), who lists thirty such characteristics. The level description for 'exceptional performance' in the attainment target of the National Curriculum for history (DfE, 1995) also helps us to identify pupils who are particularly able in the subject, by characterising their performance in various aspects of history. The following characteristics of able pupils may be listed as follows:

- the ability to use a greater amount of detail; accessibility to greater complexity of language, wider vocabulary and use of lengthier reading;
- the ability to move from the concrete to the abstract, the specific to the general, to develop higher-order skills and to make use of material not immediately in front of them;
- the ability to see the relevance of a topic, and the issues that emerge, to today's world.

TASK 7.7 IDENTIFYING ABLE PUPILS IN THE HISTORY CLASSROOM

With the permission of your mentor, when you have become reasonably familiar with one of your teaching groups, make a conscious attempt to identify any pupils who you feel may be particularly able in history, by examining their work and talking to them. What is it about their work and their oral responses which indicates exceptional ability? Consider the following characteristics, and see if your observations reveal any others:

- powers of concentration;
- critical judgement and evaluation of evidence;
- ability to argue logically;
- attention to detail;
- easy concept formation;
- originality and imagination;
- fluency and sophistication of extended writing.

There are a number of strategies which can be employed to assist the history teacher with more able pupils. Open-ended and research-based questions can give them the scope for work which is characteristic of the demands of the A level personal study, and allows them to read and analyse sources which would not be appropriate for general classroom use, and to use their powers of conjecture and hypothesis in reponse to particular historical questions (see Figure 7.2) Many history teachers keep an 'archive' of newspaper and journal articles on historical topics which can be given as extension work or homework. Able pupils can also be asked to classify and categorise information for themselves where this stage of the exercise has been organised by the teacher with other pupils. In the same way that publishers have attempted to provide

---

Some questions permit all pupils to offer suggestions, but ones which will operate at very differing intellectual levels of response. Some of these questions may be appropriate for the whole class, others might be better suited to extension activities for the able.

- In 1851, Britain was arguably the greatest power in the world. Many people feel that this is no longer the case. How do we measure the 'greatness' of nations, and why do you think that Britain is less 'great' than she was in 1851? [For those who feel that the subject of British decline is not an appropriate topic for school history, the question might allow for a discussion of whether Great Britain has declined or not.] One interesting statistic is that in 1904, Britain won over fifty gold medals in the Olympic Games; in 1996 she won only one. What reasons might pupils suggest for this change?
- How was it that William the Conqueror's army of no more than 20,000 men managed to conquer a country with a population of over 1 million?
- In what ways and to what extent was life in England different in 1485 from life in 1065?
- William the Conqueror, Richard II and Henry VIII all had to put down revolts against their governments. Which of them faced greater difficulties in crushing the revolts and why? Would it be easier or harder to put down revolts today? Give reasons for your answer.
- Why did William the Conqueror succeed where Philip II (1588), Napoleon (1805) and Hitler (1940) failed?
- Why did people stop building castles?
- Was King John a good or a bad king? What are the criteria for good government today? What does the ordinary person want from the government? How much do the answers to the above questions apply to the medieval period?
- What happened to poor/old people in (a) Elizabethan Times, (b) in the years before and after 1834, (c) in the period 1908–14, (d) after 1945. What was the attitude/policy of the government with regard to poor/old people at these times?

Figure 7.2 Questions for able pupils

materials for less able pupils, the 'Fast track' series (Aylett, 1993) attempts to provide extension tasks for able pupils.

Differentiation is again the key to successful teaching with this group of pupils. Above all, you need to encourage able pupils and provide opportunities for them to proceed at their own rate. Whilst pressures in school may make it difficult for you to give as much attention to able pupils as to the other special category pupils in the early stages of your ITE course, you must address this agenda when you have become confident and comfortable in the classroom, and identify and attempt various extension strategies. If their needs are not met, there is the same danger that able pupils will lose motivation for the subject as with less able pupils. This situation would obviously be a dereliction of the basic responsibility of teachers to do their best for all the pupils in their care.

SUMMARY AND KEY POINTS

Consideration has been given to appropriate preparation of differentiated learning materials and various teaching strategies and methods to enhance learning for pupils with SEN. The route to successful support is therefore through good differentiation. Emphasis has been placed on your duty to plan thoroughly and imaginatively to provide modified materials to meet the needs of pupils with SEN. Support is available in schools through liaison with other history teachers and the school's SENCO. Ultimately, the onus is on you to make the curriculum accessible to all the pupils you teach. As a committed teacher you need, above all, to guard against adopting the defeatist attitude that history is too difficult for a certain type of SEN pupil. You must also try to teach history in such a way that all pupils, including those with SEN, *want* to learn history.

FURTHER READING

Association for Teachers and Lecturers (1994) *Practical Information and Ideas on Teaching Pupils with Special Educational Needs in Mainstream Schools and Colleges*, London, ATL.
   This short booklet is an excellent and concise guide to SEN of all types.

Byers, R. and Rose, R. (1996) *Planning the Curriculum for Pupils with SEN: A Practical Guide*, London, David Fulton.
   A very detailed and easy to use guide to practical approaches in SEN.

Montgomery, D. (1994) *Educating the Able*, London, Cassell.
   Not history-specific, but useful.

Sebba, J. (1994) *History for All*, London, David Fulton.
This is a good introduction to various SEN teaching strategies in history teaching.

Wilson, M.D. (1990) 'History: Issues to Resolve', *British Journal of Special Education*, Vol. 17, No. 2, pp. 69–72.

8 The use of new technology in the history classroom

INTRODUCTION

Twenty years ago, history teachers who regularly incorporated the use of computers into their classroom teaching were regarded as eccentrics, and by no means all history teachers accepted that early computer applications for history were 'real history', or had much to offer beyond entertainment value. Even now, and in spite of the development of much more sophisticated and varied information technology (IT) applications for history, not all history teachers regularly incorporate the use of computers into their classroom teaching (DfE, 1995a).

It would be difficult to overstate the importance which has recently been attached to this aspect of classroom teaching. Politicians of all parties have tended to think of computers as a sort of educational miracle, which will help Britain to bridge the perceived educational gap between Britain and Pacific Rim countries. Whatever the innate and potential benefits of new technology for teaching and learning in history, there is now significant pressure on history teachers to use IT in the classroom. Some have gone as far as to suggest that teachers who cannot adapt to the advent of IT will, like dinosaurs, disappear, or survive only as limping and outmoded pedagogically crippled relics of the pre-information technology age. In the words of Peter Cochrane, 'There will be two types of teachers, the IT literate and the retired' (*TES*, 23 June 1995). To what extent is this true, and how should student teachers of history respond to such claims?

The National Curriculum for History states that 'Pupils should be given opportunities where appropriate, to develop and apply their IT capability in their study of history' (DfE, 1995b). In the light of advances in history IT applications over the past ten years it has become increasingly difficult to claim that there are no appropriate opportunities. History teachers are thus statutorily required to investigate possible uses of IT within their subject (Jones, 1995). The Dearing Report stated that for the age of 7 upwards, all subjects should contribute to the development of capability in IT (Dearing, 1994). Competence in IT is also one of the competences stipulated by DfEE *Circular 10/97* (DfEE, 1997). IT proficiency is a common topic in questions at interview, and in some cases the department expressed the hope that the NQT appointed would be able to take the lead in developing the use of IT in history. It is difficult to dispute the proposition that pupils leaving school in the twenty-first century will need to be equipped to make use of new technology, and that school history should take account of this and think carefully about how technology can be used to improve the quality of teaching and learning in history. All these pressures have made it increasingly difficult for history teachers to shy away from the question of how IT might best be used to improve the quality of teaching and learning, or to reject IT applications as 'unhistorical'.

Another important point to note is the distinction which can be drawn between new technology in general, and information technology. For the purposes of this chapter, information technology is taken to mean the use of computers. There are other (comparatively) new technologies which have had a significant impact on the history classroom, such as the use of the video-recorder and video-camera. Although personal proficiency in the operation of television, video-recorder and video-camera is not as problematic as the development of wide ranging proficiency in the use of computers, it is still very important that you give consideration to fully exploiting the potential of non-computer based applications for enhancing the quality of teaching and learning in history.

There are thus two distinct (but complementary) agendas with relation to history and IT. In the words of Eraut, 'Goals which were expressed in statements like "through IT you can teach xxxxx better" are being replaced by those which try to answer questions like, "Where are you developing IT competence?"' (quoted in McDonald, 1993).

Whilst remaining aware of this double agenda, a fundamental question which you should be thinking of right through the course is in what ways new technology might be used to enhance the quality of teaching and learning in the history classroom. Advances in new technology offer the opportunity to deliver the history curriculum, and develop pupils' understanding of the past, in a more vivid, varied, active and engaging way than was possible twenty years ago. You will need to consider in what ways you can make this proposition a reality in your classroom teaching, and in addition consider how the study of history can contribute to the development of the 'Key' skill of proficiency in the use of IT.

For all these reasons, IT is no longer an optional extra for history teachers – you *must* develop a solid foundation of competence in the use of IT in the classroom. You *should* try to make as much progress as you can towards proficiency in as broad a range of uses of new technology as possible. The 10/97 standards stipulate that you must be able to exploit opportunities to improve pupils' basic skills in IT, and make good use of IT to enable teaching objectives to be met (DfEE, 1997).

OBJECTIVES

By the end of this chapter you should:

- be aware of the importance of IT competence for your professional development;
- be aware of the range and breadth of new technology applications which might be relevant to the history classroom;
- be aware of the various aspects of developing competence in IT, particularly the difference between personal proficiency and classroom experience;
- understand that with many aspects of new technology there is a continuum in terms of the degree of relaxed assurance and effectiveness with which you are able to use new technology to enhance the quality of teaching and learning in the classroom;
- have a better understanding of the potential benefits and possible problems of using IT in the classroom, and of the classroom management factors which influence the effective use of IT;
- have clear ideas about how IT can be used in the history classroom.

A STRATEGIC APPROACH TO THE DEVELOPMENT OF COMPETENCE IN IT

As the Trotter Report points out, initial training courses attempt to lay solid foundations to build on, they do not produce experts (Trotter Report, 1989). It is important to be realistic about what can be achieved in initial teacher education, where you have many other areas of competence to develop. It is also important to stress that objectives should not be limited to the development of *personal* proficiency in IT. Research has shown that there is little correlation between personal expertise in IT and subsequent classroom use (HMI, 1988; Downes, 1993). Objectives might helpfully be divided into four discrete areas. You have to consider all four areas if you are to be in a position to use IT effectively in your NQT year.

1 You should try to develop a reasonable 'base' of personal proficiency in the use of IT. It may not be possible to develop assured mastery of a comprehensive range of applications, but you should think about what might constitute a foundation which would give you access to a wide range of

eminently usable and realistic opportunities for using IT in the history classroom in your NQT year.

2   You should be aware of the breadth of IT applications and ideas which can be used in the history classroom, even if you do not have time to explore fully the potential of all applications. In part, this can be achieved by systematically going through the major software catalogues for history, but it is also important to keep abreast of new developments and ideas by reading the regular sections on IT in *Teaching History*, the *TES*, and other relevant journals. The National Council for Educational Technology (NCET) and the Schools Curriculum and Assessment Authority (SCAA) are also important sources of information. Details of some of these publications are given at the end of the chapter.

3   You must bear in mind that in all facets of competence in IT there is a continuum between ignorance and inadequacy on the one hand, and expert levels of proficiency and knowledge on the other. Ideas for progression in competence in some of the domains of IT are suggested later in the chapter. The important thing is not to see competence as a line at which your development stops once you have achieved basic levels. A clear grasp of levels of expertise to aspire to, and a commitment to getting there are important attributes, even if you do not attain expert levels in the course of your training. In the words of Campbell and Davies, 'It is expected that students should demonstrate development within an ipsative framework which allows for all to go beyond what might be described as threshold performance, rather than aim for the achievement of one standard level of competence' (Campbell and Davies, 1997).

4   Perhaps the most important – and challenging element – is to develop a depth of classroom experience in the use of IT. No matter how sophisticated your personal levels of expertise in IT, it is only when you can successfully incorporate that expertise into your classroom teaching that IT can enhance the learning experiences of pupils. In the words of Bridget Somekh, 'It is only by trying out their new knowledge and skills in a classroom that student teachers can be adequately prepared for using IT in their first teaching post (Somekh, 1992). This is in some ways the most problematic of the four areas There are few history rooms which have three modern computers in the class, vast ranges of subject-specific software, an IT coordinator in the room to give you a hand, a perfectly docile set of pupils who will sit patiently and quietly if there are any logistical difficulties, and a history department whose members all have an encyclopaedic knowledge of history software. For these reasons you will need to adopt a flexible and proactive approach, and use your own initiative to make progress in the use of IT in the history classroom.

All history teachers are somewhere on the continuum shown in Figure 8.1. Very few of them are at either extreme of the continuum. Your overarching objective in this area of competence should be to be as far as possible towards the right hand end of the continuum as possible by the start of your NQT year.

```
┌─────────────────────────┐      ┌─────────────────────────────┐
│ Teacher is unaware of, or│      │ Teacher is able to fully exploit│
│ unable to use IT to improve│ ──▶ │ the potential of IT for improving│
│ the quality of teaching and│    │ the quality of teaching and │
│ learning in history        │    │ learning in history.        │
└─────────────────────────┘      └─────────────────────────────┘
```

Figure 8.1 Developing competence in IT: a continuum

ATTITUDES AND RESPONSES TO IT

A recent survey of PGCE students revealed that most students are keen to develop their competence in IT, both in terms of personal skills in IT and in terms of the use of IT in the classroom (Haydn and Macaskill, 1996). For a variety of reasons, not all student teachers get as far as they would wish towards mastery of the various facets of IT capability. Before looking at practical ways forward in IT, it would be helpful to consider some of the factors which have been found to influence the use of IT in the classroom. In spite of the exhortations of politicians, a majority of history teachers do not routinely use computers in their classrooms (DfE, 1995a; Haydn, 1996; HMI, 1988; NCET, 1994; OFSTED, 1994). If computers are such a wonderful aid to teaching and learning, why isn't everyone using them? An understanding of the factors which influence the use of computers in the classroom may be helpful to student teachers who are keen to develop proficiency in the use of computers but who have an understandable reticence about their first tentative steps towards this. Several research findings indicate that there is little correlation between technical levels of expertise in IT and extent of classroom use (Byard, 1995; Downes, 1993; Easdown, 1994; HMI, 1988). Barton (1997) found that the most significant influences on student teacher use of IT were seeing their supervising tutors using IT, and encouragement and support from school and university staff. Your attitude to progression in teaching competence is more important than your level of technical expertise in IT. You do not require sophisticated levels of technical IT knowledge to use computers in the classroom. Nor is there necessarily any correlation between the level of sophistication in IT and the potential for developing historical understanding in pupils. Very simple and basic exercises, in terms of the level of IT competence involved, can open up the possibility of quite complex and ambitious learning outcomes (Martin, 1996).

Research on the learning gains made possible by the use of IT in school history is neither definitive nor abundant. It has been suggested that the pace of technological change has exceeded teachers' ability fully to assimilate advances into their pedagogy, but there is a substantial amount of research evidence to suggest that the use of IT increases pupil motivation, can improve attitudes to school and pupil behaviour, and can be used to improve presentation and pride in work (Askar *et al.*, 1992; Barber, 1995; Underwood and Underwood, 1990). These are not inconsequential considerations for you as a student teacher. The evidence of gains in historical understanding through the use of IT is more equivocal, but it is interesting to note that even those condemning progressive practices in education have been careful to exempt the use of computers from their lexicon of denigration.

In the long term, what matters is not how much you use computers in the classroom but whether they are used in a way which enhances the quality of learning in your lessons. It is likely that you will only use computers as an integral part of your teaching if you are convinced that this is feasible *and* if you have got to the stage where you feel relaxed and comfortable about using computers in the classroom. In order to get to this desirable state of affairs, you need to go through the awkward and uncertain phase of acclimatising yourself to the use of computers in the classroom. Graeme Easdown notes the negative preconceptions of some PGCE students in the early stages of the course, including one student who remarked that 'Computers are becoming increasingly important in education, and I'm afraid it's going to get worse' (Easdown, 1996). The process of developing classroom ease in the use of IT is in some ways akin to learning to ride a bike or learning to change gear in a car – effortless and enjoyable once proficiency has been acquired, but nerve-racking and requiring a degree of will and determination to persevere in the first stages. What is important here is that a climate of learning is created in which you are not afraid to experiment, to take chances, and even to 'fail' in some lessons, as long as this is not done with cavalier disregard of the needs of the pupils in your care. (Although reckless overdosing on IT by student teachers is a comparatively rare phenomenon.) Short-term agendas of 'That was a reasonable lesson', need to be balanced against the longer-term consideration of developing a complete range of pedagogical skills and methods, so that you do not arrive at your NQT post having employed cautious and 'survival-orientated' teaching techniques before going on to inflict a staple diet of worksheets and wordsearches for the rest of your teaching career. Because of this it is better to attempt the incorporation of computers into lessons, and risk the possibility of everything not working out perfectly on the first occasion, than not to use computers at all. Given the variables in facilities, expertise, and attitudes to IT in different schools, departments and by university tutors, your progression towards mastery of technology in the classroom will depend to some extent at least on your use of initiative and the time you make for developing IT skills over the course of the year.

TASK 8.1 INVESTIGATING ATTITUDES TO IT

Consider the following propositions and questions with other student teachers and, if possible, with the colleagues you work with in schools.

- The use of new technology in history teaching can have negative as well as positive effects on the quality of teaching and learning.
- Why do history teachers tend to use the television and video–recorder more frequently than computers? What are the comparative advantages and disadvantages of the two types of technology?
- The limited use of computers in history teaching derives from uncertainty and lack of information, training and opportunity rather than a considered rejection of IT on pedagogical or philosophical grounds.
- The use of new technology is often peripheral to the development of pupils' historical understanding.
- IT can be used to develop children's historical understanding. (If this is true, what examples can be found?)
- History teachers' consideration of classroom IT is due more to pressure from OFSTED and other outside agencies, rather than a conviction of its merits for teaching and learning.
- An inability or refusal to use IT in the classroom limits the effectiveness of the history teacher, and the breadth and quality of learning that can occur.

DEVELOPMENT OF PRACTICAL COMPETENCE IN THE USE OF IT

TASK 8.2 WHAT IS YOUR IT QUOTIENT?

If you are to arrive at your NQT post as a technologically enabled history teacher, you will have to get to grips with a wide range of new technology applications. Part (but only part) of this agenda is your own range and depth of expertise in being able to use new technology. The following exercise was designed to get student teachers to think about what there is to think about in terms of the ontology of new technology – exactly what do you have to think about in terms of becoming technologically competent.

1 Work through the questions and try to give an honest answer as to your current state of technological competence according to these criteria. The idea is that when you add up the scores you will get some idea about whether your present IT quotient is above or below a notional and arbitrary average of 100, as in IQ tests. The test has *not* been trialled on thousands of NQTs to establish that a score of 100 represents what the average NQT can do when they start in their first teaching post; it is designed primarily to get student teachers to consider where they stand in terms of general technological proficiency, and to give some idea about the agenda for development of competence in IT.

2 It is important to bear in mind that the 'bottom line' in terms of new technology is not that you become personally proficient, but that you are able to use new technology to enhance the quality of teaching and learning in your history lessons. Some of the applications mentioned may have less relevance to the history classroom than others. Data logging, for example, is an important aspect of science teaching but of peripheral relevance to the history teacher. Look through the list of applications and consider which offer the most potential for the history teacher, which may be of some use or interest, but less important, and which are tangential or irrelevant to the teaching and learning of history.

1 Video-recorder

I don't know how to use a video–recorder: **0**
I can use a video-recorder to tape and replay TV programmes: **2**
I can use advance timer on VCR to tape a TV programme: **4**
I can use advance timer to tape several TV programmes at a time: **6**
I can do tape-to-tape editing of videoed programmes: **8**
I can use an editing suite to edit and add my own sound track to videoed
  extracts: **10**

2 Video-camera

I don't know how to use a video–camera: **0**
I think I know how to use a video–camera; might need a quick revision
  session: **4**
I am confident in the use of the video-camera: **7**

cont . . .

3 Film strip/slide/carousel projector

I don't know how to use any of them: 0
I'm OK on ones that I'm familiar with, but not all models: 3
I feel confident in using any of this equipment: 5
I even know which way the slides go without having to do it by trial and
  error: 7

4 Overhead projector

I don't know how to use an OHP: 0
I can use one, but I'm not sure about how to do all the adjustments
  (focusing etc.): 3
I am completely confident about all aspects of OHP use: 5
I even know how to change the bulb if one blows: 7

5 Making transparencies for OHP

I don't know how to do this: 0
I can make them using OHP pens, hand-written: 2
I can make them using a computer graphics package and photocopier: 4
I can use computer slide presentation packages (Powerpoint etc.) to do
  them using the computer, OHP and LCD machine: 8

6 Photocopier

I don't know how to use one: 0
I can make simple single or multiple copies: 2
I can also enlarge/reduce: 3
I also know how to do back-to-back copies: 5

7 Computers – range of hardware platforms

I don't know how to use any computer hardware system: 0
I can only confidently use one computer hardware system: 4
I am confident using more than one system: 6
I am confident using PC, Apple, and Acorn/Archimedes systems: 10

8 Computers – level of technical capability

None: 0

Very basic – can just about get round the system but sometimes get stuck: **3**

Quite confident; I know how to do most things (file management, multi-tasking, integrating and transferring bits and pieces from different applications: **7**

All this, plus can usually reconfigure and fix the system without having to send for the mendy-person when something won't work: **10**

9 Concept keyboard

Haven't got a clue: **0**

I can use one if it has been set up for me: **4**

I know how to use several concept keyboard packages: **6**

I can construct my own concept keyboard exercise: **8**

10 Word processing

I can't word process: **0**

I can do basic word processing (moving and adjusting text, saving and printing, etc.): **3**

I am confident and accomplished in word processing and can do most things: **5**

I can do all this on a variety of word-processing packages: **9**

11 Data handling

I don't know what data handling is: **0**

I know what it is but I don't know how to do it: **2**

I know how to use a data-handling package or commercially produced datafile: **5**

I know how to construct my own datafile using a data-handling package: **7**

I feel confident that I could teach/demonstrate how to construct a datafile to a group of students: **9**

I could do all this using a variety of data-handling packages: **12**

12 Spreadsheets

I'm not sure what they are and what you can do with them: **0**

I know what they are but don't know how to use a spreadsheet application: **2**

I know the difference between a database and a spreadsheet: **4**

I know how to use a spreadsheet application: **6**
I know how to use a range of spreadsheet applications: **8**

13 Desktop publishing

I'm not sure what this is: **0**
I know what it is but can't use a DTP application: **1**
I have a basic grasp of a DTP application: **5**
I have a fluent grasp of a DTP application: **7**
I know how to use several DTP packages: **10**

14 CD-ROM

I'm not sure what they are: **0**
I know what CD-ROM means/stands for: **2**
I can use a CD-ROM: **5**
I am confident in the use of a range of history CD-ROMs: **8**

15 Authoring packages
(Hypercard/Toolbook/Illuminatus/Hyperstudio, etc.)

I'm not sure what they do: **0**
I know how to find my way around a presentation which has been made: **4**
I can use one of these packages to construct my own multimedia
    presentation: **7**
I am confident in the use of several of these applications: **10**

16 The Internet

I'm not sure what it is: **0**
I know what it is but have not used it: **2**
I have surfed cyberspace on the World Wide Web: **4**
I have some idea about where I'm going and how to find my way around
    cyberspace: **6**
I can use telnet, ftp, newsgroups and all that stuff: **8**
I know how to put my own stuff up on the web: **10**

17 E-mail

I know what it is: **1**
I know how to send and receive simple e-mail messages: **3**

I know how to send and download attachments: **5**
I know how to do nicknames and pass messages on: **7**

18 Graphic calculator

I know what it is: **1**
I know what it can do: **2**
I can use one: **4**

19 Scanner

I know what it does: **1**
I know how to use one: **3**
I know how to use both flat-bed and hand-held versions: **5**

20 Data-logging

I know what it is/means: **1**
I have used data-logging software: **3**
I have used it in the classroom with real pupils: **5**

(max. proficiency = 160)

Remember that your personal proficiency in IT is only part of the learning agenda. You also need to think about which of these applications will be useful to you as a history teacher, in what ways you can make use of the applications, and what are the classroom management implications of their use. Discuss with your mentor and with other student teachers which IT applications you should prioritise in terms of developing your IT competence for the history classroom.

If you are at the start of your course, you may well have a limited grasp of the ways in which some of these applications can be used in the history classroom. Word processing and data handling, for instance, are areas where a substantial amount of development work in history and IT has been focused (see NCET 1997). A particularly important facet of your development in IT competence is to investigate how these applications can be used in the history classroom.

THE USE AND ABUSE OF NEW TECHNOLOGY: TELEVISION AND VIDEO

'That passed the time.' 'It would have passed in any case.'

Samuel Beckett, *Waiting for Godot*

The development of new technology offers a wide range of opportunities to history teachers and has had a profound effect on the way in which history is taught. It is also important to bear in mind that with nearly all applications there is a continuum between 'I don't even know what it is and what it does', and 'I feel confident that I can fully exploit the potential of this technology in my teaching'. Nearly all student teachers know how to use a photocopier, but not all of them know how to do back-to-back copies, reductions and enlargements, etc. (It is also important to find out departmental norms and conventions on photocopying and be aware of its costs to the department.) Similarly, nearly all student teachers will use the television and video-recorder in the course of their teaching, but not everyone will start their NQT year with an accomplished and relaxed assurance in the use of the video-camera in the classroom. A more developed version of this continuum is given in Figure 8.2.

IT can also be interpreted in a broader sense than merely applying to the use of computers. It is important to note that with most areas of new technology, continuums of competence exist. You may be able to use an overhead projector, but could you change the bulb if necessary? You might be able to use e-mail, but do you know how to send attachments?

In addition to developing in terms of depth of technical proficiency in the use of television and video, you will also become aware of the *breadth and range* of ways of incorporating video extracts into your lessons. There are more imaginative ways of using video as a resource than simply sticking on a schools broadcast and playing through the whole series, over consecutive lessons. There is also the question of whether and when to use the pause button, to ask questions, and when it might be appropriate to give the pupils things to do that will reduce the 'passive' nature of watching the television. Figure 8.3 gives a summary of some of the reasons for the use of video and television in the history classroom.

For student teachers in the first stages of their practical teaching, the television can seem like a godsend, particularly with difficult classes. For under-standable reasons, for some, the perfect 40-minute lesson with 9Z on a Friday afternoon would be to show an episode of *Blackadder*, set a worksheet or home-work on it, and wait for the bell to go. Although part of the agenda of learning to teach is about becoming relaxed and comfortable in the classroom, learning to talk to pupils in an appropriate manner, and learning about 'survival' and coping strategies, even in the early stages of practical teaching thought needs to

Acquisition: is dimly aware that video can be used in history lessons.

Novice: is able to operate the machine and play department video resources as part of a lesson.

Advanced beginner: is able to use department video resources selectively and discerningly, intelligently selecting appropriate excerpts, and incorporating them adroitly into the lesson as a whole to enhance the quality of teaching and learning.

Competence: contributes to department resources by using initiative and forethought to tape suitable material; is able to plan the lesson to make maximum use of extracts; always watches and selects before use in class and uses to a clear purpose; doesn't use as an 'anaesthetic' or to pass the time.

Proficient: builds up coherent collections on topics/themes and is able to edit materials to maximise their efficiency, enhancing department resources; can use video-camera in the classroom as part of lesson activity to enhance quality of teaching and learning. Handles classroom management implications of such exercises skilfully and without chaos and disruption.

Expert: makes maximum use of material available to build up collections of skilfully edited and effective extracts, and deploys them to maximum effect in the classroom. Accomplished and appropriate in use of video-camera and able to use an editing suite to make polished final versions of material.

Figure 8.2 Progression in competence in use of television, video and video–recorder

1 To engage the pupils' attention.
2 To cover broad stretches of content quickly.
3 To provide an 'enabling' task, example or analogy.
4 To make a point more vividly or forcefully.
5 To 'break the lesson up'.
6 To provide directed questions for pupils to note and then discuss.
7 To engage pupils' emotions.
8 To get pupils to guess what followed on from the extract shown.
9 To get pupils to supply their own 'script' for an extract.
10 To illustrate a concept.
11 To compare two different versions of events.
12 To help make history interesting and accessible.
13 To enable pupils to watch a video role-play they have made.
14 To pass the time with a difficult class.
15 To get out of actually having to teach the pupils yourself.

Figure 8.3 Ways of using the television and video–recorder in history

be given to the question of using resources so that they maximise effective learning for pupils. Television can be used as an 'anaesthetic', or to pass the time, but this is clearly bad practice. You need to think about how you will use the video extract to promote effective learning by pupils. There may be some excerpts and programmes which 'stand on their own', and do not require follow-up and interpretation. One example of this is the practice of showing the *World at War* programme on the Holocaust, from start to finish, with no introductory or follow-up remarks from the teacher. Some history teachers feel that this is the most powerful and effective way of getting pupils to think about the Holocaust. Usually however, the extent to which the video excerpt promotes historical understanding in pupils will depend on what is said and done afterwards – on the quality of the follow-up work by you, the teacher, whether this is in the form of teacher exposition and questioning or pupil activities. It is important to remember that in spite of the claims made for the use of new technology in the classroom, whether involving the use of computers or other forms of new technology, there is no *automatic* learning dividend in using IT; the use of new technology can have negative as well as positive effects on learning; it depends how adroitly and thoughtfully it is used. In the words of Stuart Watkinson, 'A computer is like any other piece of equipment. The inspiration comes from you, the teacher, it is not in the machine' (Watkinson, 1990).

TASK 8.3 USE OF VIDEO EXTRACTS

One commonly used extract is the 'What have the Romans ever done for us?' extract from the film *The Life of Brian*. Although the pupils may well find the extract amusing, and it will hopefully have served the purpose of engaging their attention in the past, what might the history teacher do to derive the maximum benefit from the extract after showing it?

Select a video extract which you might use as part of a lesson, and explain what you and/or the pupils would do after you have shown the extract, and what you hope the learning outcomes will be. Discuss the use of video resources with your mentor.

WHAT IS THERE TO CONSIDER IN TERMS OF NEW TECHNOLOGY AND THE HISTORY CLASSROOM?

In addition to noting that there is more to new technology in the classroom than the use of computers, you will need to develop a clear understanding of what sort of things you can do with computers, and which applications lend themselves to the development of pupil learning in history. Remembering the 'double agenda' for IT – how it can be used to promote learning in history, and how history lessons can support the development of IT capability – the guidance from the National Council for Educational Technology reminds teachers that there will be times when the development of subject capability is the main learning objective, with consolidation of IT proficiency as a subsidiary aim, and times when subject capability is a secondary learning objective.

The National Curriculum non-statutory guidance for IT identified five separate 'strands' of IT:

• communicating information;
• handling information;
• modelling;
• measurement and control;
• application and effects (awareness of implications and uses of IT outside school).

As all secondary teachers have a responsibility for the development of pupils' proficiency in IT, it is important be familiar with the National Curriculum requirements for IT (SCAA, 1995). As you become familiar with the range of IT applications which are available you will realise that some of them have more potential than others for use in the history classroom. Data logging, for example, is frequently used in science classrooms but has no obvious utility for history.

What sort of IT applications lend themselves to use in the history classroom?

Any attempt to provide a comprehensive list is doomed to instant obsolescence, given the pace of recent innovation in IT, but Figure 8.4 gives a list of some of the most commonly used applications.

Formulating an agenda for the development of IT competence

The development of personal and classroom proficiency in IT has time management implications. You cannot have it instantly transferred, or injected into you; there is no substitute for spending time becoming familiar with applications and software. As you have to balance developing competence in IT with other demands, you will probably have to prioritise your agenda for IT. You cannot reach expert levels in all the above areas. Are there any guidelines or principles on which to construct an agenda for development in IT?

As you are at different stages in terms of personal expertise in IT, and work in a variety of school contexts, it is not sensible to lay down a template or formula for developing competence in IT. Much depends on what your school

Application	Brief description
Word processing exercises	Text can be moved around to do sequencing exercises which develop pupils' grasp of chronology, or highlighted to detect bias, fact or opinion, etc. Essays can be revised and improved, documents edited to change the 'slant', tables constructed to categorise information.
Data-handling exercises	Pupils look at datafiles (a set of records with information categorised into several different fields) in order to find patterns and test hypotheses. Commercially produced datafiles can be purchased, or you can compile your own, or the pupils can construct them from information which you give them.
Desktop publishing	Pupils produce newspaper front pages, perhaps with different interpretations of the same historical event, or versions produced for propaganda purposes.
CD-ROMs	Pupils conduct an enquiry or investigation into questions they have been asked, from sources on a CD-ROM. Information can often be downloaded (printed out) to present the results of the enquiry.
Time-line packages	Pupils construct or interrogate time-lines, compare developments in different fields, answer questions on chronology.
Concept keyboard	When pupils touch different points on a concept keyboard overlay the computer gives them information about the picture/map/detail, or asks them questions about the detail they have touched.
Simulations	Pupils role-play a historical situation and make decisions as to what steps they would take in an unfolding historical event. These can be 'counterfactual' – if Harold makes the right moves he wins the Battle of Hastings – or the end result constrained to what happened in the past.

Databases	Banks of information, sources, maps, statistics, about a particular historical topic, which can be accessed in different ways, interrogated, or added to.
Multimedia authoring packages	Pupils create a presentation using text, pictures, sound, etc. to report back on a historical investigation.
Newsroom simulation	The pupils respond to periodic computer briefings about an unfolding historical crisis.
The Internet	Teacher uses the World Wide Web to find interesting documents and resources; pupils conduct searches for information on a particular historical topic; pupils contact and correspond with pupils from other schools on historical projects.

Figure 8.4 The use of IT in the history classroom

experience provides in the way of software, which strands of IT are most commonly used in the schools you work in, which aspects of IT have attracted your interest, etc. Personal competence in IT probably constitutes a necessary but not sufficient element of the demands of standards 10/97. If you start your training with no knowledge or experience of using computers, it is important that you acquire a basic grounding in the general use of a computer. Beyond that, in one sense it doesn't really matter which applications you develop personal and classroom competence in, as long as you are in a position to make use of a reasonable range of applications when you start your NQT year.

There are, however, some applications which might be given priority because nearly all schools possess the necessary software. 'Generic' applications (which are not subject-specific) such as word processing and data handling are particularly helpful in that they can be used in a wide variety of contexts. You can devise your own, cost-free activities, and there are an increasing number of examples of activities and help booklets which have been circulated by NCET and SCAA in order to promote the use of IT in history. A minimum agenda of competence in word processing, desktop publishing, data handling, the use of CD-ROM, simulation/role-play applications and the Internet would give you access to a wide range of potential activities in the history classroom. If this seems a rather limited and conservative agenda, it should be borne in mind that not all history NQTs have developed a relaxed and assured fluency in these areas when they start their NQT year. Classroom applications in IT vary to some extent across curriculum subjects. Newsroom simulation packages, simulations and role-play software are more suited to history than some other subjects; data-logging exercises are mainly confined to science and technology, but it is reasonable to suggest that there is a central core of IT applications which are particularly useful, and which offer a wide variety of potential uses. Although it might be arbitrary and unnecessarily exclusive of some valuable developments in IT, the identification of some 'essential' core of IT applications would have the advantage of setting out a common agenda which could be targeted and monitored throughout the year. Accepting that hypertext packages, concept keyboard, simulations and modelling, and quiz/revision/information packages can be just as valuable as IT applications, an essential core might be Word Processing, Desktop Publishing, Data Handling, CD-ROM, the Internet, and the use of simulations/history computer role-plays. You should try to reach at least basic levels of proficiency in these areas if you are to have a sound and broad base for using IT in your NQT year.

If you are starting your course with absolutely no knowledge of IT, the following might be stages of competence to consider over the course of the year – phases which you might move through if you were determined to become accomplished in IT by the end of the year.

The idea of progression in competence from novice to expert levels which follows is based on the model of progression in competence currently being developed and trialled by the Science Department at the Institute of Education, University of London.

GENERAL

1   Mastering basic operations on a computer – how to turn it on, access applications on the hard disk, load floppy disks, close down programs, etc.
2   To be able to use the computer network at the school you are working in.
3   To be able to negotiate your way around at least one sort of computer (IBM, Nimbus, Apple Mac, Acorn/Archimedes). This doesn't mean that you have to know how to use every application on the network, but that at least you can find your way round and get in and out of various applications. This means learning things like double-clicking the mouse to open programs, and using the mouse to 'drag' things around the screen.

WORD PROCESSING

1   To be able to write something on the computer, save it on either the hard disk of a computer or a floppy disk, and print it.
2   To acquire basic proficiency in word processing and type up your assignments

using a computer. To be able to word process some of your lesson materials on teaching practice.

3   To explore the various ways in which word processing and text manipulation can be used in task design in history lessons – highlighting text, moving text round, changing bias, writing propaganda, improving essay work, etc. so that you are able to use computers as a small part of some lessons, even if it is just letting some pupils write up some of their work using the computer.

4   To be able to work your way through a desktop publishing package and incorporate a part-manufactured front page as part of your teaching; for instance, to develop understanding that there are different interpretations of the same historical event.

5   To be able to incorporate a word processing exercise in history into one of your lessons. To manage lessons where some pupils work on the computer, doing word processing tasks, text manipulation, creating newspaper front pages, while others get on with non-computer based tasks. To reach a stage where some of the display work which your classes generate is computer produced.

6   To be able to devise your own ideas and materials for word processing exercises which help to develop historical understanding and improve essay technique. To reach the stage where you have built up a repertoire of desk-top publishing ideas which you can slot into your lessons, and you become relaxed and assured about using IT as part of the lesson.

DATA HANDLING

1   To find out about databases and spreadsheets, even if it is just at the vague level of knowing what they are and what sort of things you can do with them in history lessons.

2   To look at the data handling applications which are available in the school you are working in, and, if possible, observe someone at school or at the university using a data-handling package in order to get a basic idea of how to use it.

3   To be in a position to use printouts and information from data-handling programs or databases as part of a lesson.

4   To be able to use a database or data-handling package which you are familiar with as part of a lesson.

5   To develop and use in class, a data-handling exercise which you have devised and put on disk yourself.

6   To be sufficiently assured and confident in the use of data-handling packages that you can use your lessons to teach the pupils how to compile a history datafile and interrogate it.

CD-ROM

1   To know what CD-ROMs are and how to access them on a computer.
2   To become familiar with and able to 'find your way around' a history CD-ROM.
3   To be able to use a history CD-ROM as part of a lesson.
4   To develop your own lesson materials to support the use of CD-ROM in one of your lessons and work out a pupil activity to go with them.
5   To become familiar with a range of history CD-ROMs, and have used them on several occasions. To have taught pupils how to use them purposefully and devised activities which have led to a successful and well-managed lesson using CD-ROM.

THE INTERNET

1   To be able to access the World Wide Web and look round cyberspace.
2   To be able to find usable resources for your lessons.
3   To know how to use e-mail.
4   To be able to use the Internet as part of a teaching session.

SIMULATIONS/ROLE-PLAY

1   To be aware of the existence of these, and have a sound grasp of what they do/their potential/how they are used in the classroom.
2   To have seen one used in class and assisted with small groups; to have gone through one on your own in staff room/IT lab.
3   To have used one in class as part of a lesson.
4   To have used more than one example in class or to have used one example on several occasions and felt confident, relaxed and assured about doing so.
5   To be able to incorporate simulation/role-play software into your lessons in an assured and relaxed manner and in a way which enhances the quality of teaching and learning in some ways (increases pupil motivation, effectively develops pupils' historical understanding, etc.). To be aware of the advantages and limitations of the package/exercise, to be able to develop classroom materials to complement and make the most of the software. To be able to distinguish between good and poor examples of software.

It is important to think of these frameworks as levels to aspire to rather than summits which all have to be reached by the end of your course. There will be few teachers, even including those who have taught for many years and have an interest in IT, who have attained mastery of all aspects of IT. Not everyone will reach the top levels in all of these applications, but you should try to get as far along the continuum as possible.

CLASSROOM MANAGEMENT CONSIDERATIONS

Developing classroom confidence in the use of IT

However accomplished you are in terms of personal IT capability, it is not as useful as also having developed your classroom experience, using IT with real, live pupils. This can only be done in school. One of the most important aspects of competence is being relaxed and confident about using it in your teaching. There are some general considerations which make this easier.

1 When they first use IT in the classroom, most student teachers (and most teachers) do so with a degree of trepidation about how it will go, whether everything will work, whether the pupils will do everything they are supposed to, whether you will get through everything in the time available etc. One way to minimise these concerns is to use computers in such a way that they are merely an incidental part of the lesson – rather than the delivery and success of the lesson being entirely dependent on IT. It is generally more stressful if you have booked the IT suite for an 'all singing, all dancing' computer extravaganza, rather than simply letting them have a quick look at the timeline on *Encarta*, or getting them to print off a couple of documents to work on back at their desks.

2 Try to find out about, and use, quick, simple and reliable programs/ exercises. Some applications are useful, not primarily because they are brilliant at developing children's historical skills and understanding but because they are easy to use and therefore build up your confidence and faith in the use of IT. You can get onto the ambitious stuff when you've (hopefully) got a few successful IT lessons 'under your belt'.

3 It's not cheating to ask for help and support, even if it's just asking where an IT literate person will be that lesson in case you need a hand with some technical hiccup. Find out if there are any members of staff or fellow student teachers with an interest in IT. If there is no one in the department who is seriously into IT, see if the IT coordinator is able to help in any way, and talk about your IT interests with the school tutor, who may know the right channels and contacts for developing your IT capability. It may also be possible to observe other members of staff using computers, even if it's not in history.

4 Use IT with a teaching group that you feel reasonably comfortable with. Not 9Z on a Friday afternoon, and not a class where your control of proceedings might be a bit shaky at the best of times.

5 Have a 'Plan B', so that if there is a problem you can simply say, 'Never mind we'll do something else and get on to that next week', or 'Here's one I printed out earlier'.

6 Try to have mastered the software in rehearsal if possible so that you can concentrate on the classroom management implications of the lesson (throughput of pupils for example).

7 Think carefully about the planning of the non-computer aspects of the lesson. Devise work that is accessible and that will last a reasonable length of time so that you are making life as easy for yourself as possible.

8 School IT suites are usually free at some point in the week; try to make use of them, and your fellow students, by 'sub-contracting' the task of finding out about different areas of IT and sharing the expertise you develop over the course of the year.

9 Make the most of your school placement to develop your IT experience. This is often a propitious time for working with small groups of pupils, or developing support materials for the software which the school possesses, or simply developing your familiarity with various items of software. In some cases it is an opportunity for the student teacher to repay help and support rendered by helping the department with its IT needs and policy.

10 'Throughput' considerations: some IT applications are excellent but very time-consuming. Some of the simulation packages which are helpful in enticing the pupils into an enthusiastic commitment to finding out about the past (for example, *Arcventure*, or *Victorian Time Detectives*) take several hours to work through from start to finish. One of the challenges facing history teachers in deploying the use of IT is to think of activities where the use of the computer can be integrated into the lesson so as to provide quick, effective and eminently practicable activities which do not take up massive amounts of curriculum time.

11 Problems of access: not all schools possess the facilities to provide everyday access to computers. Part of the challenge of training to be a teacher is learning how to make the best of what is available and the art of the possible. Developing proficiency in the classroom use of IT is partly about your resourcefulness, initiative, patience, diplomacy and tenacity. Even if you have to do things at lunch time, after school, or with small groups of pupils rather than whole classes, try to fit in work with pupils if at all possible. Doing it in the staff room, with fellow student teachers, or at your ITE institution is not quite the same as doing it with pupils.

12 Work out a basic checklist before the lesson, such as the one suggested below:
   • Are you familiar with the software?
   • How will you put the software into the context of the history topic you're doing?

- How long will it take each group of pupils on the computer (through-put)?
- What exactly will they do (support materials?)?
- What will the other pupils do?
- What will you do if the computer doesn't work?
- How will you arrange the groupings?
- What work will they do/what points will you make after they've been on the computer?

It is important to remember that different applications of IT are helpful and valuable in different ways. With some applications, the principal benefit might be the enthusiasm it elicits in pupils and the extent to which it draws them into an enthusiasm for learning about the past, even if the extent to which it develops intrinsically historical understanding is marginal. With others, it might be the development of knowledge, skills and understandings which are part of the attainment targets for IT; with yet others, the main benefit may be an enhanced understanding of historical processes, concepts, knowledge or skills. Sometimes applications are helpful because they are easy to use and to incorporate into classroom use, and thus help to develop the teacher's confidence in the use of IT – in the short term they might benefit the teacher more than the pupils but this may result in a longer-term 'pay-off' for pupils who will be working with teachers who are comfortable with a broad range of IT applications. It will be unusual to come across an application which possesses all of these attributes; the important thing is to have a clear awareness of what (if any) benefits are being bestowed by the use of IT.

The development and implementation of any competence model for IT needs to keep firmly in mind certain important factors. Differences between individual schools and departments will mean that it will be easier for some student teachers to develop IT competence. Some of you will work in schools where use of computers in the classroom is highly developed, with easy access to computers; others in schools where, for various reasons, this is not the case. Some may well have a subject supervisor who is heavily committed to IT, and to some extent acts as a 'personal trainer'; others will have to be very much more reliant on their own initiative and the hardware and software resources of the ITE institution in order to make progress. If your department or your tutor isn't heavily 'into' IT you will have to use your initiative more in order to make progress.

Important though it is, IT competence is not an overriding priority for student teachers, who have to balance a number of competing claims on their time over the course of the year. If you are experiencing severe problems with classroom management (or whatever), this may well have to take precedence over aspiring to advanced levels of IT competence; indeed, it would be difficult to develop classroom proficiency in IT without having attained a reasonable working atmosphere in the classroom.

Developing proficiency in IT is time-intensive. There is often no substitute for spending substantial amounts of time becoming familiar with software programmes. It is important to be realistic about what can be achieved in the course of training. It is probably not realistic to expect student teachers to move from novice status to mastery of all facets of IT in this period. What is essential is that when you start your NQT year, you are in a position to use computers, and new technology in general, in your teaching.

TASK 8.4 SUPPORTING EVIDENCE OF COMPETENCE IN IT

Before the end of your final block of teaching experience, examine your teaching experience file and look for evidence to support the claim that you have been able to select and use information technology appropriately in your teaching. If there is little or no evidence to support this claim, try to plan, teach and evaluate a lesson which focuses on this area of competence.

Using word processing exercises in history

Figures 8.5 and 8.6 illustrate word processing exercises which might be given to Key Stage 3 pupils. These are simply sequencing and organising exercises which can be done more quickly through the manipulation of text on a word processing package than by writing them down or cutting and pasting them. It is comparatively easy to make them harder or easier according to need. The idea would be to build in progression by making such exercises increasingly more complex as their overview of British history builds up over the course of the Key Stage.

TASK 8.5 DEVISING WORD PROCESSING EXERCISES FOR THE HISTORY CLASSROOM

*   After considering the examples given in Figures 8.5 and 8.6, construct a word processing exercise of your own which addresses Key Element 1 (chronology).
*   In what ways might word processing exercises be used to address other Key Elements of National Curriculum history?

Fact or Fiction? Activity 1

Divide the following list of 'people' into two columns: those who existed in real life and those who exist only in stories and fairy tales. Then delete the record of those who you have decided are not real people.

Peter Pan, Adolf Hitler, Queen Victoria, Robin Hood, King Arthur, Roger Rabbit, William the Conqueror, Winston Churchill, Oliver Cromwell, Margaret Thatcher, Superman, Batman, Asterix the Gaul, King Henry VIII, Guy Fawkes, Alfred the Great, Florence Nightingale.

Fact or Fiction? Activity 2

Look at the list of 'real' people that you have got left on your list. Try to put them in **chronological** *order (the order in which they lived – furthest from the present day first on the list, nearest to today at the end). Try to make a rough guess as to when they were alive.*

Before AD 1066
AD 1100
AD 1200
AD 1300
AD 1400
AD 1500
AD 1600
AD 1700
AD 1800
AD 1900
AD 2000

Figure 8.5 Word processing exercise in history (1)

Desktop publishing exercises also lend themselves to work in the history classroom, particularly with regard to the Key Element of 'Interpretations'. Pupils can be asked to report on historical events from different perspectives: for instance, a Norman and Saxon report on the Battle of Hastings, German and British front page coverage of the Battle of Britain, pro- and anti-suffragette reports on the death of Emily Davison and so on. It is important, however, to

Medieval Realms: a summary. Using 'drag and drop' with the mouse, rearrange the boxes so that they are a summary of some of the main events in British history, 1066 to 1485			
Monarch	*Date*	*Event*	*Significance*
Henry II	By 1296	signed the Magna Carta,	ending the Wars of the Roses, the civil war which had weakened England for over thirty years, and establishing a strong and stable Tudor dynasty.
Richard II	In 1066	defeated the Peasants' Revolt,	to assert his power over the Church, and especially the Church courts. After this, the Church tended to support the monarch.
Henry VII	In 1264	won the Battle of Hastings,	this showed that there were limits to the king's power. A strong king might claim that there was a system of absolute monarchy, but a weak one might face challenges to his authority from the barons.
John	In 1485	ordered the killing of Archbishop Becket,	after much hostility and tension, in the centuries to come, Wales, Scotland and Ireland fell under English control to form 'Great Britain'.
Edward I	In 1154	had gained control over much of Wales and Scotland,	the first step in his conquest and rule of England, setting up the feudal system and a strong unified state under Norman control.
Henry III	In 1381	was defeated by Simon de Montfort, leader of a barons' revolt,	after public resistance to his attempts to impose a poll tax. One of the first instances of popular revolt against the monarch.
William I	In 1215	won the Battle of Bosworth Field,	this led to the setting up of parliament. Although De Montfort, leader of the barons, was later defeated and killed, parliament was to play an important part in Britain's history over the centuries.

Figure 8.6 Word processing exercise in history (2)

make sure that you build in 'real' history into the process, to ensure that it does not become simply an exercise in English or presentation. This can be done by referencing details to source materials used by pupils, and explaining to pupils the nuanced techniques of propaganda, with examples and discussion of real newspaper front pages.

DATA HANDLING IN HISTORY

Computers enable us to manipulate, interrogate and test hypotheses on information much more quickly than would be the case of having to read through and take notes on information provided. Task 8.7 incorporates an extract from the roll of honour of those killed in the Second World War in Luton (*Luton News*, 1947). It is the sort of information which might be used as a datafile which pupils could interrogate in order to discern patterns and test hypotheses about the war. What questions might be asked of this information?

TASK 8.6 CD-ROM IN THE HISTORY CLASSROOM

CD-ROMs are aesthetically very attractive on screen, and they do exciting things (compared to blackboards), but their use is not unproblematic in terms of classroom use – you still need to be able to devise a workable classroom activity which asks pupils to do something useful with the information on the disk, instead of just finding things and downloading them. Explore a history CD-ROM and try to devise a pupil activity which would be appropriate for Key Stage 3 pupils, focused on one of the Key Elements of the National Curriculum. Bearing in mind considerations of 'throughput' of pupils, and the fact that you may have only one computer for a class of about thirty pupils, try to devise an activity or enquiry which might enable seven or eight groups of 3–4 pupils to each spend between 5 and 15 minutes using the CD-ROM, so that all pupils in the class had used a CD-ROM over the course of no more than two history lessons. How can you structure an enquiry or investigation using a history CD-ROM which goes beyond information retrieval and develops pupils' understanding of the past as well as their knowledge of it? The British Library's structured investigations for their *Medieval Realms* CD-ROM offers some excellent ideas on this.

Try to familiarise yourself with a range of history CD-ROMs; to what extent do they offer the opportunity of 'interactive' learning (and what exactly do we mean by the term 'interactive'?)? Are there any possible disadvantages of CD-ROM as a learning resource?

TASK 8.7 A DATA-HANDLING EXERCISE ON THE SECOND WORLD WAR

Chamberlain, Marion. Killed by enemy action at Luton, October 14th, 1940.

Chambers, Alfred, 101, Cpl., R. Norfolk Regt. Killed in action, Battle of Imphal Road, Burma, June 9th, 1944.

Chambers, Frank, Killed by U.S. bomb lorry explosion, Offley, January 8th, 1945.

Chambers, George, Killed by enemy action at Vauxhall Motors, Luton, August 30th, 1940.

Champkin, Douglas, Sgt. F/Engr., 460 Squadron, RAF. Killed on operations, buried at Lahr, Germany, April 27th–28th, 1944.

Chance, Philip Cptn., Light AA Batty, R.A. Died at sea while a prisoner of Japanese, November 13th, 1942.

Chappell, Peter, P/Officer, RAF, Bomber Command. Killed on operations, Abingdon, July 28th, 1941.

Cherry, Harold, Lieut., R.A., att. Tactical Air Force. Killed in Italy, February 26th, 1945.

Cherry, Kenneth, L/Cpl. Died of wounds, Greece, December 27th, 1944.

Chesham, Amelia. Killed by enemy action at Luton, October 14th, 1940.

Cheshire, Sidney, Trpr., Reconnaissance Regiment. Killed on active service, April 24th, 1942.

Chote, Arthur, F/Sgt., 14 Squadron, RAF. Killed on active service, near Chester, August 3rd, 1942.

Church, Frederick, A/Seaman, H.M.S. *Isis*. Died on war service from exposure at sea, July 20th, 1944.

Claridge, Albert, F/Officer, RAF. Died May 31st, 1944.

Claridge, Cyril, Pte., 4th Battn., Suffolk Regt. Killed in action, Singapore, April 22nd, 1942.

Claridge, Sydney, Pte., Suffolk Regt. Died as prisoner of Japanese, Japan, February 3rd, 1944.

Claringbold, Leon, A/Seaman, R.N. Lost at sea, May 23rd, 1941.

Clark, David, Sgt. (O) RAF. Killed on active service, Scotland, December 10th, 1941.

Clark, William, F/Sgt., Security Police, RAF. Accidentally killed on active service, Burton on Trent, February 18th, 1945.

Clarke, Brian, Sgt., W/Op. 576 Squadron, RAF. Killed on operations, Kollerbecke, near Detmold, Germany, January 14th, 1944.

Clark, David, Sgt./Observer, RAF, Bomber Command. Killed on active service, December 10th, 1941.

Clark, John. Died India, 1941.

Clark, Ronald, Pte., Royal Scots. Killed on active service, May 1945.

Cleary, Albert, Sgt., RAF. Missing presumed killed, South Atlantic, August 17th, 1941.

Clinton, Basil, P/Officer, RAF. Killed on active service near Cape Hotham, Australia, July 31st, 1945.

Clough, R.A. Died as a result of enemy action at Vauxhall motors, Luton, August 30th, 1940.

What fields would be suitable for a datafile on this information, and what might pupils be able to find out about the Second World War from the information? What are the advantages of using a computer data-handling application to analyse the information rather than simply using it in text form?

(Exercise devised by Isobel Randall)

(Of what use to the historian . . . ?) Pupils can be asked what we could find out about the Second World War from this information, and once it has been put on a data-handling package, pupils can create bar charts and pie charts which enable them to see significant patterns in the data. It is possible to buy commercially produced history datafiles. Once you know how to use a data-handling package, you can put your own datafiles on to a computer; some pupils will be able to construct a datafile and then interrogate it to test hypotheses.

THE INTERNET

The Internet – with the World Wide Web, networks of special interest groups and the possibility of communication by e-mail – has been hailed by some as the most important communications breakthrough since the printing press. What are you to make of it as a student teacher? What does it offer in terms of the potential to enhance the quality of teaching and learning in the classroom?

The first point to stress is that few history classrooms are 'online', so the regular live use of the Internet within the history classroom is still not an option for most history classes. As a teaching resource however, and as something important which you ought to be familiar with, it has much to offer. As an absolute minimum, you should try to ensure that you know how to access and search the World Wide Web, and that you know how to use e-mail. Searching the web for resources can be time-consuming, and it might be helpful to heed the advice of Durbin (1996) and have something to read, or a set of books to mark, while you are trawling through cyberspace for resources. One way of saving time hunting down resources for yourself is to go to organisations which have already done a search for usable history resources. One of the best of these is the BBC Education History site, which provides an introductory guide to the potential of the Internet for teaching history, access to BBC history resources, including the scripts to *The People's Century*, and some interactive investigations which go beyond simply accessing and downloading information and resources (BBC, 1997). There is also an online tutorial on the use of the Internet written by Howe (1997) which is designed particularly for history student teachers.

SUMMARY AND KEY POINTS

Developing competence in IT in a way that fulfils the requirements of *Circular 10/97* (DfEE, 1997) means that you not only need to develop personal proficiency in IT but must also have a clear grasp of the ways in which IT can contribute to effective learning in history. You must make every effort, whatever the circumstances of your school placements, to get as much experience in the use of IT applications as possible; *classroom* experience is particularly helpful. You also need to consider the classroom management factors which influence the successful use of IT, and to be able to evaluate the impact of the use of computers in the classroom. It is not a question of how much you use computers, or the breadth of applications used; what matters most is how effectively you are able to use new technology to improve the quality of your lessons. With many applications, it is not a question of competence, but of levels of expertise. You will also need to think about which IT applications have most potential for use in the history classroom.

FURTHER READING

HABET (1994) *Teaching National Curriculum History with IT*, London, Historical Association.
   An outline guide of the different ways in which IT can be used.

NCET/Historical Association (1996) *History Using IT: A Pupil's Entitlement*, Coventry, NCET.
   An adroit summary of some of the ideas and applications which can help to introduce eminently usable classroom activities.

NCET/Historical Association (1996) *CD-ROMs for History*, Coventry, NCET.
   A brief description of the main features of some of the most appropriate of the rapidly increasing range of history CD-ROMs designed for the history classroom.

NCET (1995) *Approaches to IT Capability*, Coventry, NCET.
   Deals with general issues of technical competence, the range of applications which impact on the classroom, and strategies for developing competence.

NCET (1997) *History and IT: Improving Pupils' Writing in History Through Word Processing*, Coventry, NCET.
   Contains a wide variety of ideas about using word processing in the history classroom which do not need high levels of IT expertise, and attempts to make the point that simple IT can be used to address quite complex historical ideas.

Schick, J. (1995) 'On Being Interactive: Rethinking the Learning Equation', *History Microcomputer Review*, Vol. 11, No. 1, Spring.
   This is useful for leading on to what computers might add to the learning process in history if problems of access, attitudes and technical competence are surmounted.

School Curriculum and Assessment Authority (1995) *Information Technology; the New Requirements*, London, SCAA.
   Puts into perspective the whole curriculum implications of IT competence.

9 The use of resources in the teaching of history

INTRODUCTION

The National Curriculum for History (DfE, 1995) leaves the teacher in no doubt that 'using a range of sources of information, including documents and printed sources, artefacts, pictures, photographs and films, music and oral sources, buildings and sites' is not just valuable, but necessary in the teaching of history. The introduction of the National Curriculum has made more explicit the range of possibilities and opportunities for teaching with resources in history and has stimulated a broader understanding of the subject in schools. Delivering the National Curriculum in history therefore depends largely on adequate resourcing, and the quality of history teaching depends in part on the history teacher's expertise in providing and using a varied and stimulating range of resources. You will be expected to use a variety of teaching methods which include a wide variety of resources. Once you have decided what is to be taught (the content) and how it is to be taught (the teaching strategy) you need to secure the tools necessary (the resources) to ensure and maintain pupil interest and learning, although as noted in Chapter 3, there may be occasions when the discovery of an exciting or unusual resource might be the starting point for the planning of a lesson. History teachers need to be competent in the use of resources and, in particular, they must be able to produce, select, adapt, and retain resources for use in the classroom. You will need to develop a knowledge and understanding of the range of resources and skills in the use of primary sources. You also need to know what these skills are; their range; the progressive level of difficulty and the implications for differentiated work.

It is vital that you not only understand resources in history teaching but are equipped to produce, collect and arrange the required resources in your teaching. OFSTED (1993a, 1993b, 1994) has been critical of much of the quality of the resources used by teachers in history classrooms. In particular, OFSTED has criticised the use made by teachers of textbooks, computer technology, artefacts and worksheets, and this chapter will raise these as issues. This chapter therefore examines the variety and use of resources most commonly available to the history teacher, including the place of primary sources in the classroom, the use of textbooks and worksheets, and school visits. The chapter should be read in conjunction with Chapter 4.

OBJECTIVES

At the end of this chapter you should be able to make a personal evaluation of the suitability of resource material for the teaching of history by recognising its relevance and appropriateness. You should have increased your confidence in handling resource material and have understood its potential and limitations in enhancing the quality of your teaching. This chapter aims to:

- define resources and provide a theoretical framework for their understanding;
- examine the variety and range of resource material used in history class-rooms;
- consider the place of primary sources in teaching history: textbooks, worksheets, field trips and managing resources;
- provide practical suggestions on the use and management of resource material.

It is not possible, in one chapter, to provide a comprehensive survey of the potential use of resources in the history classroom. You should therefore follow up the references for each of the areas which are briefly covered in this chapter for a more detailed look at particular resources.

THEORETICAL BACKGROUND

The term 'resource' should be understood as anything that can serve as an object or stimulus for pupils and which a history teacher can effectively use to enhance or extend the teaching or learning of history. Danks (1994) identifies fifteen different uses of resources for the history teacher and divides them into three categories: 'teaching resources', 'teaching aids' and 'teaching methods'. Teaching aids relate to the use of equipment or mechanical devices such as OHPs, blackboards, flip charts and television. Whilst teaching methods and teaching aids are certainly resources in our definition, this chapter will focus on what Danks terms the 'teaching resources' which include: historical sources, field trips, worksheets, oral history, textbooks, computer programs, etc. In other words, items which are used to enrich or enhance the understanding of pupils and the development of historical skills. Teaching with these types of resources often involves an active and investigatory mode of learning and can be a very effective way of developing skills that are transferable to different kinds of activity. Many basic skills associated with information acquisition and communication, measuring, sorting and classifying can be developed through the teaching of history with resources. They are a way of helping pupils to 'do history' rather than simply receive it. The first area of 'teaching resources' which we need to consider relates to the framework we might use to understand the use of historical sources in the history classroom.

There is a wide variety of historical or primary sources which can be used, or adapted for use, in the history classroom. However, in order to appreciate the importance of primary sources and their validity as part of schools history it is necessary to have a clear understanding of what history is. Marwick's (1984) definition of history, as described in Chapter 2, leads us to believe that the use of primary sources is fundamental to 'history' and that if any school subject is to be termed 'history' it must involve the use of primary sources. This is exactly what the National Curriculum History encourages, for it advocates that pupils should have the opportunity to investigate historical issues through the use of historical sources. Sources, according to the National Curriculum Guidelines, are to be used to enable pupils to find out about the past either through illustrating change over time or by exploring a period in time. The National Curriculum does not therefore prevent you from developing your own ideas and approaches to the use of primary sources. There are, however, opponents of this view who would argue that children are unable to attain the levels of thinking necessary for historical enquiry through the use of primary sources. Those who hold this view base it on Piagetian ideas of children's cognitive development. Denis Shemilt (1987) has researched adolescent ideas about the use of primary sources in school history and has concluded that school pupils have become accustomed to handling primary sources of various kinds and to coming to conclusions from them about the past. He describes problems of understanding which pupils invariably have in handling primary sources, but details four stages of pupil conceptualisation: (1) knowledge of the past is taken for granted; (2) evidence = privileged information about the past; (3) evidence is a basis for inference about the past; and (4) awareness of the historicity of evidence. Shemilt explains:

> At stage I historical knowledge is seen as a *given*; at stage II it is
> something to be *discovered*; the stage III thinker sees it as having to be
> *worked out* by rational process; and at stage IV written history is
> beginning to be recognised as no more than a reconstruction of past
> events, a reconstruction, moreover, which makes visible connections and
> continuities, moralities and motives, that contemporaries would not have
> perceived, nor perhaps have understood.
>
> (Shemilt, 1987)

The argument here is that school pupils can proceed to stage 4 and that the use of primary sources is invaluable in attempting to move pupils on through the four stages.

Whilst further research on how children understand and make sense of historical sources is ongoing, it would seem clear that pupils should be given some insight into the 'rules' and methods of the professional historian. The view, described by Richard Aldrich (1989), that there were many who felt that it was 'the job of the university historian to determine the historical record, and the "job" of the school teacher to receive such wisdom and present it in simplified form to school pupils' is no longer tenable. As Fines (1994) says: 'Using source-material and tackling the problems of evidence give a feeling of reality which second-hand history can rarely give.' Using primary sources helps children feel for the topic they are studying.

Whilst acknowledging that our responsibility as history teachers is to present historical knowledge as 'tentative, constructed and problematic', and to select sources which enable us to explore these attributes, Hake and Haydn (1995) suggest that we need to keep in mind the balance between narrative and sources in history teaching. They point to the fact that National Curriculum textbooks consist almost exclusively of a series of double page features on a particular historical topic, dominated by four to six sources and questions focused on these sources. Student teachers of history sometimes model their own materials on those used in professionally produced textbooks. This can lead to excessive use of 'the dreaded two page spread' type of lesson. They argue that inserting pictures and diagrams and breaking-up blocks of text has been at the expense of extended pieces of writing which might provide a clearer grasp of how events unfolded, and the theories surrounding those events. There is certainly a need to ensure that more detailed accounts and explanations of periods of history are not left out in the move to a more source-based approach to history teaching. You need to bear in mind that there needs to be a balance between 'traditional' teaching strategies (sometimes dismissively referred to as 'chalk and talk') and the use of sources in the classroom. As well as understanding what 'history' is, and how it is constructed, it is helpful if pupils have a coherent view of how events, wars and crises have evolved. The emphasis on sourcework in GCSE examinations means that it would be possible for a pupil to gain full marks on a question about the Second World War by interpreting, analysing, and commenting on sources appropriately, without necessarily knowing who won the war and who was on whose side. Slater makes the point that 'History pupils who appear to know little do not make a good case for its teaching' (Slater, 1984). Pupils should develop a clear grasp of how we have moved from the past to the present day in terms of political ideas, methods of warfare, economic and social organisation and so on, in addition to acquiring the skills to analyse and interpret it. Your selection and use of resources should help pupils to build up an overview or 'framework' of the past as well as providing opportunities to analyse sources in detail. Some schools broadcasts (and the recent BBC series, *The Troubled Century*) are good examples of resources which can provide an overview or general summary of developments in a particular topic over time. The other crucially important resource which can achieve this is your own knowledge and understanding of the past, in the form of the expositions and explanations which you provide for your pupils to provide a link between source-based activities.

HISTORICAL SOURCES

Historical sources encompass every kind of evidence which human beings have left, from the written word to the shape of the landscape. In looking at any potential source you need to know why you want to use it, whether or not you need to modify it, and what questions you will pose of it. It is also necessary for you to make some selection and preparation of the materials used, since it is what you do with the source in the classroom which counts. You need to guide pupils in terms of learning how to use, examine and evaluate historical sources. The busy classroom teacher cannot rely on expensively published materials which are often in short supply. More often than not you may have to supply the deficiency from your own knowledge and local sources. Sources used should be easy to handle, collect and store, for their purpose is to cut your work load, not increase it. Their use should lead to discussion and historical thinking about the topic and lead on to further exploration of the topic. The range of skills that are developed with their use will include observation, exploration, questioning, comparison, deduction, interpretation and communication, among others. Pupils who are familiar with a variety of types of sources should at least be able to begin to comprehend and to extract information from them, to evaluate and detect bias in them, and to reach conclusions through comparison with other sources. These skills should be linked closely to the many ways in which primary sources can be used in the teaching of school history. Both the teaching strategy decided upon and the resource tools used should be designed to meet the diverse needs of pupils. The primary sources listed in Table 9.1 are illustrative, rather than exhaustive of the range and scope of the type of sources that can be employed by the history teacher.

Table 9.1 outlines a variety of sources which are used to enhance the teaching of school history. For example, extracts from government documents may be used to help pupils understand particular government policies in a period (e.g. the Welfare State); diaries can be excellent ways of understanding individuals and their perceptions (e.g. Anne Frank); and oral history can stimulate interest

Table 9.1   Types of historical sources

Historical source	Description of type
Documents	Extracts of records of government, companies, churches, schools, registers, trade directories, log books . . .
Surveys and reports	Extracts from the Domesday Book, medieval chronicles . . .
Family and personal	Letters and diaries, postcards, pictures . . .
Polemical documents	Pamphlets, polemical writings, sermons, newspapers, cartoons . . .
Archaeological findings	Artefacts, objects, archaeological digs . . .
Literary and artistic	Architecture, novels, poems, plays, paintings, films . . .
Other sources (techniques)	Aerial photography, statistical analysis, oral history . . .

in school history with pupils listening to individual recollections of, say, those who lived through the Second World War. In the use of all of these sources pupils can be guided by the teacher to identify bias in documents; to ask questions about their authenticity; and to encourage empathetic feeling towards people in the past, and to explore why they were written and for what audience. The use of sources as primary evidence is an accepted part of the history teacher's role, and you need to explore their classroom use in detail. Keith Andreetti's (1993) book provides a good introduction to the use of historical sources for primary school pupils which can also be used for less able pupils in secondary school. It is important to realise that most pupils experience historical sources as an educational source. Sources often need to be packaged and edited, sometimes heavily, so that they are accessible and in a manageable form. By editing a source you turn it into an educational resource to present to pupils. Too much editing can cause problems by distorting the impression of the past given. The quality of your exposition in working through the source and explaining problematic aspects to pupils can help to resolve or at least mitigate some of these tensions. The Schools Council History 13–16 Project's *Looking at Evidence* (1976) provides a good example of how to modify sources and turn them into an edited classroom resource. The 1989 report of the Chief Examiners in history commented that the failure to adapt the language and terminology used in sources resulted in sources being inaccessible to the less able. However, the report also warned that oversimplification would mean that much of the value of the source material would be lost. You certainly need to explain any abstract language used in sources, and be mindful of the question: if I change the source will it detract from its purpose? There are clearly dangers in editing sources for classroom use and Tim Lomas (1992) details some of these. Nevertheless, if used well, Lomas believes that sources can help 'illustrate, develop imagination, clarify old questions and pose new ones, develop historical skills and concepts, help convey a sense of reality and help make inferences and interpretations'.

TASK 9.1 USE OF SOURCES

1 Many historical sources, whether originals or replicas, can be used effectively in the classroom with pupils encouraged to observe, touch and handle them. Choose a primary source object appropriate for use in the history classroom and describe (a) the teaching and learning strategy you would employ in its use, (b) the historical skills which the object would help promote, (c) the questions you would ask pupils about the object. You should firmly locate your plan of the lesson within one of the Key Stage 3 Study Units.

2 Choose a written source which you would use with a mixed-ability class and describe what steps you would take, if any, to make it more accessible to all the pupils in your class. How would you present it to them? What teaching strategy would you employ? What other resources would you use? You should read Aris's chapter on the use of resources in Brooks *et al.*, *The Effective History Teacher* (1993), which will help you reflect on these questions.

3 Design a lesson plan for a GCSE or A level class which incorporates the detailed use of an historical source. Consider the objectives of your lesson and explain how your chosen resource will contribute to these objectives. Describe the problems you might encounter in teaching this lesson. You should read Fry's (1991) short article in *Teaching History* on using evidence in the GCSE classroom, or Brown and Daniels's (1986) book *Learning History: A Guide to Advanced Study*.

TEXTBOOKS AND WORKSHEETS

OFSTED found in its survey of school inspections in 1994 that most schools use textbooks as their main teaching resource, and that in line with current requirements of the National Curriculum most recently published textbooks include extracts from primary sources which pupils are asked to examine. Nevertheless, OFSTED noted that few of the inspected schools had appropriate textbooks in sufficient range and number to support the effective implementation of the National Curriculum. This criticism may reflect the financial situation in many schools, which has resulted in the purchase of fewer books. These financial restrictions do not, however, account for the further observation that OFSTED made: that in some of the schools textbooks were used uncritically, in a way which had a narrowing effect on the quality of work in the history department. If textbooks are to be properly utilised as both a secondary source and as a provider of primary source extracts then teachers must use them selectively and critically. You need to be aware of the strengths and limitations of the textbooks you use, and understand that no textbook is perfect. As you think about the lessons you will be teaching you should look at the textbook and consider whether there are some aspects of the lesson which the textbook might deliver perfectly well, and where there are areas which will require other resources and approaches. In selecting the most appropriate texts and sources, it can be helpful to be familiar with a range of textbooks, and the reviews of books contained in *Teaching History* and *The Times Educational Supplement* should be read on a regular basis. The annual Historical Association conferences, and the Schools Council History conference include exhibitions of textbook and other resources, and are a good way of keeping up to date with what is available in terms of new resources. You need to be aware that pupils expect textbooks to provide them with much of the information required for public examinations. For other pupils books must be well illustrated, for books which have accurately coloured reproductions and good photographs, sketches, tables and diagrams will attract greater attention from pupils. Textbooks are clearly set to remain a particularly important resource for the teachers.

As well as using textbooks as a resource, especially of historical sources, you can also create your own worksheets with extracts from primary sources. Worksheets are widely used by history departments to supplement their textbook resources, although OFSTED found that they were often poorly presented and did not support effective learning. The production of good quality source-based worksheets should not be beyond the capabilities of the competent history teacher. During your school experience you will be encouraged to produce a variety of worksheets to aid your teaching. Common problems with the production of worksheets can be overcome if you consider the pitfalls beforehand. First, your worksheets must cater for the full range of ability in the classroom. This means that you need to use appropriate language. It is better to word process a worksheet rather than write it out in your own handwriting. Pupils are often more motivated by the appearance of a worksheet than by its content. If difficult words are used then you will need to explain them to the class. Indeed, it is extremely useful to use the blackboard or OHP in conjunction with a worksheet. Second, the visual layout and quality of the worksheet needs to be good. For less able pupils you should make full use of all the possibilities of presenting information visually rather than in written form. Guidelines on the use of flow charts, pictures, and diagrams in worksheets for less able pupils are provided by Judy Sebba's (1995) excellent book, *History for All*, which you should consult.

TASK 9.2 TEXTBOOKS AND WORKSHEETS

Choose a topic from your teaching experience and select a textbook for examination and use the following criteria in order to evaluate it:

1 Do the aims of the textbook correspond to the aims and objectives of the history study unit?
2 Does the textbook cover adequately the topics to be taught and does it allow for different teaching and learning styles?
3 Is the content well organised and is there progress and continuity in the text?
4 Is the presentation and language of the textbook appropriate for the range of ability you are considering it for?
5 Does the text promote the historical skills required by the National Curriculum?
6 How broad is the range of source activities included within the textbook?
7 What is the total cost of the book for your class and is it strong and long lasting? Does the text require you to buy supplementary material? Can you copy the text?
8 What are its major weaknesses? Can these weaknesses be supplemented and/or adapted for use in the classroom?
9 Is the text up to date for your present needs? When was it published? Has it been revised? Is the table of contents useful?
10 Would you recommend the textbook for continued use in your school?

TASK 9.3 HISTORY JOURNALS

Consult back copies of *Teaching History* to see how reviews of history textbooks and resources are written. What are the criteria used by heads of history and other reviewers to evaluate the quality of textbooks? Choose a recent resource for the history classroom and write a brief review of it. Consider what you might say about the textbook or resource if asked to comment on its usefulness at an interview. Remember in particular that pupils like to feel comfortable with a textbook before they embark upon reading or listening to it.

Third, there should be a sufficient variety of stimuli for pupils. Ask yourself whether you need to provide a variety of choice in the worksheet and whether or not your questions should be open or closed. Does the worksheet make reference to the textbook? Fourth, your worksheet needs to be clear about its objectives. The aims of the course need to be reflected in the worksheet. You should not encourage mindless filling in of blank spaces on worksheets. The worksheet is designed to be a genuine learning experience and you must decide what learning experiences you can derive from the use of it. Copying and colouring are almost always bad history practice and you should avoid them in your use of worksheets. Lloyd-Jones ([1985]1995) provides an excellent introduction on how to produce better worksheets, and he asks nine questions (summarised below) which are worth considering:

Are your worksheets:

- part of a planned, balanced and coherent course?
- written in language that is easily understood?

Do they:

- provide opportunities for group work and class discussion?
- require pupils to use a variety of sources and resources?
- ask for a variety of responses, including both oral and written?
- cater for the needs of all levels of ability in the class?
- provide for progression and continuity in learning?
- avoid mindless blank filling-in or colouring?
- give clear information and unambiguous instructions?

TASK 9.4 TEXTBOOKS

The efficient use of textbooks in A level history will require students to have skills in reading which cannot always be assumed by the teacher. Consider the following five reading techniques and design a lesson, with illustrations from history textbooks, of how you would teach these reading skills as part of an A level course.

- *Trial reading* – quick survey of text to decide whether it is useful;
- *Scanning* – scan particular pages to identify keywords;
- *Skim reading* – identify and read part of text with immediate use;
- *Rapid reading* – to read through chapters quickly to get a general impression of ideas;
- *Critical reading* – to read text and take notes.

TASK 9.5 WORKSHEETS

Worksheets are increasingly used in schools either to supplement textbooks or in the absence of them. Design a worksheet for a year 9 class which incorporates the points raised in this chapter about how to judge a good worksheet. In particular you should consult Lloyd-Jones's ([1985]1995) excellent book on preparing worksheets. When you have used the work-sheet with pupils, go through pupils' responses and consider in what ways the exercise has been helpful. Did it just pass the time, or did it promote pupils' understanding of what you were trying to teach? Did it provide any useful insight into what pupils do and do not understand which might inform subsequent teaching? Did the pupils work in an assiduous or desultory fashion on the task? Were some sections more helpful and successful than others? In what ways would you amend the worksheet for future use? Would you use it again?

Worksheets have the potential to enhance, support and structure the learning that takes place in the history classroom. It is your responsibility to ensure that your worksheets meet these criteria. The standard of your worksheets will say a great deal about your relationship with your class and about your commitment to teaching them.

HISTORY FIELD TRIPS

It can be argued that by giving pupils something they can actually see and touch (Piaget's 'concrete' phase?), they will be able to comprehend the use of the item, the context in which it is placed and the historical significance of both the artefact and the period of time to which it relates. Teachers have used this argu-ment to theorise that there is a much greater sense of learning with a single site visit than with the use of a large number of textbooks in class (see Anderson and Moore, 1994). Pond (1985) has questioned whether there is any basis for justifying museum and site visits on these Piagetian grounds. Pond does not advocate the abolition of field trips in history, but rather that their justification needs to be changed. He suggests that teachers should take children on field trips because they *need* to understand a historical concept, not because they *will* understand it. Teachers need to be realistic about the strengths and limita-tions of site visits. Nevertheless, if one of the aims of school history is to give pupils an understanding of what history *is*, and how it is constructed, they need to experience history outside the classroom, and teachers therefore must look beyond the classroom in their planning. This allows pupils to experience resources in a stimulating environment, whether it be historical sites or museums.

TASK 9.6 FIELD TRIPS

Think of a specific field trip or museum visit which would be feasible for a group of pupils (this might be a major national museum you are familiar with, or a museum or site which is within easy visiting range of your school placement), and draft an outline plan of what your objectives would be for the visit, and what activities you would devise to make the experience worth while.

TASK 9.7 PLANNING VISITS

In addition to the question of the 'historical' validity of a site or museum visit, there are important logistical considerations which need to be borne in mind. You need to be aware of the possible effects of the visit on the school as a whole, on parents of pupils involved, and on other members of staff.

You have been requested by your mentor to investigate and plan a possible field trip for a year 7 class to the local cathedral as part of their 'Medieval Realms' study unit. You need to complete a short report on the feasibility of such a visit, particularly addressing the following questions:

- How would your plan affect the school timetable?
- How many staff would be involved on the day?
- How much would the visit cost pupils?
- Could all the pupils pay? If not, where would the money come from?
- How many pupils would attend and would permission from parents be necessary?
- Have you considered the school policy on outside visits? Is insurance necessary?
- Does the site have adequate toilets, parking and eating facilities?
- What is the justification for the visit? Does it have a clear focus?
- Would the focus correspond to the aims of the study unit?
- Is there an educational officer based at the site? Do you need to contact him/her?
- Does the site produce its own materials for school visits? Will you use them?
- Do you need to plan a worksheet? What would it contain?
- Do you intend to follow the visit up with subsequent lessons on the topic?
- What other questions would you ask yourself? Are there any other steps you could take to ensure that the visit does not cause problems?

Participation in history field trips can increase awareness of the nature of history through exposure to a rich variety of sources.

Planning a field trip is essential and will often involve you in extensive enquiries and preparation. You need background information before the visit and an understanding of the disruption and cost to the school. History field trips need to be planned well in advance, they are not spur of the moment ideas. A preliminary visit to the site by the teacher organising the proposed visit is usually vital to check any arrangements and to plan the focus of the visit. You need to contact museum staff or any educational officer at the site before you visit. These officers can provide invaluable information and often they cater for groups of pupils from schools. Coach parking, and toilet and eating facilities need to be checked in advance. You may wish to design a worksheet for pupils in order to focus the visit for them. However, it is important that the visit does not become a paperchase with pupils moving from one display to another looking for the right answer on their worksheets. The worksheets should be designed to encourage enquiry and self-discovery on the part of the pupils – closed questions will not extend the investigatory skills of pupils. You also need to consider how the visit will be followed up for the maximum learning potential of the visit to be achieved. Pupils could gather evidence together to be used in a number of subsequent lessons. Adams and Millar (1982) provide some good examples of how to use artefacts on site visits, whilst Anderson and Moore (1994) and McKinley (1984) provide some excellent advice on planning and preparing for field trips. Table 9.2 gives some idea of the range of visits and the type of focus they may have.

Table 9.2 Visits and their focus

Visits	Focus
Locality/town	Street names, town planning . . .
Landscape/sites	Battle sites, outline of town walls . . .
Archaeological remains	Ruins of old buildings . . .
Buildings	Cathedrals, castles, manor houses . . .
Museums	War museums, local history museums . . .
Art galleries	Second World War paintings, medieval paintings . . .
Theatre/cinema	Historical plays/films/music . . .

MANAGING RESOURCES

Whilst the National Curriculum outlined what study units were to be taught it left the school to devise an answer to the problem of resourcing them. Brierly and Parsons (1993) have advocated that computers be used for searching for resources and also to obtain an evaluation of their usefulness. The BBC's Education site on the World Wide Web is an example of the potential of this approach, which saves you having to trawl through cyberspace using your own, time-consuming searches (BBC, 1997). Perhaps the most important point is one of approach and attitude. Most schools do not possess a wide range of resource facilities, nor do they all have resource centres. Local education authorities have reduced the number of resource centres for history in recent years to such an extent that resource centres with indexed collections of resources specifically for history are now rare. This places even greater emphasis on the history department to establish and maintain a resource collection, however humble. *Initiative and imagination are essential attributes of any history teacher wishing to play a full part in the development of the department's resources.* Some student teachers tend to be over-reliant on the resources which the history department possesses. Although this is understandable in the first few weeks of school experience, as the course progresses, you should increasingly be finding and developing your own resources and materials, and feeding them into the departmental stockpile. One of the factors which may well be influential in the department's assessment of your level of competence is the extent to which you have made a positive contribution to the department's resources in the course of your school experience. This can also include contributions to display work and site and museum visits. It is also important that you are careful to look after departmental resources. Text and topic books are precious and costly resources; if you give them out, make sure that you count the books in, and don't lend departmental resources to pupils without clearing it with the department and taking all appropriate administrative measures.

Each history teacher needs to manage his or her resources and learning experiences. Therefore, you need to be aware of the opportunities to create new resources from cheap and easily obtainable materials. Resources should be easy to handle, collect and store and you could begin your personal collection by the use of envelopes and file boxes to store modest amounts of resources. Nevertheless, your teaching strategies can often be your best resource. You should learn to make full use of the white/blackboard with different coloured pens/chalks. You need to direct pupils to reference texts and public libraries. 'Talk, textbooks and note-taking' can be excellent resources and must not be underestimated or over-used. The use of role-play, simulations and games in the history classroom need not be excluded, especially as they can encourage enjoyment, cooperation and a sense of involvement among pupils. Whilst Farmer and Knight (1995) make an extremely good case for the use of games, simulations and drama in history you need to bear in mind whether or not it is history. Such activities can be useful on occasions, but not as a basis for teaching history.

Often, such activities need to be complemented by sessions which clarify and consolidate factual detail and overview. Remember that *ideas* for teaching are also a form of resource, as well as materials. Television, radio and the press are also potentially valuable areas for augmenting resources for the history classroom. Newspaper articles on present-day problems such as nationalism, poverty, warfare and government are often effective ways of linking the present with the past and giving history more explicit relevance in the eyes of pupils.

TASK 9.8 LOOKING FOR RESOURCES: NEWSPAPERS AND TELEVISION

Over a period of several days (a week would be ideal), look through the newspapers and cut out any articles which you might be able to use in your teaching. Look through the listings for television programmes for the week and make a note of programmes which might be of use or relevance to the history teacher, other than school broadcasts for history.

History projects are often popular among pupils and can result in pupils searching out their own resources, but usually only with clear guidance from the teacher. When appropriately and skilfully structured they can make a valuable contribution to Key Element 4, historical enquiry, but without careful thought they can also result in much low-level copying and cutting and pasting work. This can also be helpful preparation for GCSE work, where part of the public examination is assessed through course work. Projects can be a sophisticated area of research, and pupils will need to be introduced to basic research methods, including the use of libraries; even interview techniques can be very valuable. Parsons (1996) sheds light on some of the problems of oral history and how they can be minimised. Computer technology can also encourage learning and has much potential for the history classroom. OFSTED reports on history claim that the potential of IT is often not fully exploited by history departments (OFSTED, 1993a). History teachers need to be aware of the opportunities which new technology offers, and you will no doubt be introduced to information technology as part of your course. The knowledge you acquire on your course should be applied directly in the classroom whenever possible, and you should be aware that there is a growing amount of computer-based materials for use by history teachers on the market, such as CD-ROMs and computer simulations. This technology is expensive and often beyond the reach of some history departments, but it should be understood and used whenever the opportunity arises. You should read Chapter 8 for more detailed consideration of these resources.

The question of how to evaluate what is collected is also important. Is the format and layout of your resources attractive? Is the language used appropriate for the ability range? Do the sentences flow? Are the illustrations clear and related to the text? Are they varied? Is the content accurate? Is it suitable for existing study units? Do the viewpoints expressed give an appropriate range of historical perspectives? Each department needs to establish guidelines on the use of resources and how to monitor and evaluate such use. It is also important that you evaluate your own use of resources in class lessons during your school experience.

TASK 9.9 MANAGING RESOURCES

You have arrived in your second school placement and you need to make a quick assessment of the resources available to you within the history department and school. In consultation with your mentors compile an audit of these resources. In your audit remember to include:

- the expertise of members of staff;
- the range of textbooks used for each year group;
- the classroom facilities (blackboard, display areas, wallcharts, etc.);
- historical sources (pictures, objects, music, etc.);
- Teaching aids (OHP, TV, cassette, camera, etc.);
- Library (school resources centre, photocopying, reference books for staff);
- Cross-curricular (access to other materials held in other departments);
- Outside visits and speakers (what is available in the local community?);
- Information technology provision, in terms of computers, software and current departmental use.

CONCLUSION

There is no necessary correlation between the sophistication and expense of the resources used and the quality of the learning experience for pupils. It is important that pupils experience a variety of resources and teaching methods, but a lesson which involves no more than teacher talk and pupil talk may be more successful than one involving an array of technological aids. The most important resource of all is you, and the skilful and effective use of the teaching strategies you decide to employ. Often the main resources used by the teacher are talk, the blackboard, displays and the use of paper and notebooks. Books, source materials in books, and worksheets are also widely used, but slides, videos, role-play, games, artefacts, computer technology, TV, museums, and field trips are not always feasible in terms of everyday use – access, finance and school organisation often place limits on what can be attempted. Your task is to do the best job possible in the circumstances. Foresight, initiative and imagination are part of the art of using resources effectively, and a sureness of touch in working out 'fitness for purpose' is something which should accrue from increased experience and reflection.

You need to remember Shemilt's (1987) research findings that many pupils use sources in the same way as textbook narratives. You need to be appraised of the problems pupils have in understanding historical sources and consider how best to use sources at different levels as classroom resources. Resources certainly help pupils to be active in their own learning and can often play a significant part in motivating them to do well in history. A greater understanding of the past should be possible when you use a variety of resources in your teaching. The intelligent use of resources will ensure that history teaching does not focus on a narrow range of activities.

FURTHER READING:

Brooks, R., Aris, M. and Perry, I. (1993) *The Effective History Teacher*, London, Longman.
Mary Aris's chapter on resources is a good basic introduction to the use of resources.

Danks, E.J. (1994) 'Theory and Practice Essay: The Use of Resources and Teaching Aides in the Teaching of History, with Particular Reference to Year Eight, *Teaching History*, October, No. 77.

Lloyd-Jones, R. ([1985] 1995) *How to Produce Better Worksheets*, London, Stanley Thomas.
An excellent general guide to designing worksheets.

10 Assessment in the classroom

INTRODUCTION

The organisation of a book about teaching which considers assessment in a separate chapter – and that towards the end of the book – could in itself send out an incorrect message. For it is fundamental that if assessment is to be used successfully by the classroom teacher it must be integrated within the whole process of planning. The well-worn maxim that 'effective assessment depends on effective planning' is as true as ever. Consequently, the way in which you provide feedback to your pupils' and both record and report on their progress, will be very much related to the clarity of your teaching and learning objectives, together with *your* choice of learning experiences.

This important relationship between planning, methods and assessment means that the vast changes in the teaching of history in the last thirty years have also had a considerable impact on how learning in history is assessed. A generation ago the principal concerns were to assess the recall of knowledge, to reward the ability to select information relevant to a question and to deploy that knowledge in standard English. Differentiation was achieved in the accuracy, quantity and literary quality of the answers.

With the evolution of the 'new' history, teachers and examiners have to consider how to assess pupils' progress in their use of sources, their under-standing of key concepts, of past ideas and attitudes and, more recently, of historical interpretations and representations. Such changes made it even more imperative that the concept of progression in historical understanding was researched and applied to the assessment of that understanding. The devel-opment of 'levels' marking schemes at 16+, and the later TGAT model with its ten levels for the National Curriculum, implied the existence of a generally acceptable model of how pupils' historical understanding progresses. It may be argued that the problems experienced in the early years of both the GCSE and the National Curriculum were in part related to the limited and inconsistent application of any theoretical basis, and the lack of a universally acceptable model which would explain pupils' progression in historical understanding.

More recent developments suggest such issues are now being addressed, and the difficulties of defining 'levels' in history more clearly acknowledged.

The diversity of approaches and resources now available to the history teacher encourages the need for a corresponding variety of assessment procedures. You will notice how some pupils perform better in some situations than others: some are good orally while not so good with written work; some work well in small groups but not so well in whole-class situations; while some produce good work if given time and the opportunities for redrafting mentioned in Chapter 4. So you will need to be aware of that variety of assessment possibilities which extends beyond written responses, but also includes oral assessment together with other more ephemeral, yet significant, evidence of understanding that will occur. John Fines (1994) emphasised the point when he wrote, 'We must not allow assessment to cut out all the children with literary problems and we must be ready to see at any specific moment in the classroom, high achievement when it is happening. We must find time to stop and record them and honour it.'

OBJECTIVES

At the end of this chapter you should have:

- become aware of some of the key issues which affect the assessment of history;
- understood the recent recommendations for the use of both the formative and summative assessment of pupils' progress at Key Stage 3;
- gained some guidance about the setting of tasks and the marking, recording and reporting on pupils' progress.

KEY ISSUES IN THE ASSESSMENT OF HISTORY

The introduction of the GCSE in 1988 and the National Curriculum for history in 1991 have had a major impact on the way historical knowledge and understanding has been assessed. Teachers who have been working through the last decade have experienced a period of almost continuous change as original practices and advice have been reshaped and refined. The revised versions of both the National Curriculum (1995) and the GCSE (1998) have benefited from reflection on that hectic period of development and should bring about more consensual and user-friendly approaches to the assessment of pupils' progress. The nature of the changes means that some parts of the textbooks and teaching materials of the pre-1995 period will now seem obsolete. Such publications specifically refer to the original attainment targets and the assessment objectives. Nevertheless, although approaches may change and different procedures be advocated, there are some underlying and interrelated issues relating to assessment in history that you need to consider whatever the current emphases may be. Such issues involve (1) the use of knowledge, (2) progression, (3) differentiation, and (4) the validity and reliability of your assessment.

The role of knowledge

The role of historical knowledge in assessment has become the subject of much debate. There has taken place what to many would seem to have been a rather artificial debate which sought to place the advocates of knowledge (traditional history) against those of skills (new history). Most history teachers accepted that the learning of history required both skills and knowledge. Assessment which attempted to test skills without reference to the historical context was as arid as the recall of information without understanding was of limited value. Recent developments in both the National Curriculum and the GCSE have attempted to restore a balance. This has involved an attempt to increase the emphasis to be given to historical knowledge.

The challenge for you is to determine how that knowledge is to be used. Some pupils gain great satisfaction and a real sense of achievement when they are able to recall information, and there is a place for this in your assessment – particularly with the younger pupils. The ability to commit some information to memory is still an important skill, in life as well as in examinations. The danger is, of course, that history is once more seen as a subject whose prime objective is the memorisation of facts. Two issues may be highlighted:

• What is historical knowledge?
• Are there gradations of historical knowledge?

How you respond to these questions will influence your thinking about how to assess your pupils.

What is historical knowledge?

If you are trying to assess historical knowledge you need to have a clear understanding of what this means. To those listening to general knowledge quizzes, the answer may seem obvious – the ability to recall historical facts with accuracy. Others may settle for the ability to describe a historical event in some detail. For either of these, short-answer objective tests or requests to 'write all you know about' would be suitable forms of assessment and were indeed familiar features in the history classroom a couple of decades ago. (There may be still a case for the interim testing of factual knowledge, but this is seen as securing the basis for further applications of that knowledge.) So, while accepting the need to be able to deploy accurate information, if this is done without also demonstrating understanding, such assessment has little educational value. The issue thus becomes: how can you assess historical knowledge in a way that enables the pupils to show understanding as well?

It is now generally accepted that historical knowledge is much more than factual knowledge and also includes knowledge of explanations of events, changes and issues, and knowledge of the historical process; for example, what procedures do you adopt for analysing evidence or what questions should you ask when confronted by differing interpretations? The issue then is how can you assess such aspects of historical knowledge while still rewarding factual knowledge.

Are there gradations in historical knowledge?

If assessment were to be based solely upon historical knowledge what would be the basis for discrimination? Traditionally, the answers would have centred upon quantity and accuracy. These characteristics continue to feature in criteria for assessment, but the problems of a narrow focus on factual knowledge were increased when 'levels of reponse' mark schemes began to appear in the early 1980s, and even more so with the National Curriculum Attainment Target levels. If history was to have an Attainment Target assessing knowledge, what knowledge would characterise level 1 and what level 10? Such a question seemed only to emphasise the limitations of such assessment, and, not surprisingly, specific knowledge is not included in the Attainment Target statements.

But can we be so dismissive about the relative value of historical knowledge? It is possible to argue that knowledge will be rewarded *either* for the way in which it is acquired *or* for the way in which it is used. Your pupils' historical knowledge is likely to be worthy of praise if it has been acquired as a result of the use of initiative and the use of enquiry and reference skills. Higher rewards are also likely to be available for knowledge not immediately available to the pupil or candidates in sources or descriptions of a context. Should that knowledge be used to demonstrate the wider significance of a topic, to make links, connections and perhaps generalisations, then again this is likely to be graded more highly. Within a levels marking scheme what often pushes a mark to the top of a level is the extent to which knowledge is used to support that level of understanding. The real requirement is for pupils to be able to *apply* their knowledge to inform their opinions and judgements.

Even though due attention is paid to the use of knowledge, there will often remain the need to maintain a balance between rewarding the use of knowledge and the relationship between knowledge and levels of understanding. For example, supposing you were to set a task, the main purpose of which was to assess the pupils' understanding of historical interpretations. Pupil A *described* in detail the differences between the two interpretations and used plenty of factual information to support the answer. Pupil B was able to make some attempt at *explaining* the differences, with some (but not a lot of) factual support. Who gets the higher mark? This question of balance has again been a feature of the debate over the last ten years and remains a key issue. What is important is that you continue to *think* carefully about the relation between knowledge and understanding. Lee has pointed out that

> learning history is difficult, and does not take place in a flash at 18 or even at 25. It is a gradual process of developing ideas, in which pupils need a great deal of help. A substantial part of what is learned has to be *knowing-how*, not just *knowing-that*. Some of what children have to learn is not in itself historical knowledge at all, but provides crutches and tools for assisting them to acquire that knowledge.
>
> (Lee, 1994)

TASK 10.1 THE ROLE OF HISTORICAL KNOWLEDGE

1 Discuss with the subject teachers in your school how they encourage their pupils to recall and use their historical knowledge. On what occasions are the pupils required to recall their historical knowledge (a) orally, and (b) in writing? Do they have a different emphasis for the ability to recall and use historical knowledge for Key Stage 3 pupils in comparison to GCSE pupils? Consider how the responses might influence the objectives you formulate and the tasks you set.

2 With two different age groups (e.g year 7 or 8 and year 10), ask the pupils the following question, 'If a pupil is "good at history?", how do we know?' Compare their answers to your own answer to this question. What do the pupils answers tell you about their understanding of history?

3 Present a group of year 7 or 8 pupils with two pictures, relating to a topic they have covered, for comparison (e.g. a motte and bailey castle and a concentric castle). Ask the pupils to draw two columns, one headed 'How they differ' and the other 'Why they differ'. Ask them to try to complete the columns. When assessing their reponses, consider the role of knowledge in your final judgement. Are you rewarding the quantity or the quality of the knowledge used?

PROGRESSION

The issue of progression raises fundamental questions which will influence your whole approach to teaching and setting tasks for pupils. Two of the elements of competence in subject application stipulated by *Circular 9/92* were 'to ensure continuity and progression within and between classes and in subjects', and 'to set appropriately demanding expectations for pupils' (DfE, 1992). Standards for progression in *Circular 10/97* are detailed in Section B, a, i–v (see Appendix). Without some understanding of progression it will be difficult for you to fulfil the demands of these competence statements, and to set tasks which will provide the information to enable you to assess pupils of differing abilities. Lomas (1990) emphasises the point when stating that without an awareness of progression, 'there is a real danger that pupils will be faced with tasks beyond them or below their capabilities, may not provide a challenge, have to jump unevenly between stages and repeat too many ideas they are already clear about'.

So what does the concept of progression mean in the context of learning history? More factual knowledge? Extended vocabulary? Better literary skills? If progression is related to historical understanding, what characterises better understanding of key concepts such as causation, change and the attitudes of differing past societies? How can we identify progression in the development of source skills and in the ability to handle historical interpretations? Much has been written to help you to understand the basis for progression in the learning of history. Together the work of Hallam (1972), Watts (1973), Shemilt (1976), Booth (1983) and Dickinson and Lee (1984) cover much of the debate about how children's historical understanding develops and its implications for teachers. Opinions have varied about the age at which pupils are able to understand the complex relationship between factors and events, are able to hypothesise, use abstractions and formulate generalisations. Problems have been identified when progression is limited to those aspects of history requiring analysis, interpretation and evaluation to the exclusion of activities which require imagination, creativity and historical empathy.

Nevertheless, Lomas (1990) has demonstrated that it is possible to identify certain signposts for progression in history which you can apply to the setting and marking of your pupils' work. Lomas has listed several interrelated criteria (which not surprisingly have similarities with the characteristics of the able pupil in history described in Chapter 7):

- greater historical knowledge with which to substantiate statements and judgements;
- ability to categorise, see patterns, summarise and generalise, a grasp of essentials from a mass of detail;
- ability to make connections and links between issues, problems of different

periods including the present; the ability to focus on the more significant issues; an increasing awareness of the relevance of the topic and its wider significance;

- ability to move from the concrete to abstract concepts;
- ability to explain rather than just describe;
- ability to be precise, a concern for accuracy and the limitations of accuracy indicative of clarity of thought;
- an independence of thought, ability to pose questions, hypothesise, devise ways of finding answers;
- to have an informed scepticism, an inclination to qualify statements with elements of uncertainty, yet still be prepared to reach conclusions.

Your skill as a teacher is therefore quite crucial, for if pupils are to demonstrate the extent to which they are making progress, then they need the kind of tasks and experiences which will reveal such development.

More recently, SCAA (1996) have produced a chart which describes progression in the Key Elements of the National Curriculum (see Figure 10.1). Whatever theories of progression you employ in the assessment of pupils' work it is important they are not applied too rigidly. Pupils' responses will differ according to the context and the nature of the task so that they may appear to be regressing at times.

TASK 10.2 IDENTIFYING PROGRESSION IN HISTORY

You will find it useful to see how various notions of progression have influenced the National Curriculum and the GCSE.

1 Ask the history department in which you are placed if you may look at the original documentation for the 1991 Orders. Look carefully at all three Attainment Targets and try to identify any principles that underpin the level statements.
2 Compare these statements with those in the single Attainment Target for the revised 1995 Orders. Extract those sentences which are comparable (e.g. causation, interpretations, use of sources). How much do they differ? Note the key words in the new Orders, 'describe', 'explain', etc.
3 Ask your history department if they possess any of the marking schemes produced by a GCSE Examination Board. Again analyse these to identify any principles of progression which underpin the levels of response.
4 Finally, compare what you have found out with Figure 10.1.

Range and depth of historical knowledge and understanding

Chronology (1a and 1b)
- Sequencing events and objects, using everyday terms
- Using a simple chronological framework, using dates and terms which describe the passing of time
- Using a wider chronological framework, using dates and conventions which describe historical periods
- Making links and connections, using chronological understanding to evaluate change and continuity

Key features (2a)
- Making a distinction between past and present
- Describing characteristic features
- Making links, connections and comparisons
- Describing the diversity of past societies
- Analysing and explaining relationships between features

Reasons and results (2b)
- Recognising and describing reasons and results
- Describing and making links between reasons, events and changes
- Analysing reasons and results of events
- Setting analysis in wider historical context

Making links and connections (2c)
- Identifying similarities and differences within and across periods
- Describing and making links between features of societies and periods
- Analysing relationships between events, people and changes
- Setting analysis in wider historical context

Ascribing significance (2d)
- Assessing the significance of events, people and changes

Interpretations (3a and 3b)
- Recognising answers to questions from a source
- Describing and giving reasons for different representations and interpretations
- Describing and analysing interpretations
- Analysing and evaluating interpretations in relation to their period

Historical enquiry (4a and 4b)
- Finding answers to questions from a source
- Asking questions, selecting and combining information from sources
- Evaluating sources as part of an enquiry
- Evaluating sources and reaching conclusions as part of an enquiry
- Carrying out enquiries and reaching independent substantiated conclusions

Organisation and communication (5a, 5b and 5c)
- Communicating information
- Structuring accounts, making use of dates and terms in response to questions
- Selecting and organising information, making use of dates and terms to produce narratives, descriptions and explanations
- Producing structured analytical narratives, descriptions and explanations, making use of dates and terms, supporting valid conclusions with evidence

Figure 10.1 Progression in the key elements

DIFFERENTIATION

A further issue, linked to progression, is that of differentiation. It is possible to argue that setting differentiated tasks is one of the most difficult activities in teaching. OFSTED (1995) comment on the general lack of differentiation. 'At worst this saw classes doing the same work which was unchallenging to some of the pupils and inaccessible to others.' In history teaching, any such differentation must be based on a clear understanding of those factors which make a task easier or more difficult, hence again the importance of progression. It is important to be aware that there are many factors influencing the extent to which the learning of all pupils can be maximised (see Lewis, 1992; Biggs and Moore, 1993), but two of the commonest approaches to differentiation in the history classroom are 'by outcome' or 'by task'. 'By outcome' means that the whole range of pupils in a class, year or examination cohort are given the same assessment exercise or examination paper with questions set in such a way that pupils can respond according to their ability. The revised History GCSE continues to use this approach to differentiation even though there are criticisms of this method, well articulated by Checketts (1996). The GCSE approach may well have encouraged its overuse in schools, as indicated in the OFSTED inspectors' advice on differentiation in the Hampshire County Council publication *History Matters: 13*. There the inspectors felt that inappropriate use can become frustrating to pupils who need a more structured approach to enable them to give of their best. 'Differentiation by outcome' is more likely to work well for tasks which require creativity, imagination, investigations and empathetic reconstructions, when the pupils have a clear idea of the assessment criteria. 'By outcome' has been described as the more 'comfortable' option by OFSTED, and this is because differentiation 'by task' is generally regarded as being more difficult. Planning work which addresses different levels of conceptual understanding is a skilful business. You need not only to know the abilities of the individual pupils but also to understand the nature of progression in history. You must also remember that another important part of differentiation is the pupil's attitude to the task. If pupils are to perform to their 'personal best', to borrow a phrase used in athletics, it helps if they want to do well and are enthusiastically engaged in the process of learning. As Hallam (1996) notes, 'If you can't motivate the student, you will lose everything.' Hallam also stresses the importance of the following factors:

- valuing and encouraging all pupils – including the clever ones and the quiet ones;
- allowing pupils to make mistakes;
- making learning objectives explicit and explaining the criteria for doing the task well;

- providing accurate and positive feedback;
- taking into account that pupils have differing preferred learning styles when planning teaching and assessment activities.

(Hallam, 1996)

Your methods of assessing pupils' achievement in history should keep in mind all these factors.

Applying differentiation to your assessment

Setting written assessment topics to take account of different abilities requires the consideration of issues such as:

1 *Making sure your pupils write as fully as they can.* This can be helped by giving *precise indications* of your expectations. For example, instead of 'give reasons for' ask 'Give at least *five* reasons for'. With younger pupils you might, where appropriate, suggest they write 'at least 10 lines' for their answer.

2 The extent to which *you will provide a structure* for the pupils' answers. This might include the use of several short questions in a helpful sequence leading to the main question, or giving some indications about the required content. For example, providing some causes of an event for comment and then asking pupils to add to this list before writing a full response. In other words, helping the pupil by breaking down the task into manageable parts or providing the first sentence of a response. An issue of differentiation arises if you give too much help to the more able pupils, who would be better assessed with a more general or open-ended task.

3 *The format of the tasks* can involve differentiation. This could involve the extent to which you want to include objective items. Such items often require more limited writing and may be appropriate for some pupils. Consequently, you might find some place for making lists, labelling, the completion of sentences, sequencing exercises and, at times, the use of multiple-choice questions. All of these considerably reduce the amount of writing, but should also prompt you to keep asking what you are assessing. While there are exceptions, the use of short, objective test items could encourage the assessment of knowledge without understanding and, of course, be inappropriate for the ability of many pupils. Another useful 'rule of thumb' is that the more you reduce the number of sources and 'variables' involved in a task, the more likely you will be to make it more accessible to pupils of lower abilities.

4 A further issue is the relationship between the use of differentiated assessment and norm-referencing. If pupils are set tasks according to their ability so that they can demonstrate what they can do, you may need to have some

sensitivity in making the less able pupils aware of the limitations of their success. Otherwise they may hold unrealistic notions about their level of performance when compared with others and assessed against the levels of the Attainment Target. Similarly, you need to take into account the level of support provided when assessing the quality of your pupils' responses.

TASK 10.3 ASSESSMENT AND DIFFERENTIATION

Choose a topic which you know you will be teaching on your placement to a class with a wide range of ability. When you have familiarised yourself with the content and the available resources, select as a target a Key Element or part of a Key Element for which that content and those resources present an appropriate vehicle.

Plan *three* different task-sheets for the different abilities, taking into account the following: (a) the use of language involved for both the instructions and any sources; (b) the appearance of the sheet (where possible making use of IT facilities); (c) the use of abstract concepts; (d) the number, variety and nature of any sources used; (e) the range and progression of skills you wish the pupils to employ; (f) your expectations about the amount of knowledge you wish them to use; and (g) your expectations about the length and format of their responses.

Try to ensure that there is a very noticeable difference in demand between the tasks for the ablest and the least able pupils.

Discuss your task sheets with the teacher and, if convenient to the department, use them.

The validity and reliability of your assessment

In assessing your pupils you need to be constantly aware of the factors that can affect the validity and reliability of the information you acquire. A task may be said to be valid if it achieves what it is intended to do; if it measures what you think you are measuring; if it clearly addresses the assessment targets you have in mind. Several factors can limit validity.

First, one of the most common reasons for a test being of limited validity is *because the question has been poorly formulated*. That could mean that the pupils are confused about what they have to do; that it is ambiguous and your instructions are unclear and you may be asking the pupils to try to read your mind and guess what it is you want. Alternatively the question you have devised is actually testing a different set of objectives than you thought. Finding the best words and phrases for a question or task is much harder than you might initially believe and usually needs plenty of thought and time. Because of this, if you do create or find tasks that work well store them away for future use.

Second, if the tasks are dependent on sources, as many are, then you need to make sure the *sources are not inaccessible* but are appropriate for the ability level.

Third, you also need to consider whether the pupils have access to the *amount of knowledge* they will require for a good answer. Also, a test loses validity if the pupils are being assessed on content, skills or concepts which they have not been taught. In the SCAA (1996) Optional Tests and Tasks, the question is constantly asked 'Are the pupils ready for this assessment?' and invites consideration of the knowledge of the content and the understanding of historical concepts required of the pupils if they are to attempt the task with any degree of success. There are implications here for situations where there are several history teachers teaching different classes which are all given the same test or examination. Should your pupils not be given sufficient time to complete a task, this will again affect the validity of any assessment made.

A task is considered to be reliable if it is as likely as possible to produce the same results again. Once more, there are many situations which can adversely affect reliability and some you may well be able to do little about. These can include the physical conditions in which the pupils work (the light, temperature and noise). Other factors include the opportunities for help or copying and the effect of nerves, when attempting a formal summative test.

A task is potentially less reliable if there are several teachers involved in the marking. Hence the need for clear mark schemes which can be consistently interpreted and the identification of clear criteria for the marking. This helps to diminish the subjective aspects of marking, such as your opinion about an individual pupil's attitude to history, his or her usual behaviour, or the clarity of the writing.

Assessment and the National Curriculum

With some anguish, much has been learned by history teachers and their advisers about the mechanics of assessing National Curriculum History in the last five years. The New Order that has emerged from that experience is more holistic, less divided into discrete skills and concepts and generally more user-friendly. As such it is more likely to promote good practice in the classroom. (For a more detailed analysis of the impact of the TGAT 10-level scale on assessment in the history classroom, see Booth and Husbands, 1993; Haydn, 1994.)

The onus is now placed on history departments to plan schemes of work which, across the Study Units, cover all the Key Elements. Within such schemes pupils will be required to produce work from which their progress in the Key Elements can be assessed. Some of the tasks could well cover more than one element (e.g. chronology is often subsumed within the concept of change). Over a period of time you will need to gather a selection of pupils' work covering the range of the Key Elements and also including a range of tasks and a variety of contexts. Only when such a collection has been acquired are you asked to use the level descriptions as a basis for a summative judgement about a pupil's performance. Figure 10.2 may help to summarise the process. The shaded tasks, covering a range of Key Elements, are those retained for the summative assessment.

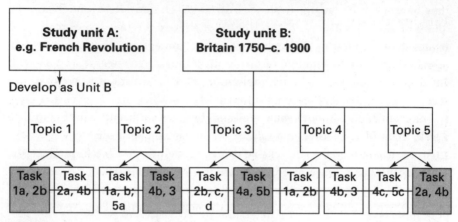

Figure 10.2 Using the level descriptions as a basis for summative judgement of a pupil's progress

Bennett and Steele (1995) emphasise the point that level descriptions were not designed as teaching and learning objectives to be used for what is to be assessed on a day-to-day basis. Where such practice was used it 'sometimes resulted in pupils having a fragmented and artificial experience of history'. In making summative judgements you will be looking for the 'best fit' description to identify the level of a particular pupil. Such judgement will also be augmented by other evidence such as oral contributions, work with groups and any other ephemeral evidence which you may happen to notice. The SCAA (1996) publication, *Exemplification of Standards in History: KS3*, together with the four units of optional tests and tasks, will help you and your colleagues achieve some consistency in your assessment. What is important is the need to develop worthwhile activities and appropriate tasks to produce the data from which to make such judgements. This re-emphasises the importance of anticipating the needs of assessment in your planning.

Although only one or two tasks from an individual topic will contribute to your *summative* judgement of a pupil, the remainder still have an important function in your day-to-day teaching, the *formative* assessment of pupils' progress. Such tasks enable you both to give the pupils feedback on their work with pointers for further development and to gain further information about the effectiveness of your teaching. The marking methods you will use will usually follow the school and department policies of the school in which you are working. There is plenty of evidence to show that pupils welcome early feedback on their work, which is likely to increase their motivation. Again, what you are not advised to do is to try to relate the assessment of individual pieces of work to the attainment target levels.

Linking a scheme of work to assessment

Figure 10.4 is a scheme of work on the Black Death. This is not set out in the established format but in a way which shows the clear links between the objectives, the content, the learning experiences and the materials which the pupils will produce which will contribute to their assessment. While it is not necessary to cover all Key Elements within a scheme of work or indeed a unit, you may find it helpful to construct an assessment grid, which shows how the Key Elements are linked to the content. The grid in Figure 10.3 shows the distribution of the elements within the scheme of work on the Black Death.

Content/Issue	1a	1b	2a	2b	2c	2d	3a	3b	4a	4b	5a	5b	5c
What was the Black Death? What were the symptoms?	x		x										x
What were the causes?				x					x		x		x
Why are there different interpretations of the causes?				x			x						x
What can we learn about the attitudes of people at the time from the study of the Black Death?		x	x										
What were the results of the Black Death?				x				x	x		x	x	
How does the Black Death fit into a chronological overview?	x				x								x
What is the significance of the Black Death?	x				x								x

Figure 10.3 Assessment grid for work on the Black Death

Enquiry	Learning Experiences	Resources, materials	Product
To enable the pupils: 1 To be able to describe what the Black Death was and to describe its symptoms [Key Element: 5 (c)]	Presentation involving video, textbook or information sheet. Pupils to draw own pictures of the symptoms	Video, textbooks, information sheet	Brief description plus drawings Produce 'Health Warning' brochure using only contemporary ideas
2 To give reasons for the outbreak of the Black Death [2b] To evaluate sources on the Black Death and to consider their utility for an enquiry into the causes of the Black Death [4b]	Source work: pupils are presented with a set of sources and the dates of the sources from which they are asked to identify the causes [group activity] Categorisation of sources – divide between contemporary and modern	Sets of sources for pair/group work and/or class teaching Exercise books	Creation of sets of causation cards Creation of a spray-diagram with contemporary explanations on one side and more modern on the other
To explain how and why different explanations have been produced over the years [3]	Class teaching – discuss the utility of the sources in turn and ask pupils to prioritise. Discuss reasons for the differing opinions offered by the sources	Sets of blank cards	Written paragraph explaining the differing explanations
3 To understand the attitudes and beliefs of people at the time of the Black Death as a feature of a past society [2a]	Radio play – reading; question and answer and then second reading. Select a character from the play and write to a relative about the plague, showing attitudes which were prevalent at the time	Duplicated set of teacher-written 'radio-plays' Exercise books	Piece of empathetic writing

Objectives	Key question	Teaching activities	Resources	Outcomes
4 Tc acquire some understanding of the results of the Black Death [2b] Tc develop further their use of general and subject-specific concepts e.g. *feudalism, serfdom, supply and demand for labour, commutation (able only)* [5b] To select and organise historical information [5a]	What were the results of the Black Death?	Group work. Pupils given textbooks, some recent, others which have been around some time, and asked to make lists of what they think were the results of the Black Death. Encourage to consider (a) short-term and (b) long-term results	Range of textbooks	Creation of a two-column chart, divided between short-term and long-term results Write an account explaining the results
5 Tc be able to show the effect of the Black Death on the size of the population and be able to relate that to a wider demographic overview [2c] Tc place the Black Death in the history of plagues [1a; 2c]	How does the Black Death fit into a chronological overview? • of demography? • of the history of plagues?	Draw time-charts, making links showing the rise and fall of the population and the history of plagues. Those able to research information about plagues abroad and over a wider period of time.	Blackboard or OHP Completion charts	Time-charts Written descriptions of what the charts tell
6 Tc identify why the Black Death was a significant event in history [2d]	What was the significance of the Black Death?	Group work: choose FIVE reasons why the Black Death was important in history	Decision sheets	Written accounts of why the Black Death was a significant event in history

Figure 10.4 Scheme of work on the Black Death

Of the pupils' work which results from such a scheme, only one or two pieces from each pupil will need to be retained for the purposes of summative assessment. Which you choose may well depend on the pieces to be used from other topics and also on your impressions about the validity and reliability of the tasks you have set. Thus, predictably, your skill in setting tasks becomes an important part of assessing pupils' progress. Again the SCAA (1996) documents mentioned above give helpful examples of successful practice.

TASK 10.4 ASSESSING THE SIGNIFICANCE OF AN EVENT

One of the more challenging, though welcome, features of the Key Elements is 2d, by which pupils should be encouraged to assess the significance of events, people and changes. This is difficult for pupils because they lack the widespread knowledge and the abstract levels of thinking which are needed to achieve this requirement. For some pupils you may feel that this particular requirement is too difficult with many topics. Pupils also need to know the difference between the results of an event and its significance. Not without reason is this final part of Key Element 2 pushed to the 'difficult' end of the progression scale (see Figure 10.1) showing progression in the Key Elements. For example, using textbooks, it is relatively straightforward to identify the results of the Black Death, but what of its significance?

Consider the following approach.

1 Discuss with the pupils why we need to understand the significance of an event. Why was it important and how does it help us in our understanding of history? Why can some events in history be said to be more important than others? In order to judge the importance of an event, we need to look at not only what happened immediately after but sometimes centuries later. We can at times ask: how has that event affected our lives today?

2 Having dealt with all the usual aspects of the Black Death, try this activity with a year 7 class and find out just what they are capable of understanding.

3 Begin with a brainstorm, have they got any ideas why the Black Death might be an important event in history? (It will be interesting to note whether they mention any of the points on the worksheet. They may have others which are as good! One can never afford to underestimate what pupils are capable of, given the opportunity.)

4 Distribute a copy of the worksheet to each pupil. (See note on differentiation, '5' in this list.) Explain the layout and then go through

each item in turn; explain the meaning but try not to give too much away.

5 Explain their task. In groups they are to find out information from the selection of textbooks, some old, some new, and other information that might be available (e.g a print-off from a CD-ROM on the Black Death). The pupils have then to try to find out events and other information which supports (backs-up/substantiates) the statements on the left-hand side of the sheet. The pupils then fill in the box on the right-hand side. To help them they will need to be told to look for 'key words' in the contents pages and index, such as 'feudal', 'monasteries', 'wars or quarrels' with the king. Differentiation may be achieved by giving some pupils precise page references, while the very able could be encouraged to be critical of the statements presented and, if possible, make some suggestions of their own.

6 Feedback from the groups. Use the board to gather all the points, adding anything omitted yourself. Pupils to complete any gaps on their own sheet.

7 Set the final task. To use the information on the sheet to write a piece of extended writing (at least one side) as an answer to the top of the sheet, 'Why was the Black Death an important event in history?' Encourage them to use the 'back-up' information to support the general statements. Encourage the able to use their initiative to include extra information or additional reasons for the event's importance.

SIGNIFICANCE: Why was the Black Death an important event in history?

Using the textbooks and any other reference material available, try to complete the boxes on the right with information which supports the statements on the left.

The Black Death was important because:	*Back-up information*
It helped to bring about the end of the Feudal System.	
It led to the decline of the monasteries – monks were particularly hard hit (easier to take away their lands).	
It encouraged increased criticism of some people in the Church (though not	

of its teachings), as it was difficult to replace educated priests.	
It led to disputes about land, which increased the quarrels between the barons and the king and reduced his control and respect.	
It shows how people's explanations of the causes of events are affected by the ideas, beliefs and the knowledge of that time.	
It showed the extent of trade routes in the fourteenth century	
It led to the desertion of many villages, the extent of which has only been discovered since the use of aerial photography.	
It showed the contribution of economic factors to changes in history: e.g wages rise if there are fewer workers; prices rise if fewer goods are available.	

Marking, recording and reporting on pupils' progress

In their review of inspections OFSTED (1995) considered that the quality of record-keeping by history departments was 'highly variable'. It was accepted that the problems history teachers had experienced with the assessment of the 1991 National Curriculum had contributed to this. Systems vary from intensely detailed and time-consuming recording of every task, targeting discrete statements of attainment and placing ticks in boxes, to a broader, more holistic approach to give an overview. As indicated earlier, current policy would favour not using the Attainment Target statements for your formative assessment but placing more emphasis on diagnostic comments on the pupils' work, about what they have achieved and what they might achieve. Any marking scheme for a task would need to reflect the progressive levels of understanding appropriate to the objectives of the tasks and the use of relevant knowledge. The challenge is to achieve a balance in your recording of pupil work that is not excessively complex and time-consuming, yet is sufficiently detailed to enable you to build up a profile of a pupil's progress related to the Key Elements in a way that high-lights strengths and weaknesses. In addition it would be helpful to be able to supplement your records of written work with notes of that ephemeral evidence such as that which accrues from oral contributions, contribution to group work and the use of initiative in pursuing historical enquiries. It is often this type of evidence which is more easily communicable to parents. Remember, there is no requirement to determine a level of attainment for pupils until the end of the Key Stage; in the main your assessment should therefore be formative in nature.

TASK 10.5 THE MARKING, RECORDING AND REPORTING OF PUPILS' PROGRESSION

Marking and recording

In your placement schools, find out if there is a policy for: (a) the whole school; (b) the Faculty; and (c) the history department.

Discuss with your mentors the main features of any policy – purposes and procedures. Does the school use Records of Achievement (ROA), profiling, pupil negotiation, review and self-assessment? Make notes on the procedures and ask to talk to pupils about their own ROA. You will find it useful to read Chapter 3 of D.S. Frith and H.G. Macintosh (1984) *A Teacher's Guide to Assessment*.

History subject marking

How is this achieved? What use is made of the pupil's exercise book? How do the teachers organise and use their mark book? Do they reflect the Key Elements of the National Curriculum? Is it possible to identify the strengths and weaknesses of individual pupils in their ability to apply knowledge, use skills and understand concepts?

What use is made of ephemeral evidence – oral responses, contribution to group work, use of initiative in historical enquiries?

Reporting

How is the recorded information translated into material for reporting?: (a) to pupils; (b) for the school records; and (c) to parents.

What are the means by which the parents are informed of their child's progress?

SUMMARY AND KEY POINTS

There is more to getting better at history than simply accumulating factual information about the past. The Key Elements help to define some of the ways in which pupils make progress in history. The assessment of pupils' progress in history is a highly sophisticated and extremely challenging aspect of your teaching. Although it is acknowledged that assessment is always an imperfect procedure, it is important that you are familiar with some of the pitfalls and aware of some of the strategies to improve the validity and reliability of your assessment. You benefit from having a good understanding of the key issues involved in the assessment of history, and of the need to integrate assessment into your planning. Such planning should make sure that the Key Elements are covered by the range and diversity of the tasks you offer to cater for the different abilities and aptitudes of your pupils.

It helps if you make sure you are assessing what you think you are assessing, if you have a clear idea about your expectations and if these in turn are clearly communicated to the pupils. By working out in advance the kind of responses you are expecting and checking these against your objectives for the exercise, you are more likely to concentrate on these criteria when you come to mark your pupils' work. This will add to the reliability of your assessment by making it more objective and less dependent on 'impression' marking. Do not despair if you find it hard to devise activities and assessment tasks which provide both access and challenge for all pupils, in every lesson. As Stenhouse (1983) remarked, 'It is, like all tasks of high ambition, a strategy in the face of an impossible task.'

FURTHER READING

Bennett, S. and Steele, I. (1995) 'The Revised History Order', *Teaching History*, April.
A succinct and lucid guide to interpreting the implications for assessment of the revised history orders.

Dickinson, A. (1991) 'Assessment, Recording and Reporting Children's Achievements: From Changes to Genuine Gains', in R. Aldrich (ed.) *History in the National Curriculum*, London, Kogan Page, pp. 66–92.
The concluding section provides a summary of some of the principles which *should* underpin assessment in history.

Frith, D.S. and Macintosh, H.G. (1984) *A Teacher's Guide to Assessment*, Cheltenham, Stanley Thornes.
This remains an excellent introduction to the principal issues in assessment and is particularly useful for history teaching because history provides so many of the examples.

Lee, P. (1994) 'Historical Knowledge and the National Curriculum', in H. Bourdillon (ed.) *Teaching History*, London, Routledge, pp. 41–52.

SCAA (1997) *Key Stage 3 Assessment Arrangements: Non-core Subjects*, London, DfEE.
In four pages, summarises the statutory requirements for assessing and reporting at the end of Key Stage 3.
Effectively dispels the idea that pupils learn the facts first, and then start thinking about them.

White, C. (1992) *Strategies for the Assessment and Teaching of History*, London, Longman.
Although related to the unrevised GCSE and National Curriculum, it retains much that is of value.

There are a host of books and articles which accompanied the first versions of the GCSE and the National Curriculum which still have value; they do not, of course, include the more recent changes noted in this chapter and Chapter 11.

11 Teaching for external examinations

TEACHING GCSE HISTORY: INTRODUCTION

An examination designed for all 16-year-olds, the GCSE was introduced in 1988. This replaced the earlier O level examination, intended for the most able 20 per cent, and the CSE, which targeted the next 40 per cent of ability. So the GCSE was not just amalgamating the two existing examinations but was extending its candidature to *all* abilities. The concept of a common examination at 16 had been promoted for many years before 1988. Schools Council (1966) publications were discussing the possibility not long after the CSE had begun in 1965. An increasing number of teachers came to see its introduction as a valuable advance, not least because it reduced the teacher's dilemma about which exam to enter pupils for. Continued delays in the introduction of the common examination led to joint ventures by the O level and the CSE Boards to produce 16+ joint examinations in the 1980s, thereby pre-empting the advent of the new examination. The Schools Council History project produced its own 16+ examination and much of that experience was to inform the principal features of the History GCSE. These were, briefly, two written papers, one of which was to assess source skills and the other a combination of concepts, skills and knowledge. All candidates would produce coursework, which had to meet precise assessment objectives, and this was carefully moderated by newly created Regional Examination Boards, four in England, one for Wales and one for Northern Ireland. There were well over thirty different syllabuses from which schools could choose, and the coursework component ranged from 20 per cent to 50 per cent of the whole examination. Although there were some modifications, these syllabuses were to run for a decade until the revised format was introduced for 1998. Thus, you will be preparing candidates for this revised examination, which includes some significant changes from the original examinations; changes which reflect some of the debates arising from the experience of the original examination and the introduction of the National Curriculum.

OBJECTIVES

At the end of this chapter you should have:

* become familiar with the recent developments in the GCSE history examination;
* learned of possible approaches you may adopt when given a GCSE class to teach;
* become familar with recent developments in the teaching of A level history;
* learned of possible approaches you may use when asked to teach an A level class.

THE PRINCIPAL CHANGES IN THE REVISED GCSE

Coursework continues to be recognised as a form of assessment which can suitably complement the end of course examinations, and now it is intended that such coursework should build on the knowledge, skills and concepts which candidates have developed in their Key Stage 3 history. Schools continue to be allowed to construct their own coursework tasks, under the guidance of an exam board, to fit their own schemes of work and resources. However, coursework can now contribute only a maximum of 25 per cent of the total assessment of the examination. This usually means the completion of two coursework assignments, each often subdivided to cover different objectives. This reduction has resulted from some concern about its supervision and authentication, together with variable factors such as home background. Thus, one finds, for example, the NEAB (1996) advising that 'as much coursework as possible must be conducted under the direct supervision of teachers' and that 'if candidates undertake activities outside their supervision, some work associated with the activity must be undertaken under the direct supervision of teachers to allow the teachers concerned to authenticate each candidate's work with confidence'.

There have been some significant changes to the assessment objectives. The new objectives for the revised GCSE are as follows:

Candidates should be able to demonstrate the ability to:

1 recall, select, organise and deploy knowledge of the syllabus content;
2 describe, analyse and explain

    2.1 the events, changes and issues studied;
    2.2 the key features and characteristics of the periods, societies or situations studied;

3 in relation to the historical context

    3.1   comprehend, analyse and evaluate representations and interpretations of the events, people and issues studied;

    3.2   comprehend, interpret, evaluate and use a range of sources of information of different types.

The new objectives try to reflect a less fragmented approach than did those formulated in 1988. Source skills are assessed within the context of prescribed content, so the 'unseen' source paper of the SHP examination has been discontinued. A major change is the exclusion of the earlier objective which required candidates to show 'an ability to look at events and issues from the perspectives of people of the past', commonly known as the 'empathy' objective, which usually contributed to the coursework. As noted elsewhere 'empathy' has given rise to sometimes acrimonious discussion. This has been replaced by that newcomer to the National Curriculum, Key Element 3, 'historical interpretations and representations', which formed the major part of Chapter 6. Consequently, how to assess pupils' understanding of such interpretations will be the next challenge for both teachers and examiners.

    There are some indications of a reversion to some of the emphases of the pre-GCSE examinations. There is likely to be a *greater emphasis placed on candidates' historical knowledge*, but pupils will still be required to apply such knowledge rather than simply recall it. As indicated in the previous chapter, the challenge to both teachers and examiners is how to accommodate knowledge with levels of response marking schemes. The new syllabuses also place *more emphasis on 'extended writing'*: not quite the return to the O level essay, but a chance for candidates to use their knowledge to substantiate their judgements. The presence of such questions, carrying a substantial percentage of the marks for the paper, will influence the way you prepare your pupils for the examination. They will benefit from the occasional class essay on a prescribed topic, in which they are given about 25 minutes to complete an answer without reference to books or notes. As Husbands notes, it is not primarily the length of the written work which matters, but

> the provision of written tasks as culminations of historical enquiries which extend pupils' capacity to think historically . . . they should be challenging in the ways they ask pupils to complete the move from the accumulation of material, through the sketching of relationships, to the presentation of a statement about the historical material which they have explored.
>
> (Husbands, 1996)

Some syllabuses offer short courses, covering about half of the full requirement, which can be taken alongside short courses for other subjects. These short courses have the same assessment objectives. There are also syllabuses for which it is possible to sit a third examination paper as an alternative to the coursework.

An additional 5 per cent will continue to be available for spelling, grammar and punctuation; as noted in the common requirements of the statutory orders,

> pupils should be taught to express themselves clearly, both in speech and writing and to develop their reading skills. They should be taught to use grammatically correct sentences and to spell and punctuate accurately in order to communicate effectively in written English.

(DfE, 1995)

PLANNING A SCHEME OF LESSONS FOR A GCSE CLASS

On at least one of your school placements you should find that you are responsible for some GCSE teaching. This is more likely to be year 10 than year 11. Here are some suggestions for the preparations you can make for such teaching:

- Study carefully the specific syllabus for which the pupils are to be entered, noticing how the assessment objectives are being met by the terminal examinations and the coursework.
- Once you have been told the content areas you have to cover with a class, find out in which part of the examination – coursework or the examination papers – that content will be used.
- If it is for the examination, find out what are the chief emphases of that particular examination paper – concepts, interpretations, sources. This will influence to some extent the way you approach the teaching of the topics you have been given.
- Examine the resources which the department uses for the teaching of that content; find out which books the pupils may take home.
- If the content area is one you have not recently studied, do some background reading to ensure that you are not only familiar with the detail but also that your knowledge is wide enough to consider associated causes, consequences and the significance of events.
- With guidance from the teacher, begin to create a scheme of work for the series of lessons. Make sure that the main emphases of that element of the examination to which the content contributes is well represented in your scheme; that is, if sources form a major feature, include source work within the scheme.
- Whatever the paper, the pupils will need to support their answers with relevant knowledge. To this end there will be some lessons, usually the earlier ones in a scheme, when you will need to consider how the pupils are to gather

and record that knowledge. How much will you tell them; how much will they find out for themselves? Remember that there are tensions here: it is often quicker in terms of syllabus coverage to use teacher exposition; on the other hand, one of the aims of school history is to enable pupils to find things out for themselves.

• Remember, there are many ways of recording information, and there is no reason why a year 10 class should not experience the variety of approaches used at Key Stage 3.

TASK 11.1 STUDYING PAST PAPERS

Another useful preparatory task is to study the past papers and/or specimen papers of the syllabus you are to teach. Look closely at the questions and the associated marking schemes. Consider what teaching and learning strategies you could employ to enable you to be able to tackle such questions.

• What do the pupils need to know?
• What skills do they need to employ?

How will your answers to these two questions affect your planning and choice of teaching strategies?

• Devise a question of your own that you feel would be appropriate for a GCSE exam. With the permission of your mentor, set the question for a class and think about its effectiveness and limitations.

COMMON MISTAKES AND MISCONCEPTIONS OF GCSE CANDIDATES

Technique. As a result of your own experience of examinations, you are already familiar with some of the guidance teachers need to give to candidates for external examinations. Advice about *the need to look carefully at the precise wording of a question* and to note that the number of marks available for a question will determine how much time should be spent on it. Your pupils should be familiar with the requirements of the paper and its rubric by having sight of an earlier paper. There are some candidates who fail to do themselves justice because they do not follow the rubric or do not read the question properly. Encourage them to look for and understand the *meaning of the key words in a question*, such as 'explain', 'compare', 'useful', 'reliable' and 'give reasons for'. They should clearly understand how such words will guide their answers.

Source skills. A common practice with some weaker candidates is to para-phrase the sources on the paper in the hope that such words will contain the answer. This may result from a limited understanding of the content of the source, or from familiarity with rather undemanding worksheets which allow pupils to copy or paraphrase without showing much thought.

There are times when pupils faced with a requirement to compare sources, will, nevertheless, paraphrase or describe each source in turn but without making any comparison. It may be helpful to encourage such pupils to develop certain routines such as completing a table:

Similarities	Differences	Reasons for differences
Source A		
Source B		

There are some candidates who devote much of what might be a lengthy answer to a description of the sources when they have been asked to explain the differing interpretations presented by the sources. Similarly, some candidates give the impression that they think that assessing a source's utility means that they need to describe it.

Another common difficulty is *the inability to differentiate between the 'utility' of a source and its 'reliability'.* You might find it helpful if the pupils are encour-aged to ask questions such as 'Useful for what?', 'Useful for whom?', and to realise that some sources, which contain some inaccuracies, will still have their uses for certain enquiries. Some candidates can be too dismissive of such sources.

Again, with reliability, your pupils will benefit from being encouraged to ask 'Reliable for what?', which again may not always be determined by the accuracy of some of the details in the source. *Your pupils benefit from having set procedures for tackling both source questions and also different interpretations.*

Less common now is the misconception that because a source is a 'primary' source it must be more reliable than a secondary source. It may still be worth while to pose a question which might explore this question. (For example, 'Would it be possible for a secondary school pupil in this school to have better knowledge and understanding of what happened at the Battle of Waterloo than a soldier who fought in that battle? Give reasons for your answer.)

Use of knowledge. As discussed in Chapter 10, the role of knowledge has generated considerable debate in the first ten years of the GCSE. One of your tasks is to try to encourage your pupils to think about how they use their historical knowledge. In this they should be aware of *not relying too much on the information available on the paper, but being able to support their opinions with other*

TASK 11.2 ANALYSIS OF A QUESTION

Study the following question.

SOURCE A: Charles Dickens, *Dombey and Son*, 1848.
I left Dullborough in the days when there were no rail roads in the land;
I left in a stagecoach. I was shunted back the other day by train . . . and the
first discovery I made was that the station had swallowed up the playing
field. It was gone . . . the two beautiful hawthorn trees, the hedges, the turf
and all those buttercups and daisies had given place to stony roads; while
beyond the station an ugly dark monster of a tunnel kept its jaws open as if
it had swallowed them and was greedy for more destruction.

**SOURCE B: Edwin Butterworth, *Descriptive History of the
Manchester and Leeds Railway*, 1845.**
Almost immediately after leaving Littleborough, the celebrated Vale of
Todmorden commences. The railway, on its approach to the Summit
Tunnel, is carried along by a cutting of nearly a hundred feet at its greatest
depth. This extraordinary subterranean depth, one of the greatest
triumphs of modern skill, presents, even at its mouth, a highly impressive
appearance. Amidst piles of towering, shapeless crags, whose face and form
have been altered by the labours of man, and the blasting of gunpowder,
rises a fine massive arch of masonry, of admirable workmanship.

Compare Sources A and B. Which do you think gives the more reliable
description of the impact of the railways on a locality? Explain the reasons
for your answer.

1 Make a list of what the pupils would need to know and understand in
   order to be able to attempt this question. Consider both the content and
   the skills.
2 Make notes on how you could use this question to encourage the pupils
   to use the key words to inform and structure their answer.
3 What would you say to pupils *after* they had attempted the question to
   try and guide them to higher levels of attainment in this type of question?

relevant, accurate information. Such knowledge is likely to push a mark to the top
of the level in a mark scheme. The revised GCSE places more emphasis on
knowledge, and so those candidates who not only display a certain level of conceptual understanding but can also support the answer with knowledge will be
rewarded. The more you can encourage your pupils to make use of knowledge
to *back up* their statements and judgements the better. The more this is done at
Key Stage 3, before the GCSE course, again the better.

Concepts. While it is important to encourage candidates to use their historical knowledge intelligently, there are times when questions dealing with concepts such as causation and change are seen by some pupils as requests for lists. This illustrates one of your problems in teaching GCSE history; namely, how to achieve a balance between teaching a body of knowledge but not giving sets of prepared answers, which may or may not answer the specific question set. Such a balance is often the case with, for example, causation, where a good candidate not only recalls the causes of an event but is able to use them. A recurrent comment from examiners is that candidates need more *practice in evaluating the relative merits of different causes of events and of explaining the links between them*. In other words, try to encourage your pupils to assess and evaluate rather than merely list; thus, some of the approaches to the teaching of concepts discussed in Chapter 5 are equally applicable to your teaching for the GCSE. So, in this way your pupils will not, for example, recount lists of results without making an attempt to assess and evaluate explicitly whether the changes they mentioned were important.

SETTING EXERCISES AND EMPLOYING MARK SCHEMES

You will soon realise that many of the procedures suggested for the setting of tasks for Key Stage 3, in the previous chapter, are also applicable for your GCSE classes. This is helped by the continuity that now exists between the Key Elements and the new assessment objectives of the GCSE.

Here are two examples of types of GCSE questions with their mark schemes. They are abridged versions of the format in the specimen papers for the revised GCSE with different content. Familiarity with the kind of questions set and their mark schemes influences the emphases you make in your teaching and gives you some insight into the type of answer to encourage in order to obtain high marks.

1 This question is designed to meet the assessment objective, which requires candidates to *describe, analyse and explain the events, changes and issues studied*.

Question

There are a number of reasons which could explain the building of the railway from Liverpool to Manchester by 1830.
Read the following causes.

- high rates and frequent delays on the Mersey–Irwell Navigation and the Bridgewater Canal;
- dissatisfaction with the speed of land transport;
- skill of the engineer, George Stephenson;

- financial contribution of Liverpudlians;
- the successful trials of steam locomotives at Rainhill;
- growing demand for faster transport by the expanding cotton industry.

(a) Choose *one* of the causes from the list above.
   Explain the part which this played in the building of the railway. (4)
(b) Were any of the causes on the list more important than the others as causes for the building of the railway?
   Use your knowledge of the period to explain your choice. (6)
(c) Why was the Liverpool–Manchester Railway built? Use *all* the reasons in the list above, as well as your own knowledge of other causes, to put together a full explanation. (10)

Mark scheme

(a) Target: Explanation of the part played by a cause related to a key event

Level 1: **Gives a *narrative* answer.**
   Describes the chosen cause without relating it to the Liverpool–Manchester railway. (1 mark)
Level 2: **Gives an answer which shows an understanding of cause and effect.**
   Relates the chosen cause to the building of the railway. (2–3 marks)
Level 3: **Shows the ability to place the chosen cause into the wider context.**
   Sees contributory cause as part of a chain of events, which led to the completion of the railway. For instance, the engineering skills of George Stephenson made it possible to build viaducts (e.g. Sankey) over difficult land, build tunnels (Liverpool), and reduce inclines sufficient for the limited power of the early steam engine. All accomplished in a short amount of time. (4 marks)

(b) Target: Recognise that causes can vary in importance

Level 1: **Gives a *narrative* answer.**
   Describes the chosen cause as an event. Does not compare or assess importance to any of the causes. (1–2 marks)
Level 2: **Explains *why* the chosen cause(s) is/are important.**
   At this level the candidate concentrates on one or two causes and explains why they are important.
   Higher mark for (i) effective comparison of causes, or (ii) well-argued non-comparative answer. (3–4 marks)
Level 3: **Realises that some causes may be more important but that it is the interrelationship of the causes that led to the completion of the railway.**
   Answer must *explain* the links between the causes and the contribution of some. Quality of explanation will determine the choice of mark. (5–6 marks)

(c) Target: Demonstrate understanding of the way in which various different factors combine to cause an event

N.B. Higher levels of this question can *only* be awarded to those candidates who use *their own knowledge* in providing reasons, which go beyond those given in the question.

Level 1: Uses only the suggestions provided and gives details of some or all of them.
At this level no additional causes are suggested and no explanation is attempted as to *how* these led to the completion of the railway. (1–2 marks)

Level 2: Explains clearly how some or all of the given causes led to the completion of the railway, OR offers causes in addition to those given, but does not explain how these led to the completion of the railway. (3–4 marks)

Level 3: Offers causes in addition to those given, and explains clearly how some or all of these led to the completion of the railway.
Other factors could include the availability of a labour force to build the viaducts, bridges and tunnels, or the defeat of the opponents of the railway (canals, turnpike trusts, coach firms, landowners) after the earlier reverse in Parliament. (5–7 marks)

Level 4: Provides a full explanation, linking given and further contributory causes in a clearly argued and developed answer. (8–10 marks)

Commentary

You will notice that several features of this reflect some of the issues covered in Chapter 10. Notice the role of *knowledge* and how this is used to amplify the points being made. Notice how information not available in the question is rewarded and that in part (c) such knowledge is needed for the higher levels. What are the implications of this for your teaching? Your pupils must have a good grounding in knowledge and also be clear as to how this is to be used. In addition to knowledge about the content, the pupils also need to be familiar with the concept of causation, to have become familiar with those varied issues involved and discussed in Chapter 5. Here they need to know about the relative importance of causes and the interrelationship of causes.

You will also notice the importance of the issue of *progression*. This is made explicit in the use of levels of response. The levels are defined in terms of cognitive development and understanding (see Chapter 10), so that there is more reward for the ability to explain than to describe, more is achieved by the pupil who can draw on information which has not been provided, and higher marks are given for the ability to relate the information to the wider context and explore the significance of a cause or set of causes. *It is important to notice that it is the progression of understanding that defines the level, not the amount of knowledge, hence the use of bold type to define the level.*

Differentiation is, of course, 'by outcome' (again discussed in Chapter 10). The lower levels of response allow pupils of limited ability to gain some marks by being able to select and describe, having been prompted by the information in the question. Further differentiation both *within* the levels and *between* the levels is achieved by the degree of substantiation and the quality of explanation.

You will also notice that this is a *structured question* with three parts. This is helpful in terms of broadening access to the question. The more limited are helped by the use of information to stimulate and jog their memories. The three parts move through a clear sequence of development from the concentration on one cause, to the more important causes, and finally leading to the complex inter-relationship of causes with the requirement for the greater use of information that is not available.

2   This question is designed to meet the assessment objective that candidates should be able to describe, analyse and explain *the key features and characteristics of periods, societies or situations studied.*

Question

Study Sources A and B.
Use the sources **and your own knowledge,** to explain the different attitudes towards public health in the middle of the nineteenth-century. (10)

Source A: A letter to *The Times* newspaper, 1854
We prefer to take our chance with the cholera than be bullied into health. There is nothing a man hates so much as being cleansed against his will or having his floor swept, his walls whitewashed, his dungheaps cleared away and his thatch forced to side way to slate. It is a fact that many people died from a good washing.

Source B: From 'Housebuilding Regulations' from the Macclesfield Local Board of Health, mid-1850s

Privies and Water-closets. The Public Health Act requires that every House shall be provided with a separate Privy or Water-closet. No Dwelling or Sleeping-room will be allowed over a Privy or Ash-pit: they must be placed as far from the House as possible. Any Approach to them must be not less than Four Feet in Width.

The entrance to the Privy to have a Step of not less than Three Inches of rise. The Floor to be Flagged with an Inclination of half-an-inch to a Foot towards the Door. All privies or Water-closets to have an opening for ventilation at or near the ceiling.

Mark scheme

Target: Comparison of sources to explain characteristic features

Level 1: **Description and extraction of information.**
Describes the sources with no comparison and no analysis of the attitudes implicit in the sources. Needs to use both sources for both marks. (1–2 marks)

Level 2: **Analysis of differences between the sources.**
Includes some element of comparison; is able to note the differences of approach with some supporting analysis of the content of the sources. (3–4 marks)

Level 3: **Begins to *explain* attitudes in the sources.**
Utilises references in the sources for explanations which involve the application of additional knowledge. E.g. 'clean'and 'dirty' parties; some knowledge of the campaigns for public health; the influences of epidemics such as cholera. (5–6 marks)

Level 4: **Fuller explanation of attitudes.**
E.g. relates the sources to wider context, such as the strength of the 'laissez-faire' attitude and the reasons for its popularity contrasted with demands for increased (local) government intervention. Reasons for the demand for better public health. (7–8 marks)

Level 5: **Provides a full explanation of the differences between the sources.**
Explains the sources within the wider context of the times; uses the sources as examples of the concept of *change*; one representing resistance to change, the other pointing to increased government control. E.g. the resistance of wealthier rate-payers, builders and landlords. The panic created by the epidemics; medical advances; government enquiries and the persistence of reformers and local Medical Officers of Health. (9–10 marks)

Commentary

You will note that the target for the mark scheme includes both source skills and the ability to show understanding of the characteristic features of a period. At the lower levels of response, the candidates are rewarded for their use of source skills including comprehension, analysis and the comparison of sources. At the higher levels they make use of sources to show their understanding of the attitudes of the time. Increasingly, such understanding will need to be supported by their use of knowledge. Note, however, that knowledge is presented in the mark scheme as *examples*, indicating the type of knowledge likely to support that level of understanding. Progression may also be noted in the use of the concept of change at the highest level of response, again showing the difficulty of compartmentalising the learning of history discussed in earlier chapters.

COURSEWORK

Although coursework is now worth a maximum of 25 per cent of the whole examination, it makes a valuable contribution to the variety of learning your pupils experience. There continue to be aspects of the teaching and learning of history – for example the development of enquiry skills and the use of intiative to acquire, analyse and evaluate sources – which are more appropriately assessed away from the examination room. Coursework can also encourage different and more personal ways of organising and communicating history, consistent with Key Element 5 of the National Curriculum. As noted in Chapter 10, assessment should form an integral part of the learning process, and this is particularly true of GCSE coursework. In the words of one syllabus (1996) 'The coursework element of the syllabus is seen as a taught component which is designed to foster good practice by facilitating imaginative and innovative styles of teaching and learning, so that courses are enjoyable for all participants.' Indeed, while it is the usual case that coursework is presented in written form, the use of film and video, diagrams, models, tape recordings and photographs, if accompanied by adequate explanatory written material, is also allowed. Under the guidance of an Examination Board, and provided the assessment objectives are met, schools and colleges are given the freedom to construct their own coursework tasks.

Should you be required to help in the preparation of pupils for their GCSE coursework, you will need to be familiar with the assignments which the history department has set and the assessment targets each assignment seeks to meet. The department will have constructed a mark scheme for each of the assignments. As with the preparation for end-of-course examinations, you will need to consider what knowledge, skills and concepts the pupils need to understand before they can attempt the assignments. For many this will involve fieldwork.

TASK 11.3 PREPARATION TO TEACH COURSEWORK

During your school placement, study the coursework details of the GCSE syllabus for which the history department enters its pupils. Among the features you should note are the way the assessment objectives are applied to the coursework elements; the choice of content available; the number and length of assignments required; the guidance offered by the Board for the creation of mark schemes for the assignments, noting the use of progression for the objectives; the administration involved and how this sets the timetable for completion by the pupils; the moderating procedures and any specimen examples made available by the Board.

Then, study the coursework proposals of the school to note how these seek to meet the requirements of the Board.

You will find it likely that pupils have several opportunities to attempt similar tasks for practice before they attempt the coursework that will count towards their final grade.

TEACHING ADVANCED LEVEL HISTORY: CONSTRAINTS AND POSSIBILITIES

Background

The introduction of advanced levels (A level) into English and Welsh schools in 1951 was clearly associated with university entrance requirements. History A level in particular was believed by many to be justified on intellectual skills alone and it remained a popular subject, with 10 per cent of candidates in 1951 entered for the examination. The overwhelming majority of these candidates in the 1950s came from the grammar schools, and the end of course examination was dominated by the set pattern of two formal papers comprising a series of essay questions which demanded, apart from excellent recall skills, rigorous academic standards of achievement. Comprehensive reorganisation of schools in the 1960s broadened the ability ranges to be found in sixth form education and there was an increase in the number and variety of subjects offered for study at A level. Both these developments had the effect of reducing the overall percentage of candidates who were entered for A level history. The overall decline continued as history faced competition in the sixth form curriculum from an increasing number of new subjects and vocational qualifications offered mainly in further education colleges. By the early 1980s history was also in decline in comparison to other traditional A level subjects, which prompted the establishment of the 'History at Universities Defence Group' in 1983 in an attempt to promote history in schools.

Few students embarked upon a course of study in history at school with a view to further study of the subject in higher education. The perceived 'usefulness' of the subject by students was in assisting them with entry into higher education itself. There was a tension therefore between those who continued with history (the minority) and those who did not (the large majority), in terms of what sixth form history should provide. Teachers began to call for a clearer understanding of the purpose of A level history, and Fisher (1991) indicated that there was some concern about how teachers were expected to cope with the increasing range of student abilities in studying history. Lewin (1990) detailed two major challenges for A level history: first, the need for a different examination system; second, a growing feeling that A levels themselves were no longer appropriate. History in particular was seen by some as too narrowly academic, and there was certainly a general concern in the 1980s about the forms of assessment at A level standard. Lang (1990) claimed that history was widely perceived to be dull and badly taught, with sixth form history teaching dominated by lecture-style presentations and dictated notes. University history course structures were undergoing a process of change in the 1980s, with many adopting modular approaches and continuous assessment methods. Entry requirements to university courses were also at the same time becoming more flexible. These developments in higher education increased the pressures for change in schools.

However, A levels have been more resistant to change than other areas of the school curriculum and public examination system. Since 1987 A levels have been awarded on a seven point scale A–E, N and U. A–E are 'pass' grades, 'N' is a 'near miss' and 'U' indicates an unclassified result. There are seven General Examination Certificate (GEC) examination boards, and the requirements for history A level are set out in the syllabuses published by these boards. In 1988 the A level History Committee of the Schools Examination Council (SEC, later Secondary Examinations and Asssessment Council (SEAC), and now Schools Council Assessment Authority (SCAA), but soon to be renamed again) published a pamphlet entitled *Principles and Good Practice in 'A' Level History*. This pamphlet recommended a number of points for improving A level history without changing the framework of syllabuses. In the same year (1988) the government's Higginson Committee on A levels reported. The report recommended a 'leaner but tougher' A level system, with students studying five A levels rather than three as the norm, which is similar to the Scottish Higher system of examinations. The government rejected the recommendations on the same day they were published and committed itself to retaining A levels as the 'gold standard' of sixth form academic qualifications. Nevertheless, the government did initiate the Advanced Supplementary level qualification in 1989 to encourage breadth in the curriculum for post-16 students. The A/S level was intended to be of the same standard as the A level, but studied in half the time with two A/S levels equalling one A level. In history there have never been more than around 1,000 candidates for this examination annually. Nevertheless, the Higginson Report (1988) also recommended the need to rationalise existing provision of syllabuses and to encourage a variety of assessment forms at A level. The Report called for a broader sixth form curriculum and a system which recognised all the achievements of candidates, with opportunities to link 'A', A/S and vocational qualifications. Modular courses and credits for study and their transfer seemed real possibilities in sixth form education. In 1989 SEAC set up working parties to develop general principles to control standards, syllabus development and progress from the GCSE.

The connection between sixth form history and the National Curriculum and GCSE history was becoming closer. In 1988 the Education Reform Act had made history a foundation subject at both Key Stages 3 and 4. However, the revision of the National Curriculum in 1994 reduced history's foundation status to Key Stage 3. This revision envisaged parallel A level and vocational tracks in the sixth form with bridges linking them. History was not to be compulsory beyond the age of 14, and Taylor (1994) has commented that the revision of the National Curriculum had placed history at the periphery of the Key Stage 4 curriculum; he predicted that history will go into decline at both GCSE and sixth form level. Certainly, the revision did not please many history teachers and there appears to have been an underlying assumption that history has little to contribute to vocational courses. Nevertheless, history remains the sixth most popular subject at A level, and in recent years the numbers opting for history have begun to rise again. This may be connected with the changes which have taken place in the assessment, teaching and learning in history at sixth form level. It is therefore important to examine the claim by Kilmartin (1995) that there has been a 'sharp and growing discontinuity between teaching and learning of history before and after sixteen'.

Recent initiatives

The 1996 *Review of Qualifications for 16–19 Year Olds* provides us with some interesting insights into history in the sixth form. We see that A level history is grouped with Mathematics, Physics, French and German as being a 'more diffi-cult than average' subject. History is not only 'difficult' in the sixth form but has one of the highest entry requirements at university. In 1993 the pass rate for A level history was 82.9 per cent with a 10 per cent drop out rate, whilst for A/S level the pass rate was 62.5 per cent. It was found that A level history emphasised theoretical knowledge and skills, teacher exposition, and written examinations. History groups tended to be small, with students spending four to five hours per week split between two teachers. The most popular combina-tion was History and English Literature. History has the greatest number of options, a total of 904 across all boards and syllabuses, with English and English Literature next in line with 337 options. The *Review* found no evidence that there was a major problem with these multiple routes in history assessment. History at A level is offered at 97.5 per cent of schools with a sixth form, and it was found that student choice of A level is influenced most by GCSE results and the availability of courses in the school.

It would be misleading to suggest that all A level history courses in the 1970s ended with traditional essay-based examinations. Both the Associated Examining Board (AEB) and the Cambridge Local Examinations Syndicate Board (CLESB) had well-established personal investigations in some of their A level history syllabuses. These personal studies involved a personal historical investigation on a topic or theme from the syllabus. Martin (1990) provided a good summary of what these personal studies involve. In the same way Fines (1987) explained how the Southern Regional Examinations Board had used source-based questions at A level for some time. Nevertheless, the introduction of the National Curriculum and GCSE examinations in the 1980s accelerated changes to A level courses, and we see in the late 1980s a number of innovative pilot A level history schemes being introduced.

The Joint Matriculation Board (JMB) had the largest number of A level entries for history of any of the GCE boards, and its Committee for History produced a range of flexible new-style alternatives to existing syllabuses. The Board conducted research into the learning capacities and teaching strategies used with 16- to 19-year-olds through its History Research Project team. This team looked at source based questions, course work and personal studies which were less dependent on end of course examinations. The JMB essentially inserted new ideas into its own traditional examination format, which included more options, course content being cut, stress placed on historical skills and source materials, including topics with an immediate relevance. There was also some consideration given to themes and concepts in history. In March 1990, SEAC produced *Examinations Post-16: Developments for the 1990s*, which endorsed a number of these moves. The JMB was certainly committed to change, but other boards went further.

The AEB produced three new syllabuses, all of which aimed to place greater emphasis on historical understanding rather than on historical content. AEB syllabus 673 provided scope for extended individual studies through investigation of themes in history, syllabus 620 had a focus on the nature and methods of history, whilst syllabus 630 emphasised source material. Syllabus 673 has had a substantial increase in candidates since its introduction in 1988. Assessment in these syllabuses is 'objectives led' in that they focus on the needs of the student, giving each task more definition so that students know exactly what is expected from them. A candidate would have a number of attempts to demonstrate an ability to support an assignment with relevant evidence or produce a coherent argument. These two objectives could be separated so that the student can concentrate on the one which causes most difficulty. Assessment is therefore clearly related to the objectives of the task, and the emphasis is on defined assessment objectives and a variety of means of assessment. The London Board's Syllabus E is also 'objectives led' and has two end of course examination papers, four coursework assignments and one individual study. It is this objectives-led approach which underpins almost all of the new initiatives in A level history since 1988. This contrasts sharply with the common practice of giving essay titles from past papers as preparation for examinations.

The syllabus of the Cambridge History Project borrowed much from the Schools History Project and was piloted by the CLESB. It focused on the assessment of conceptual understanding by means of breaking down history into component skills and concepts. The recent review of A level syllabuses has cast the future of this syllabus in doubt. However, the most ambitious project was perhaps the Enquiry into Teaching History to Over Sixteens (ETHOS) which also began in 1988. Whilst the project has since been abandoned, it is worth looking at what it attempted. It was funded by the Nuffield Foundation and was based at the University of Exeter and the West Sussex Institute of Education. Its aim was to improve teaching, learning, resourcing and the assessing of history in the sixth form, and also to generate enthusiasm and excitement about involvement in 'doing history'. It aimed to encourage and measure progress rather than to categorise students through assessment methods. ETHOS was not a syllabus, but rather a process of restructuring which was offered to existing syllabuses to free teachers and students to work with each other, to manage their own learning, and to problem-solve. ETHOS recommended a conceptual topic or thematic net which would broadly cover the range of possible topics in history syllabuses, but it would not dictate the content used to examine them. ETHOS was certainly a radical attempt to change the way history teachers viewed the teaching and learning of history.

All the initiatives in A level history, whilst reducing content, actually increased the workload of teachers. ETHOS made greater demands on teachers through their active involvement in planning and assessing courses, but this did not necessarily render it unpopular, as some teachers relished the autonomy and flexibility it provided. Modular programmes in school history which utilise continuous assessment methods lessen the emphasis on end of course examinations but invariably increase the teachers' role in assessment. Nevertheless, the principles underlying ETHOS are worth revisiting, especially as the project also emphasised that history A level would continue to offer high reading and writing skills, critical reading, good scholarship and research, use of evidence to justify an argument, application of experience and common sense, the study of human behaviour and social groups, political education. It even asserts that cross-curricular issues can be most readily delivered in history. Despite the termination of the ETHOS syllabus the two directors of the project (Fines and Nichol, 1994) concluded: 'In a real sense ETHOS attempted to respond to the GCSE challenge; it is hoped that it will inform and even influence the form which post-16 provision takes in both history and other subjects from the mid-1990s.'

Many of the changes since 1988 have been successful and popular, but according to the *Review* of post-16 qualifications these innovative changes at A level history have impacted upon a minority. Nevertheless, almost all syllabuses have changed and many have given greater emphasis to investigation and enquiry; this has allowed students to produce some excellent and original work. Teaching strategies have also changed in many schools, even if we agree with Kilmartin's (1995) claim that in some schools A level history flourishes on a bed of 'traditional practice'. Students have clearly changed, and there have been varied and often successful attempts to improve their learning.

TASK 11.4 PREPARING TO TEACH AN A LEVEL HISTORY SYLLABUS

1 History A level syllabuses that are taught in schools are usually selected by the Head of Department based on three considerations: their personal preference, their expertise and the resources available to them. You will no doubt wish to share in the selection but you will first need to familiarise yourself with the variety of syllabuses available. Send for a copy of two separate syllabuses from two different examination boards. You may also send for the examiner's report for that particular syllabus. After studying each syllabus comment on the following:

- What publishers produce the appropriate course textbooks? Are they useful?
- What assessment arrangements does the board make?
- Do the assessment procedures require resources? What are they?
- Would the content of the course appeal to both teacher and student?
- What teaching strategies are necessary for the course?
- What skills are demanded from the students and how will you need to prepare them for the examination?
- Does the examiner's report help you to decide whether to recommend the syllabus?
- How would the course work/personal study be marked?
- Will you need to train the students in new assessment techniques?
- Is the course objectives led?

2 Read *Source Based Questions at A level* by John Fines, published by the Historical Association (1987), No. 54. Design a set of ten questions which might be asked about any one of the selection of sources in the pamphlet. Keep in mind that these questions are designed for A level history students. The information on pp. 10–12 of Fines's book should help you focus the questions that would be most appropriate.

Preparations for teaching an A level group

Most secondary training courses are 11–18 courses, so that you find yourself teaching not only Key Stage 3 and the GCSE but also some post-16 history classes. Even if you are teaching in an 11–18 school, opportunities to teach whole A level groups for sustained periods of time are often limited. However accomplished and conscientious you may be, schools have to be careful that involvement in ITE does not compromise the examination preparations of pupils, and have to reassure parents on this point. Because opportunities are limited, you need to take advantage of any offers available to become involved in A level teaching. This can often include observation, work with small groups, or team and collaborative teaching with the teacher responsible for the group. Often, exposure to A level classes comes later in your school placement, when you have (hopefully) become more comfortable in the classroom and have had some time to think about the challenges of teaching A level. Experienced teachers can often make A level teaching look deceptively easy. Many student

---

TASK 11.5 NATIONAL CURRICULUM AND GCSE AS A PREPARATION FOR A LEVEL HISTORY

Before considering your preparation for teaching, it may be instructive to consider the extent to which National Curriculum history and the GCSE might have prepared your A level students for their history course.

1 Ask the Head of History for the appropriate documentation related to the A level course you are to teach. This involves details of the syllabus, the department scheme of work, the assessment procedures and the examiners' reports. What are the assessment objectives for the A level course? What are the characteristics of the work of a good A level candidate?
2 Make a list of the principal characteristics and objectives and then consider the extent to which the study of National Curriculum history and the revised GCSE will have already developed the students' understanding of history in a way that the A level course can extend. Compare the A level assessment objectives with the National Curriculum Key Elements and the revised GCSE assessment objectives.
3 Consider (a) the development of pupils' skills in reading history and (b) their ability to produce extended writing. How much opportunity did pupils have to develop these skills before the A level course?

Discuss your answers to these questions with the history teachers and ask how such considerations influence their approaches to A level teaching.

teachers find A level preparation and teaching quite challenging at first, and an illuminating experience. If you do find that it is 'hard going' at first, in terms of both preparation and teaching, remember that many teachers find it to be one of the most enjoyable and rewarding aspects of teaching.

Because you are learning so much with all ages and abilities in such a short space of time, it can be helpful if the topic you are asked to teach is one with which you have considerable familiarity from your own higher education or A level experience, but as with so many facets of school experience it is important that you try to fit in with the needs of the department. It may be possible to negotiate A level experience which ties in with your subject knowledge strengths and the convenience of the department, but if this is not possible do not eschew the opportunity to get as much experience of A level as possible. You will however have to accept that preparation time will be increased if you have to work on subject knowledge in addition to subject application.

Preparation for A level teaching can be onerous and time-consuming. Because you are so conscious of the need to do your best for the students, knowing from first-hand experience the importance of grades, *there may be a danger that you allocate too much time to your A level preparation at the expense of the younger pupils.* To reduce this kind of pressure, if possible, *try to ensure that you are given as much prior notice as possible of any A level teaching commitments.* It is often better to begin your A level teaching a few weeks after the rest of your teaching, and very useful to have spent time observing the class for several lessons before you take over. In this way you will be more familiar with the prior content and with the teacher's style and approaches. There is a case for greater observation before taking external examination classes as Figure 11.1 indicates.

Your own knowledge of the topic Your first concern will be to gather together as much background information for yourself as you can. Secure subject knowledge will help you to feel more relaxed and confident about teaching the class,

Week	1	2	3	4	5	6	7	8	9	10
Year 12	Obs	Obs	Obs	Obs	T	T	T	T	T	Team Teach
Year 10	Obs	T	T	T	T	T	T	T	T	T
Year 9	T	T	T	T	T	T	T	T	T	T
Year 8	T	T	T	T	T	T	T	T	T	T
Year 7	T	T	T	T	T	T	T	T	T	T

Figure 11.1 Possible schedule for the incorporation of A level experience

and in responding confidently to pupils' questions. Dig out your own notes if you have them, but be prepared to discuss your preparation with the teachers. They will appreciate the pressures on your time and can be very helpful in indicating useful chapters and articles for you to read. Make sure you do not confine your reading too exclusively to the topic you are to teach but read around it as well. In this respect you should pursue what is also good practice for pupils; that is, to read around the subject at several levels, studying general texts, books more specifically related to the topic in question, and also articles and monographs from journals written specifically to support A level history (see 'Further Reading' at the end of this chapter). You may need to extend your reading as your preparation develops, and as your involvement with A level classes extends.

Be clear about your objectives This is just as important as for your teaching of younger pupils. In the same way as your schemes of work covered a variety of objectives and approaches with, say, Key Stage 3, the same applies to A level teaching. Different lessons will have different purposes. You need to be clear what these are, and they could include:

- to contextualise, to present a general framework of the topic;
- to identify the key issues/concepts/attitudes;
- to discuss differing interpretations;
- to develop further the students' study skills

  (a) in communication: oral, written, essay writing;
  (b) in expressing their opinions with confidence, substantiated by use of knowledge;
  (c) in reading, pursuing enquiries and note-making;

- to develop further the students' historical understanding

  (a) in the analysis, interpretation and evaluation of primary and secondary sources;
  (b) in the application of key concepts in history;
  (c) in assessing the significance of events;

- to develop an informed scepticism and an acceptance of uncertainty;

Crinnion (1987), in his presentation of the skills required of A level students, elaborated on these and encouraged the teacher new to A level teaching to use his list both to explain the value of the subject to prospective candidates and to inform the teaching techniques that you will need to develop.

Check the students' previous knowledge As you will be taking over a group during the course of the academic year, familiarise yourself with the content they have already covered. This gives you some idea about what the students may be expected to contribute and helps you to link your topic to others. You also need to find out about the abilities and attitudes of the students. With the great increase in the numbers continuing in full-time education beyond the statutory school-leaving age, you meet a quite wide range of ability in A level groups, with the result that differentiation continues to be a significant factor in your planning and teaching.

Resources You need to find out what books and other reading materials are in the possession of the students and what other books, articles and source materials are easily available to the students. Limitations on resources can be one of the more frustrating aspects of A level teaching and you need to find out how the department tries to manage, especially if there are large groups. Try as much as you can to resist the temptation to rely on an unchanged version of your own notes from previous study because of the limited availability of books. Your undergraduate notes, however assiduously compiled, may well be wildly inappropriate for the purposes of A level teaching. Find out what scope there is for the students to use their own initiative, local libraries and information technology resources such as history CD-ROMs and the Internet; whether some purchase their own paperbacks, and the extent to which they cooperate in the effective sharing of resources.

Choice of approaches

As with your teaching of the younger pupils, you need to include a variety of approaches and styles in the planning and delivery of your A level lessons. Indeed, many of the methods recommended elsewhere in this book can be applied with equal effectiveness in the A level classroom. Your choice of approach will, as ever, be determined by your learning objectives for a particular lesson. You still need to think precisely about the outcomes for the students and try to avoid the notion that your preparation is only concerned with the historical content.

Teacher presentation You will find that there are times when you have to do quite a lot of the talking in some lessons. It is useful to think about what aspects of the scheme is most appropriate for teacher presentation. Yet *it can be an interesting challenge to try to reduce the amount of teacher talk in teaching A level history*. There is a good case for teacher exposition at the beginning of a topic, to set the framework of the topic in its general context, to draw out the main issues and events, and to indicate (where appropriate) the different interpretations that have emerged. Given the range of ability you are likely to encounter, there remains a good case for the use of visual aids, charts, diagrams or duplicated handouts to assist your presentation. There is a good case for then presenting the students with task sheets and book references to help them to research the details for themselves rather than you pursuing such detail in a lengthy monologue while the students attempt to transfer your exposition to their notes.

Reading and note-making   Be prepared to allocate time in the classroom for the students to do their individual reading and note-making. This could give you time to talk to individuals, review their progress and apply some differentiation. The reading and note-making usually needs to be done within a prescribed framework and time limit with clear indication about the purposes of the reading. *The History Manual* (1985) by J.A. Cloake, V.A. Crinnion and S.A. Harrison remains one of the best and one of the most detailed guides for A level students and is particularly helpful on the key activities of reading and note-making. They make the point that often students read inefficiently and ineffectively, and so much thought needs to be given to helping them to make the most of their reading, especially as reading can be a neglected feature of the learning of history lower down the school. The new entrant to the A level course will need plenty of help and encouragement. There is a case for spending some time analysing some texts together, deciding what are the key points, what is note-worthy and how one might set out such notes. What students decide is note-worthy is often an indicator of their historical understanding. Inspection of pupils' notes can produce a useful dialogue. Cloake, Crinnion and Harrison also emphasise the need for the pupils to be involved in 'active' reading, questioning and to consciously assimilating what is being read, with reference to their previous understanding of the topic.

Source skills   The extent to which this might feature in your scheme will depend on the topic you have been asked to teach and the syllabus for which you are preparing students. With a background of the GCSE, pupils will have a familiarity with source skills in a way that many former O level candidates did not. This needs to be built upon with more advanced text and language and greater emphasis on the significance of the sources and their relationship to the wider issues. Again it is much better that such source activities are placed in the context of a genuine historical enquiry, debate or problem rather than a rather sterile skills exercise. Crinnion (1987) advocates the use of case studies, with the students being given initially a general context and framework, as advocated earlier, and then provided with a selected body of primary sources with which to analyse the historical correctness of a given statement or to discover the solution to a particular problem.

Variety of activities   Teaching A level history can offer plenty of opportunities for pair work and group work. Different groups can be set different tasks, particularly if there are limitations of resources, as a preparation for a plenary feedback. You can try to be imaginative in creating situations where the students have to make decisions; for example, comparing the treatment of a topic by different authors, evaluating interpretations or deciding which of two written responses to a question is the better. Getting the students to be able to communicate and discuss *from an informed position* requires thought and preparation, but can be both rewarding and enjoyable to properly set up and implement.

There is a good case for using role-play in A level history teaching. It will differ from similar activities with younger pupils in that it will be much more firmly rooted in the sources, both secondary and primary. Role-play could be used effectively to draw explanations of why different historians produce different interpretations. The nature of the subject also encourages the use of set debates for which the students need to use their reading to prepare a case. They can be asked to devise and explain charts and diagrams to summarise ideas.

Essay writing Setting essays, marking them and giving detailed feedback is another important part of A level teaching, especially as there may have been limited opportunities for extended writing in the GCSE. Many students find essay writing to be one of the most difficult features of their study and usually need detailed guidance and feedback, as well as encouragement. Study the examiner's reports for indications of the qualities that should be encouraged. They often give examples of good answers. Students can be encouraged to devise, perhaps in pairs, skeleton answers to questions as a basis for discussion.

Reviewing As indicated above, setting reading and other tasks can free you to talk to individuals and review their progress. With a range of ability you can try to match their individual study to their ability, suggest appropriate reading, check understanding, consider written work, including essays, and set targets. It is useful to keep your own records of such meetings.

Team teaching There are times when there is much to gained by team-teaching an A level topic with the students' usual teacher. There are many ways in which together you can present differing viewpoints and stimulate debate. There are other occasions when you and a fellow student can work effectively as a pair in teaching an A level topic.

The following list is taken from a lecture to history student teachers by Bernadette Josclin of Richmond Tertiary College, which many students found helpful.

Things to try to do:
1 Plan your classes carefully within the framework of a topic and then the overall scheme of work. Keep a close eye on *timing*. Know how long you've got for each topic.
2 Ensure that students have a clear idea of where they are going in a topic/scheme of work. (Give out a typed scheme, or plan of the topic.)
3 Remember, topics take longer at the start of the course than at the end.
4 Prepare your notes using past papers, syllabuses, key texts, etc.
5 *You* set the agenda in class, i.e. deadlines, work rate, etc.
6 Remember to explain key concepts – particularly at the start of the course.
7 Build in a variety of activities to the sessions.

8 Start from *their* knowledge and work back.
9 Build in study skills sessions – time management, essay writing, etc.
10 Organise some low-energy sessions for yourself – sessions where *they* have to do most of the work.
11 Think carefully about how the work which you do in class will translate into effective revision notes for them – clear headings etc.
12 Set them work which they can bring *to* the lesson, so they know something about the lesson beforehand.
13 Check their notes/files: keeps pupils on their toes and gives you an idea of how they are translating the work you set for them.
14 Build in *regular* checks on understanding – not just essays.
15 Constant reminders of key issues.
16 Recognise and remember that most groups are mixed ability; identify learning difficulties.
17 Be clear about deadlines and stick to them, even if this is unpopular!
18 Use the blackboard (or whatever) to emphasise key words, points, etc.
19 Look in GCSE and Key Stage 3 resources to see it there are good teaching ideas and resources which can be adapted.
20 Use source material wherever possible – try to develop historical skills.
21 Try and create situations where the pupils work/talk rather than you.
22 Be positive in the comments you make in response to pupils' efforts.
23 Give pupils lists of past questions at the end of a topic – useful for revision.
24 Always prepare a fall-back activity in case you run out of material.

Try not to:
1 talk too much; what are the pupils doing?;
2 do all the work – the pupils must do some things for themselves;
3 always have 'high-energy' sessions on your part. They are not always what is educationally best for your pupils;
4 always prioritise transmission of content at the expense of other learning objectives;
5 be sloppy in your time-keeping/punctuality to lessons, giving work back – this will only encourage the same traits in them;
6 assume that all pupils are highly motivated budding historians. Like all other teaching groups, they need motivating and encouraging;
7 waffle in class – be prepared! Admit mistakes if you don't know;
8 assume too much about pupils' knowledge and vocabulary.

(Josclin, 1995)

SUMMARY AND KEY POINTS

Assessment in history has undergone enormous changes in the last thirty years. Much of what is now established as common practice would be unrecognisable to the history teacher of a generation ago. Such changes in assessment have resulted from the acceptance that what constitutes historical understanding involves a combination of skills, concepts, and attitudes allied to knowledge. Attempts to assess these various elements have led to the use of varied types of assessment and much debate about their validity. The recent moves away from the targeting of a precise skill towards a less compartmentalised and more holistic approach indicates a probable resolution of some of the difficulties surrounding an achievement of balance between historical understanding and knowledge.

FURTHER READING

Cloake, J., Crinnion V.A. and Harrison, S.A. (1985) *The History Manual*, Lancaster, Framework Press.
This manual, intended for the A level student, gives plenty of useful advice to the teacher new to A level teaching, covering topics such as analytical reading, note-making, question analysis and essay writing.

Fines, J. (1991) *History 16–19 The Old and the New*, London, Historical Association (No. 68).

Fines, J. and Nichol, J. (1994) *Doing History 16–19: A Case Study in Curriculum Innovation and Change*, London, Historical Association.
An excellent introduction to the ideas behind much of the thinking in A level history reform.

Brown, R. and Daniels, C.W. (1986) *Learning History, A Guide to Advanced Study*, London, Macmillan.
A useful guide both for the student beginning an A level course and a trainee teacher given some A level teaching.

Journals such as *The Historian*, and *Modern History Review* contain articles which are eminently suited to A level study.

12 Continuing professional development

INTRODUCTION

The final chapter encompasses two elements of teaching history which are not part of the competences outlined in *Circular 10/97*. The first is the question of applying for your first post in teaching. It is important to realise that effective preparation for this is a separate area of competence. There is no necessary correlation between teachers' classroom teaching abilities and their skills in self-promotion and preparation for job applications. There are many excellent teachers and student teachers who do not do themselves justice in terms of job applications because they have not applied the same degree of thought and rigour to the process of application as to their classroom competence in teaching history.

The second area returns us to questions which were broached in the first chapter: how do history teachers get better at teaching, and why do some progress to higher standards or levels of competence than others?

What can you do to ensure that you are successful in your applications for teaching posts, and to ensure that your NQT year marks the start of your progress towards becoming an 'expert' teacher, rather than the end of your professional training?

OBJECTIVES

At the end of this chapter you should:

- be able to draft a letter of application or personal statement for a first post;
- be aware of the range of questions which might be asked at an interview for a first post in history;
- be aware of ways in which you can approach your first teaching post in a manner conducive to assisting your continuing professional development and prospects for career success and job satisfaction.

APPLYING FOR YOUR FIRST TEACHING POST

Advice on job applications and interviews for student teachers for all subjects is provided in Chapter 8 of *Learning to Teach in the Secondary School* (Capel *et al.*, 1995) To a large extent, this chapter confines itself to information relevant to student teachers of history.

The word processor has made it much easier and quicker to adapt personal statements and letters of application to the particular school you are applying to, and to the job and person specifications to which you are directing your application. There is a tension here between simply constructing one version and sending it to all the schools you apply for, and 'customising' the content of your letter or statement in order to fit the post advertised. This is a question of judgement; if there has been no effort to direct your response to the post as specified, this might smack of laziness or a casual attitude. There is, however, the danger that if you attempt to tailor your writing to suggest that you have always dreamed of teaching in St Swithin's, Bolton, teaching SHP GCSE syllabuses, and London 'Syllabus E' A level, your sincerity might be called into question. Most schools will accept the reality that you will be applying for a range of schools in different areas; there is therefore no need to dissemble over your reasons for applying.

The range of *periods* of history, as well as differences between exam syllabuses, poses questions about how to approach the issue of subject knowledge which perhaps go beyond those pertaining to other subjects. Very few applicants will have expert levels of subject knowledge of all optional elements of the National Curriculum, and be familiar with all examination alternatives. You can, however, 'do your homework' in terms of studying the information which the school sends to you, to have a look at the exam syllabuses which the school subscribes to, and to consider what you would suggest as your present strengths and developing interests in terms of subject knowledge. As well as being able to talk confidently about areas of history which you think you are particularly well equipped to teach, you should be prepared to talk about the ways in which you have augmented your subject knowledge in the course of your training, and your agenda for developing your subject knowledge further. Capel makes the point that there are several ways of developing subject knowledge other than reading (Capel, 1997). This might include observation in schools, talking to fellow student teachers, watching video-recordings, studying history CD-ROMs, and peer or collaborative teaching. Capel also stresses the importance of keeping a record of your developing breadth of competence in subject knowledge and other areas. If you have kept a thorough record of your experiences in the course of training it can streamline the process of constructing your letters of application and preparation for interview. If you are well organised, and make the time to record your observations, experiences and evaluations, this can also make your

NQT year much easier, and save you from having to redraft lessons from scratch instead of simply refining and adjusting what you have tried out in the course of your training.

Letters of application

Some schools will require you to fill in an application form, part of which is a personal statement in support of your application, other schools simply ask for a letter of application. It is important that you do not repeat yourself and reiterate statements that have been made elsewhere in your response – for instance, in talking about your degree details in the personal statement when they are appended in a curriculum vitae. The construction of curricula vitae and letters of application in general are described in depth in Capel *et al.* (1995). It may be salutory to remind yourself of what schools are looking for when they seek to appoint a new member of staff. Although not all schools send out both a job description and a person specification with the details for a post, it is helpful to keep in mind that there are two ways of looking at what schools want when they advertise a post. One perspective is the audit of various aspects of the job which need to be done – 'What will this person be required to do?' Another way of looking at the vacancy is to think of what qualities a person would have to possess in order to do the job effectively. Your letter of application should bear in mind both these considerations. Very few student teachers find writing letters of application an easy or edifying process. How do you indicate that you are good without coming over as bumptious or arrogant? Many applications suffer from an inability to make clear that the candidate has not merely undergone teaching practice, but has done so successfully and in a way which has developed their teaching skills and reinforced their commitment to entering the profession. As in writing history, you should attempt to provide supporting evidence for your claims, but in a carefully measured and (if anything) understated manner. One way of doing this is to incorporate brief extracts of summary reports and lesson observation notes which have been produced in the course of your placement. This is a way of avoiding having to rely solely on personal claims about your teaching competence, and can be balanced with statements indicating that you felt or believed that certain aspects of your teaching competence developed and improved as your practice progressed. If you look carefully at all the written comments which have emanated from your school experience, it should be possible to marshal the comments in such a way as to give a clear indication of the ways in which you have done well and proved to be successful, or demonstrated the potential to be a good or very good history teacher. There are obvious connections between the standards stipulated by *Circular 10/97* and the prerequisites outlined in Figure 12.1, but schools will be looking for more than

The following list may not be comprehensive, but it gives some indication of what most heads of history would be looking for when seeking to appoint a new member of staff. The first three criteria are particularly important.

1   Secure a purposeful and controlled atmosphere in the classroom and establish positive working relations with pupils.
2   Arrive at lessons equipped with materials and ideas which will provide worthwhile, stimulating and challenging learning experiences for pupils.
3   Work with colleagues in a cooperative and helpful manner and be prepared to play a full part in the life and work of the department.
4   Mark pupils' work promptly and thoroughly, with appropriate feedback and comment.
5   Set and mark purposeful homeworks according to school policy.
6   Keep an effective record of pupil attainment and progress.
7   Liaise effectively with parents, heads of year, form teachers, other members of your department and the school's senior management team.
8   Develop and maintain the state of classrooms, prepare display work, etc.
9   Contribute to the department's teaching resources and take care of resources used.
10 Be aware of, and make a positive contribution to, school policies and the life of the school in general.

Figure 12.1 What do heads of history want from a prospective member of their department?

a teacher who can adequately fulfil the demands of the competences. The four domains of competence specified in *10/97* are central to teaching competence, but they are a necessary, not sufficient condition of employability – schools are looking for teachers who have reached high levels in the *10/97* standards, but there are attributes which lie beyond this central core and can often be decisive in interview situations where more than one candidate convinces the interview panel that they possess the fundamental competences of classroom teaching.

There are other facets of classroom teaching to which departments might attach particular importance, in the light of their circumstances; the department may be looking for a new appointment who will provide a lead in the development of information technology, cross-curricular themes or equal opportunities, but the attributes outlined in Figure 12.1 are at the heart of the work of all history departments, and the first three items on the list are of particular importance. Your letter of application, and your performance at interview should bear in mind that these are the considerations which are central to the head of history's concerns. Are you the sort of teacher who will do these things well?

In view of this question, many schools draw up a person specification as well as a job description. Even where this is not the case, in addition to teaching competences, schools will be looking for teachers who possess personal and

TASK 12.1 COMPOSING LETTERS OF APPLICATION

The following details are an exemplar of a job description for a history post. Read them and then draft a letter of application which attempts to address the demands of this particular post.

'In the first instance, the successful candidate will be required to teach across the 11–16 age and ability range, at this mixed, split-site 11–18 high school. Opportunity for A level work would be considered for candidates with appropriate experience and qualifications. The person appointed would be expected to take responsibility for the teaching and organisation of history in the Lower School, under the overall supervision of the head of history. They will also be expected to teach GCSE classes, and to contribute to the department's impressive academic record in public examinations. An ability to contribute to extra-curricular activities, particularly in the areas of sport and drama, would also be welcomed. The ability to promote the development of information technology in the history department would also be helpful. Pupils study Modern World History at GCSE, and Nineteenth Century British and European History at A level. History classes are setted according to ability at the end of year 7.

The successful candidate will be expected to possess the following attributes:

- A determination to aspire to the highest academic standards for pupils.
- The ability to take responsibility and initiative in the field of curriculum development.
- Willingness to play a full part in the whole life and activities of the school.
- The ability to contribute effectively to the school's pastoral system by involvement as a form tutor.
- Expertise in information technology and its application to the history curriculum.
- Health, stamina, energy and determination.'

professional qualities which will complement technical classroom competence and subject knowledge. Your letter of application and your performance at interview will need to convince the panel that you are intelligent, conscientious, committed to working with young people, well organised and able to work to deadlines, with a sense of initiative and imagination, and that you are a 'reasonable human being' who has the interpersonal skills to work as part of a team. Probably the most important paragraph of your letter of application, and the one which should be longest, is the one which relates to your performance on school placement, and in composing it you should attempt to convey these professional attributes, as well as your classroom competence in planning, assessment, and subject knowledge. It is also important to keep in mind the importance which schools attach to the life of the school beyond the classroom. It is not unknown for one of the questions at interview to be about what you could bring to the school in addition to your abilities as a history teacher.

One final point about interview; although you are judged to some extent on the quality of your answers to the specific questions posed by the panel, your general manner and approach can have an important bearing on the outcome. If you come over as sincere, composed, intelligent, personable, and committed, this may outweigh a less than perfect answer to one or more questions. Often student teachers who have been unsuccessful at interview blame their fate on the content of their response to a particular question, and underestimate the importance of their general demeanour. Although you may feel self-conscious about the exercise, it can be helpful to tape-record your answers to some possible interview questions, and play them back to see whether you are answering at inordinate length, whether your responses come over as glib or ponderous, faltering or garbled, or simply boring.

TASK 12.2 ADAPTING LETTERS OF APPLICATION

What changes would you make to your letter of application in the light of the following job specification:

'The school is seeking to appoint a candidate who will be able to teach across the age and ability range at this 11–16 inner-city comprehensive school. An ability to teach the subject in a way that will stimulate the interest and enthusiasm of all pupils is an important prerequisite for the post, as is the ability to establish good working relations with pupils. The department enters pupils for the Schools Council History syllabus; pupils are in mixed-ability groups from year 7 to year 9. The ability to teach some Key Stage 3 Geography or RE would be welcomed, as would a willingness to contribute to the school's extra-curricular activities.

The following would be considered to be particularly important attributes for the post in question:

- Liveliness of approach and variety of teaching methodologies.
- Relationships with students and colleagues.
- Commitment to working with pupils of all abilities.
- Contribution to activities outside the classroom.
- Flexibility and resilience.'

INTERVIEW QUESTIONS

Although the details of the post which you receive along with the application form may provide some clues as to what questions might be asked (see Figure 12.2 for examples), and what are the most urgent concerns and priorities of the school, question spotting is as speculative an activity in the context of interviews as in attempting to predict what questions will be asked in written examinations.

The following list of questions was drawn up as the basis for a history interview at a London comprehensive school. Six questions were selected from the list by the interview panel. (We have added one or two questions to the list which have also featured in recent interviews for history posts.)

'What benefits has the introduction of the National Curriculum had for the teaching of history?'

'What are the implications of a wide range of assessment techniques for classroom practice and management?'

'How can history contribute to the wider cross-curricular themes and dimensions of the school curriculum?'

'How would you be able to contribute to a collaborative approach to curriculum development?'

'How would you monitor and assess your own delivery of the curriculum?'

'What do you feel are the most important issues in history teaching and learning?'

'Using specific examples, what principles would you apply when designing resources for mixed-ability classes?'

'How would you monitor pupil progress in learning?'

'Describe a lesson that you were responsible for that you feel was particularly successful and explain why?'

'If appointed to the post, what evidence might you point to in a year's time to show that you had executed the job description successfully?'

'How can we maximise the achievements of our students?'

'How can the history curriculum contribute to the school's equal opportunities policy?'

'What are your principal strengths and weaknesses as a teacher, and how will you ensure that the effects of your weaknesses are limited?'

'Given that the school's INSET budget is extremely limited, how will you seek to develop your teaching skills and subject knowledge?'

'How will you engage the interest and enthusiasm of the pupils for the study of history? Give an example of ways in which you have done this.'

'What factors enable teachers to achieve success for their pupils in external examinations?'

'In what ways might history teachers use information technology successfully in the classroom?'

'In what ways will pupils have benefited if they have been in your history lessons from year 7 to year 9?'

Figure 12.2 A list of interview questions

There may be general trends underlying which questions are 'fashionable' (information technology seems to be more prevalent than equal opportunities; differentiation and progression may have overtaken history outside the classroom), but it is probably more helpful to practise answering interview questions in general, rather than rehearse a 'set piece' answer to particular ones in the hope that you can trot out a rehearsed formula if one crops up at interview. You should also beware of trying to say what you think the panel wants to hear rather than what you feel. Interviews are not generally a test of political or pedagogical correctness, and you are more likely to talk fluently and convincingly if you believe what you are saying. It is also advisable to be measured and careful in what you claim, rather than lurching beyond what you can plausibly claim from your limited experience. You do not want to come over as dogmatic and inflexible, but neither do you want to be seem an empty-minded opportunist.

The short list for a first appointment in history is unlikely to be fewer than four candidates, and may be as many as ten. Given that part of the day will generally be given over to showing candidates round the school, introducing them to the senior management team, and meeting members of the history department, this usually leaves time for an interview of no more than 25 to 45 minutes. The former length would usually leave time for no more than five or six questions; you should be aware of these constraints, not feel the need to talk for the same length on all of them, and keep answers short if you feel you have

---

TASK 12.3 PRACTISING FOR INTERVIEW

Together with two fellow student teachers, conduct a practice interview using some of the above questions, or others which you might devise. One of you should act as observer, commenting on what they felt were the strengths and weaknesses of your responses and any idiosyncracies/habits which might adversely influence performance at interview (such as a tendency to say 'you know' at intervals, scratching the back of your neck, looking too gloomy, or evading eye contact).

TASK 12.4 FINDING OUT ABOUT INTERVIEW PROCEDURES AND QUESTIONS

Ask your subject mentor about the general procedures for interview at the school you are working in; what questions are commonly asked at history interviews; what heads of history look for in candidates; what mistakes candidates sometimes make in answering questions; and what advice he or she would give you in terms of preparation for the interview.

nothing further of value to say. Another factor which you should keep in mind is that in the course of the day the head of history will be considering whether you would be a pleasure to work with, and whether you would 'fit in' to the department, both socially and professionally. 'Reasonable human being' qualities are not central to the demands of *Circular 10/97*, but at this point in the process of entering the teaching profession they are an important factor.

TEACHING AT INTERVIEW

It has become increasingly common in recent years to incorporate some element of presentation or teaching into the selection process. Although this introduces an extra hurdle, and possibly an element of pressure and concern into the procedures, in many ways it is easier to prepare for this element of the selection process. Unlike the interview, where you will not know exactly what will be asked of you, it is usual to give candidates a clear brief of what is to be taught, and to what class. It is not likely to be the class from hell on Friday afternoon, and there will obviously be someone observing the class, so classroom management should not be a major concern. You will usually be told what topic to teach, but be given a degree of latitude in how to approach it. In effect, you should have a reasonable amount of time to prepare a single lesson; most applicants find that this is a comparatively enjoyable and relaxing aspect of the selection process, given the extent to which the candidate is informed beforehand what is required.

GETTING BETTER AT TEACHING HISTORY

In Chapter 1 we posed the question of how people get better at teaching. It is generally accepted that it is not simply a matter of accumulated experience, and that several factors are involved; including doing it, watching it being done, being instructed in it, reading about it and talking about it with fellow practitioners. Matthew Arnold, commenting on a school inspector who boasted of being an inspector of thirteen years' experience, remarked that he was an inspector of one year's experience, repeated thirteen times over. How can you avoid similar accusations being made of your own teaching career? Although the idea of reflective practice has become an influential one in recent years – the idea that teachers improve through the quality of their reflection on doing it, reading about it and so on – reflection on practice might not *per se* enable teachers to develop to expert levels. (Hamlet was good at reflecting but did not become effective at what he wanted to do.) Part of the definition of being professional is that you want to improve and are determined to do whatever is necessary to effect improvement. Initiative, determination and ambition (to aspire to the highest possible professional standards) are as important as reflection in making progress as a teacher.

Other agendas include the question of developing ownership of your own teaching. Whilst working within the framework of your department, you will hopefully develop your own ideas and style of history teaching, and generate ideas as well as assimilating those of other history teachers and tutors; one of the pleasures of teaching as a profession is that it offers the opportunity for genuinely creative and innovative practice. There is, however, the danger of what MacDonald has termed 'induction into bad practice' (MacDonald, 1984), and of being socialised into a particular brand of professional practice rather than remaining open to new ideas and suggestions (Calderhead, 1994).

The demands of your course, and your observations and experiences in the course of your training, will have made you fully aware that however diligent and accomplished you have been, you will not emerge from your training as the perfect, fully equipped 'expert' teacher. As in so many aspects of teaching, the idea of a continuum can be extremely helpful. The best teachers are aware of the continuums involved on the journey towards becoming an expert teacher and are constantly seeking to aspire to the highest possible professional standards. Progression is an issue that pertains to teachers as well as pupils. The Teacher Training Agency's emphasis on the importance of professional development, from NQT to expert teacher and on to subject and school leadership, has focused attention on the the need for teachers to continue to be learners who will refine and develop their classroom competences. Figure 12.3 shows the list of qualities which the TTA consider to be desirable in the mentoring of student teachers. It is indicative of the sort of teacher who is likely to be effective, and a good role model, in helping other teachers and student teachers to improve.

At one level, this is about refining your classroom teaching skills, as defined in the competences outlined in *Circular 10/97*. You *must* develop to adequate levels of competence in the areas stipulated by *10/97*, but you *should* aspire to excellence in all these areas, rather than settling for 'baseline' or minimum levels of competence. The framework of competences outlined by *Circular 10/97* has a continued relevance, but you should now be focusing on expert levels of competence, rather than adequacy. Thus, for instance, with standard B2 a ii, B2 k i–iv, 'keep all pupils engaged through stimulating intellectual curiosity, communicating interest for the subject, fostering pupils' enthusiasm for the subject, and maintaining pupils motivation', there is the question of the range and percentage of lessons in which you are able to arouse the interest and engagement of pupils, and there is also the degree of interest and engagement which you are able to elicit from your teaching groups. The Chief Inspector for Schools' 1996 Report comments on the 'urgency' for learning which was observed in many classrooms (OFSTED, 1997). In what percentage of your lessons do pupils leave the room still talking about what they have learned? As your experience and classroom knowledge increase, there should be more and

The ideal contributor to ITT (Initial Teacher Training) might, amongst other things, be:

- knowledgeable about teaching and learning, and still curious about them;
- knowledgeable about a subject and how to teach it;
- knowledgeable about a range of teaching methods and when and how to use them;
- always ready to reassess teaching methods in the light of research, experience and feedback (a 'reflective practitioner');
- an active listener;
- good at giving clear and constructive feedback;
- a skilful planner;
- a skilful manager of time;
- someone with plenty of enthusiasm, energy and imagination;
- someone who goes on learning throughout their career.

Figure 12.3 Qualities desirable in subject mentors
Source: TTA, 1996

more historical topics which you are able to present in a way which elicits the engagement and enthusiasm of pupils.

Whether you consider your teaching competence in terms of a continuum, between novice and expert levels of competence, or the six-level model referred to in Chapter 8, it is important to be aware that there are many areas of history teaching in which you need to continue to pose questions of yourself. Progression is something that pertains to teachers as well as pupils; if teaching is to continue to be a rewarding, enjoyable and fulfilling profession, you will need to feel that you are getting better at it and learning new skills, or acquiring higher level skills in your teaching. The range of factors involved in developing into the expert teacher and the 'complete' history person are such that, as in your training, you will have to make difficult choices in terms of prioritising your professional development. The Career Entry Profile envisaged by the TTA should provide a more formal and developed plan for mapping your professional career development. From 1998 all newly qualified teachers will be expected to bring with them to their first post an audit of 'strengths and needs' which can serve as a basis to negotiate a programme of continuing support and professional development. You still need to work on weaker areas of your teaching, but you should also give some thought to thinking about which strengths to develop to higher levels, in order to further your career and ensure that you continue to find the business of teaching rewarding. Some history teachers choose to focus on the consolidation of their subject knowledge, others on progressing to more sophisticated levels of expertise in information technology. Many find that involvement in the mentoring of student teachers is an interesting and helpful area for developing professional expertise. INSET courses, whether accredited and leading to advanced diplomas and masters degrees, or simply one-day workshops to develop new schemes of work, will not magic away all your problems and limitations in the classroom, but can serve to sustain your interest and offer some practical ways forward. The choice of ways forward will need to be negotiated with the school and department you work in, but it is important to be proactive in terms of staff development; initiative and drive are as important after QTS (Qualified Teacher Status) as before.

Figure 12.4 includes but a handful of the many questions/continuums which you should consider in the course of your continuing professional development. As you aspire to subject leadership, there are also agendas such as time management, administrative efficiency, professional relationships and effective communication which complement those of classroom teaching. You will also need to continue to develop your subject knowledge, keep abreast of new developments in history software, keep up to date with new ideas for teaching history,

---

There are many areas of history teaching where student teachers develop to levels of basic competence or beyond in the course of their training, but not to higher levels of competence. The following are 'prompt' questions, which you might consider in thinking about where you stand in terms of the continuum between adequate and expert levels of proficiency in various aspects of teaching history. With all these questions, you might consider both the percentage of lessons in which . . . , and the extent to which . . .

How effective are you at explaining to pupils what happened in the past in a way that interests pupils and in a way which they can understand?

How effective are the homeworks which you set in terms of advancing pupils' learning and reinforcing their motivation to do well in history?

How effective are you in using new technology to enhance the quality of teaching and learning in history?

How effectively do you differentiate your planning for learning in a way that provides both access and challenge for pupils in your history lessons?

How broad and accomplished is your range of teaching techniques in the history classroom?

How good are you at working cooperatively with colleagues to share ideas and good practice?

How assured is your subject knowledge in the areas you are obliged to teach?

Figure 12.4   Questions to think about in terms of degrees of competence

and ensure that you have an up-to-date knowledge of official documents relating to assessment arrangements and changing syllabuses.

Proposition: There are not enough hours in the day to do everything which might be done to become the perfect or complete history teacher (and keep a sliver of life apart from your teaching). However, if you do at least some of the things listed in Figure 12.5 the improvements in your effectiveness as a teacher will be sufficiently rewarding to justify the time and effort involved.

It might also be added that that if you possess all the characteristics outlined in Figure 12.5, you are likely to be tired by the end of term, but in recent years intrinsic enjoyment of employment has been increasingly regarded as an important element of job satisfaction. It is much more likely that you will enjoy teaching if you believe you are doing it effectively, and getting better at it.

Circular 10/97 defines the framework for your induction into the teaching profession, and the four domains of competence – knowledge and understanding;

- They continue to read history books for pleasure and pass on some of the fruits of their reading to pupils.
- They read books, and journal and newspaper articles about current debates concerning history and the nature and purpose of school history.
- They read review articles about new publications in history and new history software.
- They attend INSET courses and history conferences to keep abreast of new ideas and to develop a broader repertoire of teaching skills.
- They talk to other history teachers about their teaching, and exchange ideas and resources.
- They find time to read history journals such as *Teaching History, Modern History Review, History Today*.
- They make changes and refinements to lessons even when they have worked quite well first time with classes.
- They keep abreast of broader educational debates by reading *The Times Educational Supplement*, and the weekly education sections in the newspapers.
- They continue to try out new ideas and methods in their teaching.
- They display initiative in 'scavenging' for resources which help to make lessons more vivid and enjoyable for pupils.
- Their relations with teaching groups improve as the teaching year progresses.
- They make time to talk to and work with pupils outside formal lesson time.
- They make strenuous efforts to get the best results possible for pupils taking external examinations.
- They enjoy their teaching.

Figure 12.5 Some characteristics of improving history teachers

planning, teaching and class management; monitoring assessment; recording, reporting and accountability; and other professional requirements – remain just as central to your development as a teacher after you have gained QTS. There are, however, other models of competence which might provide insight into which teachers are likely to progress towards mastery of teaching skills and expertise. John Elliott's work on action research as an agent for teacher development has been influential (Elliott, 1991, 1993), as has the work of Les Tickle (1994). Another source of insight might be to study the weekly feature on 'My best teacher' which is now included in both *The Times Educational Supplement*, and the *Guardian*'s education section. As well as demonstrating that there are very different types of expert teacher, it is heartening to be reminded of the impact and difference that a good teacher can make. Indeed, amongst all the debates and disputes about class size, teaching methodology, league tables and OFSTED inspection, almost the only area of consensus is that the most important element of effective educational provision is a good teacher.

SUMMARY AND KEY POINTS

Your ITE course is the first stage of your development as a history teacher, not the culminating point. It is just as important not to 'plateau' after attaining QTS as before. There are still important choices and conflicting priorities in terms of the ways you are to progress as a teacher – you can't become expert at everything at once. A large measure of job satisfaction in teaching is derived from the satisfaction of doing the job well and getting better at it. You need to display initiative in your continuing professional development rather than simply waiting passively for professional advancement. This should derive partly from your own sense of adventure in the classroom, partly from reading, and partly from advice, courses, conferences and guidance from other professionals. The challenge of becoming a comprehensively accomplished history teacher is a very difficult and demanding one, requiring a wide range of knowledge, skills and personal and professional qualities; the nature of this challenge helps to explain why the profession of the history teacher is such an interesting and (potentially) rewarding one.

FURTHER READING

The annual conferences of the Historical Association and the Schools Council History conference are the most important events in terms of keeping up to date with your subject and keeping abreast of the ideas of leading practitioners, official bodies and recent research into school history. In addition to keynote addresses, a wide choice of workshops, 'drop-in' IT demonstrations, and publishers' exhibitions, it is generally exhilarating and enjoyable to meet with and talk to fellow history teachers in such a propitious and congenial environment. The conferences demonstrate that it is possible for in-service experience to be useful and enjoyable at the same time.

The main professional journal for history teachers is *Teaching History*, published four times a year by the Historical Association. There has been a conscious attempt to move towards articles which are of use and interest to classroom practitioners. There is a regular update on developments in history and IT by HABET, the Historical Association's advisory body on educational technology. *Teaching History* also contains reviews of new textbooks, topic books and history software. Subscription details can be obtained from the Historical Association, 59a Kennington Park Road, London, SE11 4JH.

The Historical Association also provides an extensive list of publications on aspects of classroom practice in its 'Teaching of History' series.

Some recent texts on the teaching of history are more user friendly than others; they are not all 'page turners', but, as Lawlor has noted, 'Very many things in life – at school and later – including the acquisition of knowledge, require effort and concentration' (Lawlor, 1989). The training process, with its taut schedules, frenetic pace and constant demands, does not lend itself to discursive reading, but after qualification you should at least have some time over the summer break to read some of the important and influential books which have shaped opinion on what school history should be, how it relates to academic history, and how it might best be taught. We have noted here only works which have not been mentioned earlier in this volume.

Appleby, J., Hunt, L. and Jacob, M. (1994) *Telling the Truth about History*, New York, Norton.
One of the most readable and stimulating contributions to the debate on the function of history in society.

Brown, R. (1994) *Managing the Learning of History*, London, David Fulton.
Contains some interesting and provocative ideas about developing a collaborative, learning culture in the history department.

Farmer, A. and Knight, P. (1995) *Active History in Key Stages 3 and 4*, London, David Fulton.
Contains many sensible ideas for teaching history to secondary phase pupils.

Hobsbawn, E. (1997) *On history*, London, Weidenfeld & Nicholson.

Nichol, J. (1984) *Teaching History*, London, Macmillan.
In spite of its age, contains interesting and useful ideas for teaching National Curriculum history.

Slater, J. (1995) *Teaching History in the New Europe*, London, Cassell.
Eclectic, and as with all Slater's work, eminently readable.

Tosh, J. (1984) *The Pursuit of History*, London, Longman.
An important and very readable text which provides insights into varieties of historical work, and a rationale for the uses of history.

Appendix
Standards for the award of
Qualified Teacher Status

Annex A to the DfEE Teacher Training Circular, Letter 10/97

SECTIONS PERTAINING TO SECONDARY STUDENT TEACHERS

Introduction

The sections apply to all trainees seeking Qualified Teacher Status (QTS) and, except where otherwise specified, should be met by those assessed for QTS from May 1998. Successful completion of a course or programme of ITT, including employment based provision, must require the trainee to achieve all these standards. *All* courses must involve the assessment of *all* trainees against *all the standards specified*.

The standards have been written to be specific, explicit and assessable, and are designed to provide a clear basis for the reliable and consistent award of Qualified Teacher Status, regardless of the training route or type of training leading to QTS. To achieve this purpose, each standard has been set out discretely. Professionalism, however, implies more than meeting a series of discrete standards. It is necessary to consider the standards as a whole to appreciate the creativity, commitment, energy and enthusiasm which teaching demands, and the intellectual and managerial skills required of the effective professional. While trainees must be assessed against all the standards during their ITT course, there is no intention to impose a methodology on providers for the assessment of trainees against the standards.

It is not intended that each standard should require a separate assessment occasion. Groups of standards are closely linked and are designed so that they can be assessed together.

A KNOWLEDGE AND UNDERSTANDING

1 Secondary

For all courses those to be awarded Qualified Teacher Status must, when assessed, demonstrate that they:

i have a secure knowledge and understanding of the concepts and skills in their specialist subject(s),[1] at a standard equivalent to degree level to enable them to teach it (them) confidently and accurately at:

- KS3 for trainees on 7–14 courses;
- **KS3 and KS4 and, where relevant, post-16** for trainees on 11–16 or 18 courses; and
- **KS4 and post-16** for trainees on 14–19 courses;

ii have, for their specialist subject(s), where applicable, detailed knowledge and understanding of the National Curriculum programmes of study, level descriptions or end of key stage descriptions for KS3 and, where applicable, National Curriculum programmes of study for KS4;

iii for RE specialists, have a detailed knowledge of the Model Syllabuses for RE;

iv are familiar, for their specialist subject(s), with the relevant KS4 and post-16 examination syllabuses and courses, including vocational courses;[2]

v understand, for their specialist subject(s), the framework of 14–19 qualifications and the routes of progression through it;[2]

vi understand, for their specialist subject(s), progression from the KS2 programmes of study;[3]

vii know and can teach the key skills required for current qualifications relevant to their specialist subject, for pupils aged 14–19, and understand the contribution that their specialist subject(s) makes to the development of key skills;

viii cope securely with subject-related questions which pupils raise;

ix are aware of, and know how to access, recent inspection evidence and classroom-relevant research evidence on teaching secondary pupils in their specialist subject(s), and know how to use this to inform and improve their teaching;

---

1 Required subject knowledge for those teaching English, mathematics and science at secondary level will be specified when the relevant ITT National Curricula are implemented.

2 This does not apply to trainees on 7–14 courses.

3 This does not apply to trainees on 14–19 courses.

x know, for their specialist subject(s), pupils' most common misconceptions and mistakes;

xi understand how pupils' learning in the subject is affected by their physical, intellectual, emotional and social development;

xii have a working knowledge of information technology (IT) to a standard equivalent to Level 8 in the National Curriculum for pupils,[4] and understand the contribution that IT makes to their specialist subject(s);

xiii are familiar with subject-specific health and safety requirements, where relevant, and plan lessons to avoid potential hazards.

B PLANNING, TEACHING AND CLASS MANAGEMENT

2 Standards for Primary and Secondary

This section details the standards which all those to be awarded Qualified Teacher Status must demonstrate, when assessed, in each subject that they have been trained to teach. For primary non-core, non-specialist subjects, trainees being assessed for Qualified Teacher Status must meet the required standards but with the support, if necessary, of a teacher experienced in the subject concerned.

Planning

For all courses those to be awarded Qualified Teacher Status must, when assessed, demonstrate that they:

a plan their teaching to achieve progression in pupils' learning through:

  i identifying clear teaching objectives and content, appropriate to the subject matter and the pupils being taught, and specifying how these will be taught and assessed;

  ii setting tasks for whole class, individual and group work, including homework, which challenge pupils and ensure high levels of pupil interest;

  iii setting appropriate and demanding expectations for pupils' learning, motivation and presentation of work;

  iv setting clear targets for pupils' learning, building on prior attainment,

---

4 Trainees may omit the 'control' element of the IT National Curriculum Order if this is not relevant to their specialist subject. This standard does not apply until September 1998.

and ensuring that pupils are aware of the substance and purpose of what they are asked to do.

v identifying pupils who:

- have special educational needs, including specific learning difficulties;
- are very able;
- are not yet fluent in English;
  and knowing where to get help in order to give positive and targeted support;

b provide clear structures for lessons, and for sequences of lessons, in the short, medium and longer term, which maintain pace, motivation and challenge for pupils;

c make effective use of assessment information on pupils' attainment and progress in their teaching and in planning future lessons and sequences of lessons;

d plan opportunities to contribute to pupils' personal, spiritual, moral, social and cultural development;

e where applicable, ensure coverage of the relevant examination syllabuses and National Curriculum programmes of study.

Teaching and Class Management

For all courses those to be awarded Qualified Teacher Status must, when assessed, demonstrate that they:

f ensure effective teaching of whole classes, and of groups and individuals within the whole class setting, so that teaching objectives are met, and best use is made of available teaching time;

g monitor and intervene when teaching to ensure sound learning and discipline;

h establish and maintain a purposeful working atmosphere;

i set high expectations for pupils' behaviour, establishing and maintaining a good standard of discipline through well focused teaching and through positive and productive relationships;

j establish a safe environment which supports learning and in which pupils feel secure and confident;

k use teaching methods which sustain the momentum of pupils' work and keep all pupils engaged through:

i stimulating intellectual curiosity, communicating enthusiasm for the subject being taught, fostering pupils' enthusiasm and maintaining pupils' motivation;

ii matching the approaches used to the subject matter and the pupils being taught;

iii structuring information well, including outlining content and aims, signalling transitions and summarising key points as the lesson progresses;

iv clear presentation of content around a set of key ideas, using appropriate subject-specific vocabulary and well chosen illustrations and examples;

v clear instruction and demonstration, and accurate well-paced explanation;

vi effective questioning which matches the pace and direction of the lesson and ensures that pupils take part;

vii careful attention to pupils' errors and misconceptions, and helping to remedy them;

viii listening carefully to pupils, analysing their responses and responding constructively in order to take pupils' learning forward;

ix selecting and making good use of textbooks, IT and other learning resources which enable teaching objectives to be met;

x providing opportunities for pupils to consolidate their knowledge and maximising opportunities, both in the classroom and through setting well-focused homework, to reinforce and develop what has been learnt;

xi exploiting opportunities to improve pupils' basic skills in literacy, numeracy and IT, and the individual and collaborative study skills needed for effective learning, including information retrieval from libraries, texts and other sources;

xii exploiting opportunities to contribute to the quality of pupils' wider educational development, including their personal, spiritual, moral, social and cultural development;

xiii setting high expectations for all pupils notwithstanding individual differences, including gender, and cultural and linguistic backgrounds;

xiv providing opportunities to develop pupils' wider understanding by relating their learning to real and work-related examples;

l are familiar with the Code of Practice on the identification and assessment of special educational needs and, as part of their responsibilities under the Code, implement and keep records on individual education plans (IEPs) for pupils at stage 2 of the Code and above;

m ensure that pupils acquire and consolidate knowledge, skills and understanding in the subject;

n   evaluate their own teaching critically and use this to improve their effectiveness.

C MONITORING, ASSESSMENT, RECORDING, REPORTING AND ACCOUNTABILITY

This section details the standards which all those to be awarded Qualified Teacher Status must demonstrate, when assessed, in each subject that they have been trained to teach. For primary non-core, non-specialist subjects, trainees being assessed for Qualified Teacher Status must meet the required standards but with the support, if necessary, of a teacher experienced in the subject concerned.

For all courses those to be awarded Qualified Teacher Status must, when assessed, demonstrate that they:

a   assess how well learning objectives have been achieved and use this assessment to improve specific aspects of teaching;

b   mark and monitor pupils' assigned classwork and homework, providing constructive oral and written feedback, and setting targets for pupils' progress;

c   assess and record each pupil's progress systematically, including through focused observation, questioning, testing and marking, and use these records to:
    i   check that pupils have understood and completed the work set;
    ii   monitor strengths and weaknesses and use the information gained as a basis for purposeful intervention in pupils' learning;
    iii information planning;
    iv   check that pupils continue to make demonstrable progress in their acquisition of the knowledge, skills and understanding of the subject;

d   are familiar with the statutory assessment and reporting requirements and know how to prepare and present informative reports to parents;

e   where applicable, understand the expected demands of pupils in relation to each relevant level description or end of key stage description, and, in addition, for those on 11–16 or 18 and 14–19 courses, the demands of the syllabuses and course requirements for GCSE, other KS4 courses, and, where applicable, post-16 courses;

f   where applicable, understand and know how to implement the assessment requirements of current qualifications for pupils aged 14–19;

g   recognise the level at which a pupil is achieving, and assess pupils consistently against attainment targets, where applicable, if necessary with guidance from an experienced teacher;

h   understand and know how national, local, comparative and school data, including National Curriculum test data, where applicable, can be used to set clear targets for pupils' achievement;

i   use different kinds of assessment appropriately for different purposes, including National Curriculum and other standardised tests, and baseline assessment where relevant.

D   OTHER PROFESSIONAL REQUIREMENTS

For all courses those to be awarded Qualified Teacher Status should, when assessed, demonstrate that they:

a   have a working knowledge and understanding of:

i   teachers' professional duties as set out in the current School Teachers' Pay and Conditions document, issued under the School Teachers' Pay and Conditions Act 1991;

ii   teachers' legal liabilities and responsibilities relating to:

- the Race Relations Act 1976;
- the Sex Discrimination Act 1975;
- Section 7 and Section 8 of the Health and Safety at Work, etc. Act 1974;
- teachers' common law duty to ensure that pupils are healthy and safe on school premises and when leading activities off the school site, such as educational visits, school outings or field trips;
- what is reasonable for the purposes of safeguarding or promoting children's welfare (Section 3(5) of the Children Act 1989);
- the role of the education service in protecting children from abuse (currently set out in DfEE *Circular 10/95* and the Home Office, Department of Health, DfEE and Welsh Office Guidance *Working Together: A guide to arrangements for inter-agency co-operation for the protection of children from abuse 1991*);
- appropriate physical contact with pupils (currently set out in DfEE *Circular 10/95*)
- appropriate physical restraint of pupils (Section 4 of the Education Act 1997 and DfEE *Circular 9/94*);
- detention of pupils on disciplinary grounds (Section 5 of the Education Act 1997).

b   have established, during work in schools, effective working relationships with professional colleagues including, where applicable, associate staff;

c   set a good example to the pupils they teach, through their presentation and their personal and professional conduct;

d   are committed to ensuring that every pupil is given the opportunity to achieve their potential and meet the high expectations set for them;

e   understand the need to take responsibility for their own professional development and to keep up to date with research and developments in pedagogy and in the subjects they teach;

f   understand their professional responsibilities in relation to school policies and practices, including those concerned with pastoral and personal safety matters, including bullying;

g   recognise that learning takes place inside and outside the school context, and understand the need to liaise effectively with parents and other carers and with agencies with responsibility for pupils' education and welfare;

h   are aware of the role and purpose of school governing bodies.

Editors' note We have included only those standards pertaining to Secondary student teachers. Those studying for Primary or Early Years courses should consult the original circular.

References

1 INTRODUCTION

Barber, M. (1994) *Guardian*, 23 August.

Bennett, S. and Steele, I. (1995) 'The Revised History Order', *Teaching History*, No. 79, April, pp. 5–8.

Burston, W.H. and Green, C.W. (eds) (1962) *Handbook for History Teachers*, London, Methuen.

Dean, J. (1995) *Teaching History at Key Stage 2*, Cambridge, Chris Kington Publishing, p. 4.

DfE (1992) *The Accreditation of Initial Teacher Training: Circular 9/92*, Council for the Accreditation for Teacher Education.

DfEE (1997) *Annex A to the Department for Education and Employment Teacher Training Circular Letter 10/97, Standards for the award of Qualified Teacher Status*, DfEE

Jenkins K. and Brickley, P. (1991) 'Always Historicise: Unintended Opportunities in National Curriculum History', *Teaching History*, No. 62, January, pp. 9–14.

Labbett, B. (1996) *Principles of Procedure and the Expert Teacher*. This is an electronic seminar paper, available on the World Wide Web at http://www.uea.ac.uk/care/edu/Main.html.

Lawlor, S. (1996) *Times Educational Supplement*, 6 September.

National Curriculum Council (NCC) (1991) *History: Non Statutory Guidance*, London, HMSO, section B1.

Nichol, J. (1995) *Teaching History at Key Stage 3*, Cambridge, Chris Kington Publishing, p. 1.

Noble K. (1995) *The International Educational Quotations Encyclopaedia*, Buckingham, Open University Press, p. 83.

Phillips, R. (1991) 'National Curriculum History and Teacher Autonomy, the Major Challenge', *Teaching History*, No. 65, October.

Schick, J. (1995) 'On Being Interactive: Rethinking the Learning Equation', *History Microcomputer Review*, Vol. 11, No. 1 (Spring), pp. 9–25.

Schon, D. (1983) *The Reflective Practitioner*, New York, Basic Books.

2 THE PLACE OF HISTORY IN THE SCHOOL CURRICULUM

Aldrich, R. (ed.) (1991) *History in the National Curriculum*, London, Kogan Page.

Batho, G. (1986) 'From a Test of Memory to a Training for Life', in M. H. Price (ed.) *The Development of the Secondary Curriculum*, London, Croom Helm.

Beattie, A. (1987) *History in Peril: May Parents Preserve It*, London Centre for Policy Studies.

Blunkett, D. (1996) BBC News, 19 October.

Booth, M. (1990) 'National Curriculum History: Interim Report', *Teaching History*, January.

Bourdillon, H. (ed.) (1994) *Teaching History*, London, Routledge.

Bracey, P. (1995) 'Developing a Multicultural Perspective Within Key-Stage 3 National Curriculum History', *Teaching History*, January.

Coltham, J. B. and Fines, J. (1971) *Educational Objectives for the Study of History*, London, Historical Association.

Conquest, R. (1969) from Cox, C. and Dyson, A. 'Fight for Education: A Black Paper', in *Critical Quarterly*, quoted in M. Ballard (ed.) (1970) *New Movements in the Study and Teaching of History*, London, Maurice Temple Smith, p.3.

Crawford, K. (1995) 'A History of the Right: The Battle for Control of National Curriculum History 1989–1994', *British Journal of Educational Studies*, Vol. XXXXIII, No. 4, pp. 433–56.

Dearing, R. (1994) *The National Curriculum and its Assessment*, London, SCAA.

Department of Education (DfE) (1995) *History in the National Curriculum*, London, HMSO.

DES (1988) *History from 5 to 16: Curriculum Matters 11, an HMI Series*, London, HMSO.

DES (1989) *National Curriculum History Working Group: Interim Report*, London, HMSO.

DES (1990) *Final Report of the National Curriculum History Working Group*, London, HMSO.

Haydn, T. (1992a) 'History for Ordinary Children', *Teaching History*, April.

Haydn, T. (1992b) 'History Reprieved', *Teaching History*, January.

Haydn, T. (1996) 'Nationalism Begins at Home: The Impact of National Curriculum History on Perceptions of National Identity in Britain, 1987–1994', *History of Education Bulletin*, April, pp. 51–61.

Hill, C. (1953) *Suggestions on the Teaching of History*, Paris, UNESCO.

HMI (1985) *History in the Primary and Secondary Years*, London, HMSO.

Husbands, C. (1996) *What is History Teaching: Language, Ideas and Meaning in Learning about the Past*, Buckingham, Open University Press.

Jenkins, C. (1995) 'Life Skills Book for Slow Learners', *Times Educational Supplement*, 1 December.

Joseph, K. (1984) 'Why Teach History in School', *The Historian*, No. 2.

Lee, P. (1994) *Historical Knowledge and the National Curriculum*, in H. Bourdillon (ed.) *History Teaching*, London, Routledge.

Lee, P., Slater, J., Walsh, P. and White, J. (1992) *The Aims of School History: The National Curriculum and Beyond*, London, Tufnell Press

Little, V. (1990) 'A National Curriculum in History: A Very Contentious Issue', *British Journal of Educational Studies*, Vol. XXXVIII, No. 4, pp. 319–34.

Longworth, N. (1981) 'We're moving into the Information Society – what shall we tell the children?', *Computer Education*, June, pp. 17–19.

Marwick, A. (1984) *The Nature of History*, London, Macmillan.

Ministry of Education (1952) *Teaching History*, London, HMSO.

NCC (1991) *History: Non-statutory Guidance*, York, NCC.

NCER (1995) *1995 Year 11 GCSE Examinations Pupil Referenced Analysis*.

Pankhania, J. (1994) *Liberating the National History Curriculum*, Lewes, Falmer.

Phillips, R. (1996) 'The Origins, Creation and Implementation of History in the National Curriculum', unpublished Ph.D. thesis, University of Wales, Swansea.

Price, M. (1968) 'History in Danger', *Teaching History*, November.

Slater, J. (1984) 'The Case for History in School', *The Historian*, No. 2.

Slater, J. (1989) *The Politics of History Teaching: a Humanity Dehumanised?*, London, ULIE.

Slater, J. (1991) 'History in the National Curriculum: The Final Report of the History Working Group', in R. Aldrich (ed.) *History in the National Curriculum*, London, Kogan Page.

Slater, J. (1995) *Teaching History in the New Europe*, London, Cassell.

Tate, N. (1996) Paper presented to the SCAA Conference on Curriculum, Culture and Society, held at the Kensington Hilton Hotel, 7 February 1996.

White, C. (1996) 'History 14–19: Challenges and Opportunities', *Teaching History*, January.

White, J. (1994) 'The Aims of School History', *Teaching History*, January.

Williams, N. (1986) 'The Schools Council Project: History 13–16, The First Ten Years of Examinations', *Teaching History*, October.

Woodhead, C. (1996) *Guardian*, 4 April.

3 PLANNING FOR LEARNING: LEARNING OBJECTIVES

Battersby, J. (1996) 'Discipline and Control', Unpublished lecture, University of East Anglia, 4 November.

Bennett, S. and Steele, I. (1995) 'The Revised History Order', *Teaching History*, No. 79, April, pp. 5–8.

Bowen, P. (1993) 'Work from the Known to the Unknown', *Welsh Historian*, No. 20, Autumn, pp. 19–22.

Burston, W.H. (1963) *Principles of History Teaching*, London, Methuen.

Counsell, C. (1996) 'Progression at Key Stage 3: What Does "Getting Better" at History Mean?', Address to the Historical Association Conference, York, 14 September.

Dearing, R. (1994) *The National Curriculum and its Assessment*, London, SCAA.

Department for Education (1992) *The Accreditation of Initial Teacher Training: Circular 9/92*, Council for the Accreditation of Teacher Training.

Department for Education (DfE) (1995) *History in the National Curriculum*, London, HMSO.

Deuchar, S. (1989) *The New History: A Critique*, York, Campaign for Real Education.

Farmer, A. and Knight, P. (1995) *Active History In Key Stages 3 and 4*, London, David Fulton.

Feiman-Nemser, S. and Parker, M. (1990) *Making Subject Matter Part of the Conversation or Helping Beginning Teachers Learn to Teach*, National Centre for Research on Teacher Education, ERIC document ED 322 135, March, quoted in M. Fertig (1995) 'Planning for National Curriculum History Lessons – the Experience of Newly-qualified Teachers', *Teaching History*, No. 78, January, p. 27.

Haydn, T. (1994) 'Uses and Abuses of the TGAT Testing Model: The Case of History and the 45 Boxes', *The Curriculum Journal*, Summer, Vol. 5, No. 2, pp. 215–33.

Heafford, D. (1990) 'Teachers Teach but do Learners Learn?', in C. Wringe (ed.) *Language Learning Journal* 1, 88, quoted in N. Pachler and C. Field (1997) *Learning to Teach Modern Foreign Languages in the Secondary School*, London, Routledge.

Historical Association (1988) *History in the National Curriculum*, London, Historical Association, p. 15.

HMI (1985) *History in the Primary and Secondary Years*, London, HMSO, p. 14.

Holt, J. (1982) *How Children Fail*, New York, Delacorte/Seymour Lawrence, pp. 176–7, 276.

Husbands, C. (1996) *What is History Teaching?*, Buckingham, Open University Press, p. 34.

Lawlor, S. (1989) 'Correct Core', in B. Moon, P. Murphy and J. Raynor (eds) *Policies for the Curriculum*, Buckingham, Open University.

Lawton, D. (1985) Education, Culture and the Curriculum, London, Hodder and Stoughton, pp. 84–5.

Lomas, T. (1990) *Teaching and Assessing Historical Understanding* (Teaching of History Series, No. 63), London, Historical Association.

MacLennan, S. (1987) 'Integrating Lesson Planning and Classroom Management', *ELT Journal*, Vol. 41, No. 3, pp. 193–6.

McGovern, C. (1994) *The SCAA Review of National Curriculum History: A Minority Report*, York, Campaign for Real Education.

Ministry of Education (1952) *Teaching History*, Pamphlet 23, London, HMSO, p. 32.

Moss, P. (1970) *History Alive 55 BC–1485*, London, Hart-Davis.

National Curriculum Council (NCC) (1991) *Non Statutory Guidance for History*, Section B1.

National Curriculum Council (NCC) (1993) *Teaching History at Key Stage 3*, York, NCC.

OFSTED (1996) *Annual Report of Her Majesty's Chief Inspector of Schools*, London, OFSTED, pp. 61–2.

Ridley, J. (1972) *Lord Palmerston*, London, Constable, pp. 171–91.

SCAA (1994) *An Introduction to the Revised National Curriculum*, London, SCAA.

Smart, L. (1995) 'The Contribution of CD-ROMs to the Development of Key

Historical Concepts with Children up to the Age of 8', Paper delivered at the CHC conference, Luxembourg, 21 April.

Thompson, D. (1962) 'Some Psychological Aspects of History Teaching', in W.H. Burston and C.W. Green (eds) *Handbook for History Teachers*, London, Methuen, pp. 18–38.

4 LEARNING STRATEGIES AND THE USE OF LANGUAGE

Arkell, T. (1982) 'How well do Readability Tests Detect Difficulties in History Texts?', *Teaching History*, February.

Barnes, D. (1976) *From Communication to Curriculum*, London, Penguin.

Barnes, D., Britton, J. and Rosen H. (1969) *Language, Learner and the School*, London, Penguin.

Barnes, D. and Todd, F. (1977) *Communicating Learning in Small Groups*, London, Routledge and Kegan Paul.

Bloom, B.S. (1956) *Taxonomy of Educational Objectives: Cognitive Domain*, New York, David McKay.

Bowen, P. (1995) 'Secondary History Teaching and the OFSTED Inspections: An Analysis and Discussion of History Comments', *Teaching History*, June.

Brasher, N.H. (1970) *The Young Historian*, Oxford, Oxford University Press, p. 7.

Brzezicki, K. (1991) 'Group work', *Teaching History*, July.

Burston, W.H. (1963) *Principles of History Teaching*, London, Methuen, p. 41.

Capel, S., Leask, M. and Turner, T. (1995) *Learning to Teach in the Secondary School*, London, Routledge.

Counsell, C. (1995) Lecture on the use of IT in the history classroom at BETT Exhibition, London, January.

Counsell, C. (1996) 'Progression at Key Stage 3: What Does "Getting Better" at History Mean?', Address to the Historical Association Conference, 14 September.

Counsell, C. (1997) *Analytical and Discussive Writing in National Curriculum History at Key Stage 3: A Practical Guide*, Teaching of History Series, London, Historical Association.

Cowie, E. (1979) *History and the Slow-learning Child*, London, Historical Association.

Curtis, S. (1994) 'Communication in History', *Teaching History*, October.

DES (1975) *A Language for Life* (The Bullock Report), London, HMSO.

Edwards, A.D. (1978) The Language of History', in A.K. Dickenson and P.J. Lee, *History Teaching and Historical Understanding*, London, Heinemann, p. 62.

Edwards, A.D. and Furlong, V.J. (1978) *The Language of Teaching*, London, Heinemann, pp. 27–8, 55, 78.

Edwards, A.D. and Westgate, D.P.G. (1987) *Investigating Classroom Talk*, Lewes, Falmer.

Fines, J. (1994) Workshop at Historical Association Conference, Manchester, September.

Garvey, B. and Krug, M. (1977) *Models of History Teaching in the Secondary School*, Oxford, Oxford University Press.

Gunning, D. (1978a) *The Teaching of History*, London, Croom Helm, p. 20.

Gunning, D. (1978b) *The History Teacher and Problems of Written Language*, Historical Association Information Pamphlet 3, London, Historical Association, p. 109.

Hake, C. and Haydn, T. (1995) 'Stories or Sources?', *Teaching History*, No. 78 (January), pp. 20–2.

Labbett, B. (1996) 'Principles of Procedure', Unpublished lecture, University of East Anglia, 8 January.

Lawton, D. (1968) *Social Class, Language and Education*, London, Routledge and Kegan Paul.

Lee, P.J., Ashby, R. and Dickinson, A.R. (1995) 'Progression in Children's Ideas about History', in M. Hughes (ed.) *Progression in Learning*, BERA Dialogues: 11, Clevedon, Multilingual Matters, pp. 50–81.

Levine, N. (1981) *Language, Teaching and Learning: History*, London, WLE, p. 109.

Lunzer, E. and Gardner, K. (1979) *The Effective Use of Reading*, London, Heinemann, for the Schools Council.

Marland, M. (1977) *Language across the Curriculum*, London, Heinemann.

OFSTED (1993) *History: a Review of Inspection Findings, 1992/3*, London, HMSO.

OFSTED (1995) *History: A Review of Inspection Findings 1993/94*, London, HMSO.

Schools Council (1978) *Writing across the Curriculum Project: Writing in Geography, History and Social Studies*, London, Ward Lock.

Sutton, C. (1981) *Communicating in the Classroom*, London, Hodder and Stoughton.

Teacher Education Project (1979) *Would You Read This? A Practical Guide to Criteria of Readability*, Leicester University.

Torbé, M. (1981) *The Climate for Learning*, London, WLE.

Wilson, M.D. (1985) *History for Pupils with Learning Difficulties*, London, Hodder and Stoughton.

5 DEVELOPING HISTORICAL UNDERSTANDING (1)

Ashby, R. and Lee, P.J. (1987) 'Children's Concepts of Empathy and Understanding in History', in C. Portal (ed.) *The History Curriculum for Teachers*, Lewes, Falmer Press, pp. 62–88.

Booth, M., Culpin, C. and Macintosh, H. (1987) *Teaching GCSE History*, London, Hodder & Stoughton, p. 21.

Cairns, J. (1989) 'Some Reflections on Empathy in History', *Teaching History*, April.

Clements, P. (1996) 'Historical Empathy – R.I.P.?', *Teaching History*, October.

DES (1985) *G.C.S.E.: The National Criteria*, London, HMSO.

DES (1990) *History in the National Curriculum: Final Report*, HMSO, p. 9, para 3.18.

Haydn, T. (1995) 'Teaching Children about Time', *Teaching History*, October, p. 11.

Lee, P.J. (1984) 'Historical Imagination', in A.R. Dickinson, P.J. Lee and P.J. Rogers, *Learning History*, London, Heinemann Educational, p. 86.

Lee, P.J., Dickinson, A.R. and Ashby, R. (1996) 'Children Making Sense of History', *Education 3–13*, March.

Levine, N. (1981) *Language Teaching and Learning: 5. History*, London, Ward Lock Educational.

Low-Beer, A. (1989) 'Empathy and History', *Teaching History*, April.

NCC (1993) *Teaching History at Key Stage 3*, York, NCC, p. 38.

Sansom, C. (1987) 'Concepts, Skills and Content: A Development Approach to the History Syllabus', in C. Portal (ed.) *The History Curriculum for Teachers*, Lewes, Falmer Press, p. 116.

Scott, J. (1987) *Medicine Through Time: a Study in Development*, Edinburgh, Holmes McDougall.

Scott, J. (1990) *Understanding Cause and Effect* (Teaching History Research Group), London, Longmans.

Shemilt, D. (1980) *History 13–16: Evaluation*, Edinburgh, Holmes McDougall.

Thompson, D. (1984) 'Understanding the Past: Procedures and Content', in A.R. Dickinson, P.J. Lee and P.J. Rogers, *Learning History*, London, Heinemann Educational, p. 178.

Wilson, M.D. (1985) *History for Pupils with Learning Difficulties*, London, Hodder and Stoughton, p. 44.

6 DEVELOPING HISTORICAL UNDERSTANDING (2)

Bennett, S. (1995) *The Teaching and Assessment of Interpretations and Representations in History: A Discussion Paper*, London, SCAA, p. 5.

Bowen, P. (1995) 'Secondary History Teaching and the OFSTED Inspections', *Teaching History*, June, p. 12.

British Library (1994) *Medieval Realms*, CD-ROM, London, British Library.

Dearing, R. (1994) *The National Curriculum and its Assessment*, London, SCAA.

DfE (1995) *History in the National Curriculum*, London, HMSO.

DES (1990) *History in the National Curriculum*, London, HMSO, p. 7, B6.

Harper, P. (1993) 'Using the Attainment Targets in Key Stage 2: AT2, Interpretations of History', *Teaching History*, July, pp. 11–13.

NCC (1993) *Teaching History at Key Stage 3*, York, NCC, pp. 50–8.

OFSTED (1993) *History, Key Stages 1, 2 and 3: The Implementation of the Curricular Requirements of the Education Reform Act*, London, HMSO.

OFSTED (1995) *History: A Review of Inspection Findings, 1993–94*. London, HMSO.

Pendry, A. *et al.* (1997) 'Pupil Preconception of History', *Teaching History*, No. 86, January, pp. 18–20.

SCAA (1996) *Exemplification of Standards in History, Key Stage 3*, London, SCAA.

Scott, B. (1994) 'A Post-Dearing Look at History: Interpretations of History', *Teaching History*, April, pp. 20–6.

Towill, E. (1997) 'The Constructive Use of Roleplay at Key Stage 3', *Teaching History*, No. 86, January, pp. 8–13.

Wilson, M.D. (1985) *History for Pupils with Learning Difficulties*, London, Hodder and Stoughton, p. 88.

7 PUPILS WITH SPECIAL EDUCATIONAL NEEDS IN THE HISTORY CLASSROOM

Aylett, J. (1993) *History Fast Track, 1750–1900*, London, Hodder and Stoughton.

Banes, D. and Sebba, J. (1991) 'I Was Little Then', *British Journal of Special Education*, Vol. 18, No. 3, pp. 121–4.

Bourdillon, H. (ed.) (1994) *Teaching History*, London, Routledge.

Clarke, J. and Wrigley, K. (1988) *Humanities for All: Teaching Humanities in the Secondary School*, London, Cassell.

Cowie, E. (1979) *History and the Slow Learner*, London, Historical Association.

DfE (1994) *The Code of Practice and the Identification and Assessment of Special Educational Needs*, London, HMSO.

DfE (1995) *History in the National Curriculum*, London, HMSO, p. 2.

DfEE (1997) *Standards for the Award of Qualified Teacher Status, Circular 10/97*, London, DFEE.

DES (1978) *Special Educational Needs* (Warnock Report), London, HMSO.

DES (1990a) *History for Ages 5–16*, London, HMSO.

DES (1990b) *Final Report of the National Curriculum History Working Group*, London, HMSO, p. 171.

Goacher, B. (1988) *Policy Provision for Special Educational Needs: Implementing the 1981 Education Act*, London, Cassell.

Hargreaves, D.H. (1984) *Improving Secondary Schools: Report of the Committee on the Curriculum and Organisation of Secondary Schools*, London, ILEA.

Harrington, S. and Chaplin, C. (1990) *History: Back to Basics*, Canvey Island, Mayday.

Hornby, G. (1995) 'The Code of Practice: Boon or Burden', *British Journal of Special Education*, Vol. 22, No. 3, pp. 116–19.

Hull, J. (1980) 'Practical Points on Teaching History to Less Able Secondary Pupils', *Teaching History*, October.

Husbands, C. (1996) *What is History Teaching?*, Buckingham, Open University Press, p. 13.

Kennedy, P. (1994) *The Making of the United Kingdom*, Oxford, Heinemann.

Laycock, S.R. (1957) *Gifted Children: A Handbook for the Classroom Teacher*, Toronto, Copp-Clark.

Lee, P.J., Ashby, R. and Dickinson, A.R. (1995) 'Progression in Children's Ideas about History', in M. Hughes (ed.) *Progression in Learning*, BERA Dialogues: 11, Clevedon, Multilingual Matters, pp. 50–81.

Lee, P.J., Dickinson, A.R. and Ashby, R. (1996) 'Children Making Sense of History', *Education 3 to 13*, March, pp. 13–19.

Lewis, A. (1992) 'From Planning to Practice', *British Journal of Special Educational Needs*, Vol. 5, No. 2, pp. 216–33.

Lovey, J. (1995) *Support for SEN in Secondary School Classrooms*, London, David Fulton.

McMinn, R. (1983) 'A Feast or a Famine?', *Teaching History*, June.

Marjoram, T. (1988) *Teaching Able Children*, London, Kogan Page.

Mason, P. and Essen, J. (1987) *The Social, Educational and Emotional Needs of Gifted Children*, NAGC, July.

OFSTED (1993) *History: A Review of Inspection Findings 1992/1993*, London, HMSO.

OFSTED (1995) *History: A Review of Inspection Findings 1993/1994*, London, HMSO.

OFSTED (1996) *Promoting High Achievement*, London, HMSO.

Price, M. (1968) 'History in Danger', *Teaching History*, November.

Robson, W. (1993) *Britain 1750–1900*, Access to History Series, Oxford, Oxford University Press.

Sebba, J. (1994) *History for All*, London, David Fulton.

Sebba, J. and Clarke, J. (1991) *Meeting the Needs of Pupils Within History and Geography*, Lewes, Falmer Press.

Shephard, C. and Brown, B. (1994) *Britain 1750–1900*, Special Needs Support Materials, London, John Murray,

Wallace, B. (1985) *Teaching the Very Able Child*, London, Ward Lock.

Ware, J. and Peacy, N. (1993) 'We're Doing History – What Does it Mean?', *British Journal of Special Education*, Vol. 20, No. 2, pp. 65–71.

Weston, P. (1992) 'A Decade of Differentiation', *British Journal of Special Education*, Vol 19, No. 1, pp. 5–9.

Wilson, M.D. (1982a) 'The History Curriculum for Slow Learners', *Teaching History*, February.

Wilson, M.D. (1982b) 'Teaching History to Slow Learners: Problems of Language and Communication', *Teaching History*, June.

Wilson, M.D. (1985) *History for Pupils with Learning Difficulties*, London, Hodder and Stoughton.

8   THE USE OF NEW TECHNOLOGY IN THE HISTORY CLASSROOM

Askar, P., Yavuz, H. and Koksal, M. (1992) 'Students' Perceptions of Computer Assisted Instruction Environment and their Attitudes to Computer Assisted Learning', *Educational Research*, Vol. 34, No. 2, Summer, pp. 133–9.

Barber, M. (1995) 'Seven Steps into the Educational Future', *The Times*, 3 April.

Barton, R. (1997) 'A Partnership Approach to IT in Initial Teacher Training', *Journal of IT in Initial Teacher Education*, Vol. 5, No. 3, pp. 283–301.

BBC (1997) *History on the Web*, http://bbc.co.uk/education/histfile/history.htm

Byard, M. (1995) 'IT under School Based Policies for Initial Teacher Training', *Journal of Computer Assisted Learning*, Vol. 11, No. 3, pp. 128–40.

Campbell, R. and Davies, I. (1997) 'History Student Teachers and the Information Superhighway', *Teaching History*, forthcoming.

Dearing, R. (1994) *The National Curriculum and its Assessment*, London, SCAA.

DfE (1995a) *Statistical Bulletin on the use of IT in schools*, London, HMSO.

DfE (1995b) *History in the National Curriculum*, London, HMSO.

DfEE (1997) *Standards for the Award of Qualified Teacher Status*, London, DfEE.

Downes, T. (1993) 'Student Teachers' Experiences in Using Computers During Teaching Practice', *Journal of Computer Assisted Learning*, Vol. 9, No. 1, pp. 17–33.

Durbin, C. (1996) 'The Use of the Internet in Teaching History', address to the BETT Conference, London, January.

Easdown, G. (1992) 'Student Teachers, Mentors and Information Technology', *Journal of Information Technology for Teacher Education*, Vol. 3, No. 1, pp. 63–78.

Easdown, G. (1996) 'History Student Teacher Preconceptions of Information Technology', in J. Lehners and A. Werné, A. Martin and F. Hendrickx, (eds) *Information Technologies for History Education*, Luxemburg, Publications du Centre Universitaire.

Haydn, T. (1996) 'The Use of Computers in the History Classroom in Britain; Myth, Reality and Some Reasons for the Difference between the Two', in J. Lehners, A. Werné, A. Martin and F. Hendrickx, (eds) *Information Technologies for History Education*, Luxemburg, Publications du Centre Universitaire.

Haydn, T. and Macaskill, C. (1996) *Making the Most of Information Technology in the PGCE Year*, London, ULIE.

HMI (1988) *The New Teacher in Schools*, London, HMSO.

Howe, M. (1997) *Using the Internet to Teach History*, http://uea.ac.uk/~m287/pgce.htm

Jones, C. (1995) Address to the BETT Conference, London, January.

Luton News (1947) *Luton at War*, Home Counties Press, appendix.

Mcdonald, S. (1993) 'Information Technology: Building Structures in Initial Teacher Training to Develop Effective Practitioners', *Journal of Computer Assisted Learning*, Vol. 9, No. 1, pp. 141–8.

Martin, D. (1996) 'Little Pain but Lots of Gain', *Times Educational Supplement*, 19 April.

NCET (1994) 'What Works In IT', Coventry, NCET.

NCET (1997) *History and IT: Improving Pupils' Writing in History Through Word Processing*, Coventry, NCET.

OFSTED (1994) *History: A Review of Inspection Findings*, London, HMSO.

Somekh, B. (1992) *Initial Teacher Education and New Technology (Project INTENT)*, Coventry, NCET.

SCAA (1995) *Information Technology: The New Requirements*, London, SCAA.

Trotter Report (1989) *Information technology in Initial Teacher Training: Report of the Information Technology in Initial Teacher Training Expert Group*, London, HMSO.

Underwood, J. and Underwood, G. (1990) *Computers and Learning: Helping Children Acquire Thinking Skills*, Oxford, Blackwell.

Watkinson, S. (1990) *The Teacher*, 23 March.

9 THE USE OF RESOURCES IN THE TEACHING OF HISTORY

Adams, C. and Millar, S. (1982) 'Museums and the Use of Evidence in History Teaching', *Teaching History*, No. 34.

Aldrich, R. (1989) 'Class and Gender in the Study and Teaching of History in

England in the Twentieth Century', *Historical Studies in Education*, Vol. 1, No. 1, Spring.

Anderson, A. and Moore, A. (1994) 'Making History Happen Outside the Classroom', in K. Andreetti (1993) *Teaching History from Primary Evidence*, London, David Fulton.

Bourdillon, H. (ed.) (1994) *Teaching History*, London, Routledge.

BBC (1997) *History on the Web*, URL, http://bbc.co.uk/education/histfile/history.htm

Brierly, M. and Parsons, M. (1993) 'Practical Evaluation of Historical Sources', *Teaching History*, January, No. 70.

Brooks, R., Aris, M. and Perry, I. (1993) *The Effective History Teacher*, London, Longman.

Brown, R. and Daniels, C.W. (1986) *Learning History: A Guide to Advanced Study*, London, Macmillan.

Danks, E.J. (1994) 'Theory and Practice Essay: The Use of Resources and Teaching Aides in the Teaching of History, with Particular Reference to Year Eight, *Teaching History*, October, No. 77.

DfE (1995) *History in the National Curriculum*, London, HMSO.

Farmer, A. and Knight, P. (1995) *Active History in Key Stages 3 and 4*, London, David Fulton.

Fines, J. (1994) 'Evidence: The Basis of Discipline', in H. Bourdillon, *Teaching History*, London, Routledge.

Fry, H. (1991) 'Using Evidence in the GCSE Classroom', *Teaching History*, April, No. 63.

Hake, C. and Haydn, T. (1995) 'Stories or Sources', *Teaching History*, January, No. 78.

Lawrie, J. (1994) 'Desperate Remedies – Inventive Resourcing for the History Classroom', *Teaching History*, October, No. 77.

Lloyd–Jones, R. ([1985] 1995) *How to Produce Better Worksheets*, London, Stanley Thomas.

Lomas, T. (1992) *Teaching and Assessing Historical Understanding*, London, Historical Association.

McKinley, R.R. (1984) 'The Adoption of an Evidence-based Approach to a Site Visit: A Case Study', *Teaching History*, February, No. 38.

Marwick, A. (1984) *The Nature of History*, London, Macmillan.

OFSTED (1993a) *History Key Stages 1, 2, 3*, London, HMSO.

OFSTED (1993b) *History – A Review of Inspection Findings, 1992–3*, London, HMSO.

OFSTED (1995) *History – A Review of Inspection Findings, 1993–1994*, London, HMSO.

Parsons, M.L. (1996) 'Lets Grab a Gran off the Street: The Problems of Oral History and How they can be Minimised', *Teaching History*, June, No. 94.

Pond, M. (1985) 'School History Visits and Piagetian Theory', *Teaching History*, No. 37.

Portal, C. (1987) *Sources in History: From Definition to Assessment*, London, Southern Regional Examination Board.

Schools Council History 13–16 Project (1976) *Looking at Evidence*, London, Holmes McDougall.

SEAC (1989) Chief Examiners' History Conference.

Sebba, J. (1995) *History for All*, London, David Fulton.

Shemilt, D. (1987) 'Adolescent Ideas About Evidence and Methodology in History', in C. Portal, *The History Curriculum for Teachers*, Lewes, Falmer Press, pp. 39–61.

Slater, J. (1984) 'The Case for History in School', *The Historian*, No. 2.

10 ASSESSMENT IN THE CLASSROOM

Bennett, S. and Steele, I. (1995) 'The Revised History Order', *Teaching History*, April.

Biggs, J. and Moore, P. (1993) *The Process of Learning*, New Jersey, Prentice-Hall, Chapter 16.

Booth, M. (1983) 'Skills, Concepts and Attitudes: The Development of Adolescent Children's Historical Thinking', *History and Theory*, Vol. 22.

Booth, M. and Husbands, C. (1993) 'The History National Curriculum in England and Wales: Assessment at Key Stage 3', *The Curriculum Journal*, Vol. 4, No. 1, pp. 21–36.

Checketts, J. (1996) 'GCSE History: A Case for Revolution', *Teaching History*, January.

DfE (1992) *The Accreditation of Initial Teacher Training: Circular 9/92*, London, HMSO.

DfE (1995) *History in the National Curriculum*, London, HMSO.

Dickinson, A. and Lee, P. (1984) 'Making Sense of History', in A. Dickinson, P.J. Lee and P.J. Rogers, *Learning History*, London, Heinemann.

Fines, J. (1994) 'Progression – A Seminar Report', *Teaching History*, April.

Hallam, R.N. (1972) 'Thinking and Learning in History', *Teaching History*, November.

Hallam, S. (1996) 'Pupil Learning and Differentiation', Unpublished lecture, Institute of Education, University of London, 17 January.

Hampshire County Council (1994) *History Matters*, 13 (OFSTED Inspector's Guidance on the use of Differentiation).

Haydn, T. (1994) 'Uses and Abuses of the TGAT Assessment Model: The Case of History and the 45 Boxes', *The Curriculum Journal*, Vol. 5, No. 2, pp. 216–33.

Lee, P. (1994) 'Historical Knowledge and the National Curriculum', in H. Bourdillon (ed.) *Teaching History*, London, Routledge.

Lewis, A. (1992) 'From Planning to Practice', *British Journal of Special Education*, Vol. 19, No. 1, pp. 24–7.

Lomas, T. (1990) *Teaching and Assessing Historical Understanding*, London, Historical Association.

OFSTED (1995) *History, a Review of Inspection Findings, 1993/4*, London, HMSO.

SCAA (1996) *Exemplification of Standards in History: KS3*, London, SCAA.

Shemilt, D. (1976) 'Formal Operational Thought in History', *Teaching History*, May.

Stenhouse, L. (1983) *Authority, Education and Emancipation: A Collection of Papers*, London, Heinemann, quoted in 'Making Differentiation Manageable', *School Science Review*, December 1995, Vol. 77, No. 279, pp. 106–10.

Watts, D.G. (1973) *The Learning of History*, London, Routledge and Kegan Paul.

11 TEACHING FOR EXTERNAL EXAMINATIONS

Checketts, J. (1996) 'GCSE History: A Case for Revolution', *Teaching History*, January.

Clements, P. (1996) 'Historical Empathy – R.I.P.?', *Teaching History*, October.

Cloake, J., Crinnion, V.A. and Harrison, S.A. (1985) *The History Manual*, Lancaster, Framework Press.

Crinnion, V. (1987) 'Some Problems and Principles of 'A' Level History', in C. Portal, *The History Curriculum for Teachers*, Lewes, Falmer.

DfE (1995) *History in the National Curriculum*, London, HMSO.

Fines, J. (1980) 'Educational Objectives and the Assessment of History at 'A' Level: A Discussion Paper', in University of Exeter School of Education, *Development in History Teaching Perspectives* 4.

Fines, J. (1987) *Source Based Questions at 'A' Level*, London, Historical Association.

Fines, J. (1988) *Question Framing at GCSE and A Level: An Introduction for History Teachers*, London, Historical Association.

Fines, J. (1989) *A Survey of A Level History*, London, Historical Association.

Fines, J. and Nichol, J. (1994) *Doing History 16–19: A Case Study in Curriculum Innovation and Change*, London, Historical Association, p. 141.

Fisher, T. (1991) *'A' Level History: More Questions than Answers*.

Higginson Report (1988)

Husbands, C. (1996) *What is History Teaching?*, Buckingham, Open University Press.

Josclin, B. (1995) 'An Introduction to 'A' Level History', Unpublished lecture, Institute of Education, 23 January.

Kilmartin, J. (1995) 'Looking Beyond National Curriculum History: Ensuring Continuity and Progress after 16', in R. Watts and I. Grosvenor (eds) *Crossing the Key Stages of History*, London, David Fulton, p. 137.

Lang, S. (1990) *'A' Level History: The Case for Change*, London, Historical Association.

Lewin, J. (1991) '"A" and A/S Levels – Present State of Play' in J. Fines *History 16–19: The Old and the New*, London, Historical Association, pp. 23–9.

Martin, P. (1991) 'Some Thoughts on Teaching the "A" Level Personal Study', in J. Fines *History 16–19: The Old and the New*, London, Historical Association, pp. 30–42.

NEAB (1996) *GCSE Syllabus for 1998: History Syllabus C (British Social and Economic History*, Manchester, NEAB.

OFSTED (1993) *GCE Advanced Supplementary and Advanced Level Examinations – Quality and Standards*, London, HMSO.

Schools Council (1966) *Examining at 16+*, The Report of the Joint GCE/CSE Committee, London, HMSO.

Swift, R. and Arnold, P. (1991) 'Breaking New Ground in Sixth Form History', *Teaching History*, April, No. 63.

Taylor, L. (1994) 'Response to the Dearing Report: History post-16', *Teaching History*, April, No. 75.

White, C. (1991) 'History 14–19: Challenges and Opportunities', *Teaching History*, January, No. 82.

12 CONTINUING PROFESSIONAL DEVELOPMENT

Calderhead, J. (1994) 'The Reform of Initial Teacher Education and Research on Learning to Teach: Contrasting Ideas', in P. John and P. Lucas (eds) *Partnership in Progress*, USDE Papers in Education, Sheffield, University of Sheffield Department of Education.

Capel, S. (1997) *Learning to Teach Physical Education in the Secondary School*, London, Routledge.

Capel, S., Leask, M. and Turner, T. (1995) *Learning to Teach in the Secondary School*, London, Routledge.

Elliott, J. (1991) *Action Research for Educational Change*, Buckingham, Open University Press.

Elliott, J. (ed.) (1993) *Reconstructing Teacher Education*, Lewes, Falmer.

Lawlor, S. (1987) 'Correct Core', in B. Moon, P. Murphy and J. Raynor (eds) *Policies for the Curriculum*, Buckingham, Open University Press, p. 68.

MacDonald, B. (1984) 'Teacher Education and Curriculum Reform – Some English Errors', Presentation to the symposium 'Theory and Practice of Teacher Education', Madrid, Ministry of Education, February.

OFSTED (1997) *The Annual Report of Her Majesty's Chief Inspector of Schools*, London, HMSO.

Tickle, L. (1994) *The Induction of New Teachers: Reflective Professional Practice*, London, Cassell.

TTA (1996) *Effective Training through Partnership*, Paper 1, London, Teacher Training Agency, p. 13.

Index